To Margaret Vogt, with enormous appreciation & gratitude for the wonderful contribution you have made to my work & to my life.

With Warmest thoughts,

[signature]

Reinventing Peacekeeping in Africa

Conceptual and Legal Issues
in ECOMOG Operations

'FUNMI OLONISAKIN
King's College, London

KLUWER LAW INTERNATIONAL
THE HAGUE / LONDON / BOSTON

A C.I.P Catalogue record for this book is available from the Library of Congress.

ISBN 90-411-1321-5

Published by Kluwer Law International,
P.O. Box 85889, 2508 CN The Hague, The Netherlands

Sold and distributed in North, Central and South America
by Kluwer Law International,
675 Massachusetts Avenue, Cambridge, MA 02139, USA

In all other countries, sold and distributed
by Kluwer Law International, Distribution Centre
P.O. Box 322, 3300 AH Dordrecht, The Netherlands

Printed on acid-free paper

Cover photo: ANP

Printed and bound in Great Britain by Cromwell Press, Trowbridge, Wilts.

This book is dedicated to Olaloye Badamosi,
my soul mate and inspiration

Table of Contents

Foreword

One of the paradoxes of contemporary international affairs is encapsulated in the idea of a 'violent peace'. For most western states, the post-Cold War security landscape has been marked by a receding threat of direct military attack on their territorial integrity. Yet, as is the case for the United Kingdom, their armed forces have hardly been idle. Indeed, to the contrary: in addition to traditional Cold War NATO roles involving the stationing of troops in Germany, they have also become increasingly focused on deployments abroad in a variety of peace support operations, such as in Bosnia and Kosovo and, much more modestly, Sierra Leone. For today's armed forces commitment to such operations brings in its train a number of problems: the 'overstretch' of personnel and equipment as well as other issues, such as how best to configure forces so that they might respond flexibly to a range of operations, whether these be war fighting or peacekeeping. Such issues will continue to preoccupy force planners on both sides of the Atlantic.

In defence policy terms, the UK is committed to 'going to crises before they come to us'. This approach is rooted in the fact that, while the West does not face direct military threats to its own borders of a 'state on state' kind, for other regions of the world – in much of Asia and especially Africa – their populations' experience continues to be marked by violent conflict, particularly forms of civil conflict and internal warfare. As in the European cases of Bosnia and Kosovo, these violent conflicts pose serious humanitarian, economic and political problems for regional – and potentially global – stability and security. This is why the nature of peacekeeping has become transformed over the past decade. Traditional or classical forms of peacekeeping presuppose inter alia, the prior consent of the warring parties, the termination of their conflict, and the presence of peacekeepers with restricted mandates – commensurate with their role of keeping a peace that has already been reached by the contending parties – normally limiting their military action to self-defence. It is important to acknowledge that such operations continue to be a significant, indeed very successful, element of the UN's contribution to international peace and security; and some have argued that this is what should remain at the core of UN peacekeeping operations.

However, contemporary crises arising from internal warfare have, for humanitarian and political reasons led to forms of military intervention that have shifted the boundaries of what have been conventionally known as peacekeeping operations. Thus, mandates have been extended to incorporate more coercive measures beyond self-defence. Interventions have taken place with levels of consent far lower than would be required in a classical peacekeeping operation, and during a phase of conflicts far short of the stage at which they had been terminated by the prior agreement of the contending parties. All of this is evident in the language that has been used to conceptualise such activities: 'conflict mitigation', 'strategic peace-keeping' and, as in the present volume by 'Funmi Olonisakin, 'peace creation'.

In this book, Olonisakin focuses on the violent internal warfare and civil conflicts in the Liberian context and the responses they have engendered. In doing so, she deals with an important series of issues that should attract the interest of anyone concerned with how such crises – whether in Africa or other parts of the world – might be managed: by neighbouring states, regional organisations, non-state actors and the United Nations. She focuses on the ways in which interventions in such crises need to be able to draw on a mix of military and non-military instruments, and considers the prospects of not simply conflict mitigation but also more longer lasting forms of peace creation and institution-building.

Now the very concept of intervention, as has been dramatised in the discussion about the legality of Nato's campaign in Kosovo in 1999, indicates that any attempt to understand the potential of the new forms of peace support operation needs to start with an investigation of the legal and normative basis of such activities. Olonisakin then turns her attention to the operational issues arising from applying a concept of peace creation to the seemingly intractable problems of internal warfare to be found in the West African context. In doing so, she highlights a number of important issues, not the least of which is the extent to which peace support operations can and should be organised – in doctrinal and operational terms – and implemented on the basis of regional security systems.

In what are complex and multi-functional peace operations, Olonisakin focuses especially on the experiences and contributions of the soldiers themselves. It is their competence and commitment that is essential to the success of such operations however firm their basis is in terms of doctrine and international law. In this kind of operation, soldiers increasingly find themselves working in situations of immense pressure. Thus junior personnel have increased levels of responsibility in complex and fast moving situations. Decision-makers have to think not just in terms of military categories but also be aware of the political, humanitarian contexts. They also need to take into account the scrutiny of their actions by the media, which for technological and political reasons, can no longer be subjected to the forms of control and censorship possible fifteen years ago. At the same time, such operations pose problems for their sense of identity as soldiers, the core of which for the great majority is the defence of their state by being prepared for war fighting.

None of these issues can be analysed without a detailed appreciation of the soldier's experience and this is one of the strengths that Olonisakin brings to bear in this book, drawing on an intensive period of research. Her work is a significant contribution to the literature on peacekeeping, regional security and international affairs. It has been supported by the Department of War Studies at King's, first when she was a postgraduate research student and more recently during her appointment as a Post-Doctoral Fellow in the Department's 'Regional Security in a Global Context' programme, which is supported by an Institutional Fellowship from the John D. and Catherine T. MacArthur Foundation.

Christopher Dandeker
Professor of Military Sociology
and Head of Department of War Studies

Preface

The euphoric cries of a peaceful and more dynamic "new world order", which followed the end of the Cold War have been silenced by the increased intensity of local conflicts around the world. The humanitarian crises resulting from these conflicts have attracted greater international attention. Perhaps even more tragic is the failure of the international community to find early effective response to these conflicts, which have profound security implications for the affected regions and have led to the collapse of state structures in some cases. The intra-state conflicts in Africa alone have claimed over one million lives since the beginning of this decade.

On the international scene these internal conflicts have created new challenges for the UN, whose efforts at dealing with these conflicts have produced mixed results, whilst international policy makers, the military and academics are faced with difficult questions. Can traditional peacekeeping be stretched to accommodate this class of conflict? If not traditional peacekeeping then what? What is the legal basis for these operations? Who should bear the responsibility for them? What are the determinants of success? How will the role of peacekeepers be changed to cope with the new crises? Quick and accurate answers are needed to these questions, as decision-makers require information upon which to draw conclusions and make decisions. It seems certain that, as the conduct of these conflicts changes and tasks change, so must peacekeeping. Post-Cold War thinking is beginning to reflect this. Attempts to answer these questions at the conceptual level have led to the development of concepts such as second generation peacekeeping, wider peacekeeping, peace support operations and strategic peacekeeping. It has emerged that there is no common view on an effective and realistic set of tools to manage these crises. Thus, it is likely that different modus operandi will emerge, which will inevitably alter the effectiveness of these operations. This is compounded by the absence of a clear legal framework to guide such operations.

Perhaps the most significant point to arise from the differing conceptual views presently is that an effective approach and sound legal basis have not been found for dealing with difficult internal conflicts in far away regions,

xiii

which are not high on the strategic considerations of the great powers. Thus, there are two broad reflections: on the one hand, there is an emerging gulf between what is desirable and political will at the global level, and on the other, a gulf between capability and what is desirable at the regional level.

The war in Liberia was not only a true reflection of the deadly and recalcitrant internal conflicts that have pervaded the post-Cold War milieu, it was also one in which a radical approach was adopted in dealing with the crisis. The measure of success achieved by this approach (albeit one with serious flaws) led to successful elections in the country on 19 July 1997. The civil war, which erupted in Liberia in December 1989 questioned the suitability of the traditional methods of intervening in conflicts, and served as an early test of the capability of the UN to respond to them. The Liberian war was among the earliest to highlight the challenges that internal conflicts would pose for the international conflict resolution machinery in the post-Cold War period and for the existing legal framework for responding to conflicts within the UN. It is estimated that this war resulted in about 200,000 deaths, and more than half a million refugees fled to neighboring states within the first year, putting severe strain on the already weak economies of these countries. The conduct of conflicting parties created real problems, as the rules of war and humanitarian law of armed conflict were blatantly violated. The Liberian imbroglio gave a hint of what Post-Cold War battle grounds would look like and it demonstrated the growing irrelevance of traditional peacekeeping and an emerging gap in terms of legal bases for the new multi-faceted operations. This was confirmed by the subsequent slide of Sierra Leone into a civil war and the crisis of May 1997, when the ousting of Ahmed Tejan Kabbah's democratically elected government in a military coup led to the Nigerian-led ECOMOG military intervention.

This book conducts an analysis of the operational approach, which achieved some measure of success that led to elections in Liberia, and later, the re-instatement of a democratically elected government, following a military coup in Sierra Leone and assesses the real challenges that confronted this approach. In particular, it asks some important questions – can Africans devise, appropriate even if radical concepts of operations, in response to recalcitrant conflict within states? Can they successfully evolve a doctrine that is *not* backed by extra-regional sources? How can their potential for planning and executing complex operations be improved? P*eace creation* is proposed as a necessary tool for dealing with difficult civil conflict. This concept, and its practical application are examined. In particular, the book conducts an analysis of the operational and legal conditions under which the concept of peace creation can be successfully applied to conflict situations and the challenges of the approach. It examines the important characteristics of the military men who will seek to implement peace creation, and the factors that will decide their effectiveness and success in the field as distinct from the demands of classical peacekeeping operations.

Three key factors set this book apart from recent works on regional peacekeeping and the Liberian conflict. First, the analysis of *peace creation* and of the activities of the peace force is based largely on a field study of the peace force in the area of operation. Second, the opinions of the military men who implemented the peace plan and their first hand account of their experiences were relied upon in drawing some of the conclusions reached in this book. The opinions and experiences of the men upon whom the successful conduct of these new operations depend are crucial to understanding the present challenges, and to developing an effective approach but they are often not at the fore-front of the considerations of many analysts. Their operational experiences, their perception of their role and of the psychological and social impact of the mission are often ignored. This book utilizes the testimonies of these soldiers in its analysis of the concept of peace creation, the social organization of ECOMOG, the African multinational force, and the socio-political factors which influence the conduct of troops seeking to create peace. Third, this book discusses an often neglected issue in regional peacekeeping: the legal basis for the conduct of missions beyond peacekeeping and the legal relationship between the UN and regional organisations, particularly in the initiation of military intervention.

This book, on the one hand, offers an analysis of a new conceptual framework for managing vicious conflicts. On the other hand, it gives first hand account of the character of a force which has attempted to apply this new approach. It is becoming a widely held view, that ECOMOG, or a regional standing force will be part of the short to medium-term future of West Africa. This suggests that ECOMOG's operational experiences must be studied closely, in order to decide on the character and composition of a future West Africa force, be it for preventive deployment, peacekeeping or outright intervention. Studying the lessons of ECOMOG will also go some way in giving direction to programs such as the African Crisis Response Initiative (ACRI), which seeks to build the capacity of Africans to respond to crisis in their region. If such initiatives are to achieve positive results, they must be based on a deep understanding of the nature of the conflicts in the region and of the experiences of the organisations that have sought to deal with the consequences of these conflicts.

Acknowledgements

This book grew out of my PhD thesis, submitted to King's College London. Researching a conflict in progress presents a catalogue of problems, which become all the more profound in Africa where even at the best of times, security information is treated with utmost secrecy. I owe a debt of gratitude to several individuals, who contributed to the process of researching this work and in preparing it for publication. First, I thank the Liberians, who showed interest in discussing with me the disaster that befell their country for seven years. In Liberia, I wish to thank in particular, Lindsay Barrett, Jo-Jo Burgess, Ruth Caesar, Ann Davies, Bill Frank Enoanyi, Clifford Flemister, Saa Kanda, and Professor Amos Sawyer. I am deeply grateful to ECOMOG and UNOMIL Officers and men. I have decided not to mention most of the officers by name, as this could paint them with the brush of association. I want to express my gratitude to them through the two ECOMOG Commanders that attended to my needs (General Ishaya Bakut and General John Inienger) and through UNOMIL Commander, General John Opande.

There is, however, an ECOMOG officer I want to acknowledge by name, not because of his professional role as a soldier, but because he is a King's College London alumnus. This is Colonel Ade Ajibade, who by pleasant coincidence was on deployment to Liberia as the Colonel General Staff of the Nigerian Contingent during one of my field trips to the country. He and his staff accommodated and catered to my needs. I am most grateful to them.

I want to thank Targema Takema and Drs. Jimi Peters, Margaret Vogt and Joy Ogwu of the Nigerian Institute of International Affairs, Mr Frank Ofei and Mrs Abimbola of the ECOWAS Secretariat, and in particular, General Ishola Williams (Rtd), who provided enormous encouragement to undertake this study in the first place. My thanks also go to the Liberian refugee women at their camp in Oru Ijebu, Nigeria, and Olivia Bennett, other Panos staff, and Bisi Adeleye-Fayemi for making my meeting these women possible.

In preparing this work for publication, several people offered useful advice and suggestions. I thank Professor Christopher Dandeker, who supervised the original work and read my drafts with enormous interest. I am also grateful to Dr. James Gow, who tirelessly offered his advice and encouragement at various stages. I thank Professor Jack Spence also for his support. To Abiodun and Ronke Alao, I am deeply grateful for their friendship and support over the years, and for putting up with my complaints and ill-timed phone calls. Comfort Ero, Jullyette Ukabiala and Iretiola Badamosi undertook the hard task of editing my work. I appreciate their interest and sacrifice. I am indebted to Kayode Fayemi, for tolerating my endless requests at very short notice. I thank Mr. Gbade Bamisaiye for his assistance in the collection of important data in Nigeria, and Tunde Adebayo for tracing other elusive material.

Gratitude of a special category goes to all members of my family and friends. The privation associated with undertaking research of this kind has been considerably assuaged by the affection and support I have received from them. I count myself very fortunate to have been raised by Tuyi and Lana Olonisakin, who taught me to persevere amidst formidable odds. With my sisters and brothers, I have known the joy of human love. I thank Yem-Yem for her unconditional love and unflinching faith in my ability, and Bisi, Tope and Adesuyi, who have never stopped being proud of me. I am grateful to Ituen Basi, for being a dear friend when few were – in times of need. My thanks also go to my 'extended family', Dokun and Tinu Badamosi, Oye, Dupe, Ifeolu and Ireti. Major Badamosi (Rtd) gave me unlimited use of his library. I am deeply grateful. I thank Kazeem and Kunle for their love and affection. Likewise, Titi and Junior, Ekaette Ikpe, Keji, Emem and Ubong Basi, for their love.

My relationship with some friends suffered during the period I spent on this work. To Jumoke, Wale, Joy and Biola, I express my sincere gratitude for their patience. I am also grateful to Ranti and Yinka, Yemi and Diran. Finally, I owe this book to the love and firm support of my other, perhaps better half, Olaloye. But for his tolerance, patience and understanding through the difficult times and field trips, this book may not have been completed.

Introduction

In recent years, the world has been confronted with the harsh reality of armed intra-state conflict. This class of conflict has been elevated to fore of international agenda as vivid images of the resulting humanitarian tragedy are beamed into millions of homes via the television. Although this is not a new phenomenon, the changes in the global political climate occasioned by the end of the Cold War, account for the prominence now accorded conflict within states. The bipolar system of the Cold War era promoted interest in inter-state and inter-alliance disputes, within which all other conflicts were often contained. The collapse of that system gave way to a different environment. Whilst the threat of nuclear holocaust could be said to have been eliminated, in the same vein, the end of bipolar politics removed what has been described as the 'mantle of cold war stability' from old regional conflicts, world-wide.[1] Armed conflict erupted in parts of Europe and other regional conflicts have easily escalated to very destructive levels. The bulk of these conflicts has occurred within state boundaries.[2] It is these conflicts that have posed a formidable challenge for the international community, in the post-Cold War era.

The dominance of this type of conflict on the international scene places immense demands on the UN. Military operations, mainly peacekeeping ones, in response to internal conflicts have numbered over a score in recent years.[3] The demands for democracy and political pluralism in eastern Europe resulted in violent conflict in some areas, with the former Yugoslavia, perhaps representing the worst example. In other regions, particularly in Africa, the demand for access to power and resources escalated the conflicts in Liberia, Somalia, and Rwanda, amongst others. On the whole, the UN efforts in dealing with these conflicts have produced mixed results. The difficulty it encountered in Somalia, and its reluctance on many occa-

---

[1]   John Q. Blodgett,   'The Future of UN Peacekeeping', *The Washington Quarterly*, (Winter 1991), p. 210.

[2]   *SIPRI Yearbook 1994: World Armaments and Disarmament*, Oxford: Oxford University Press/SIPRI, (1993), pp.81-95; and 1993, p.81.

[3]   See for example, Alan James, 'Internal Peacekeeping: A Dead End for the UN?', *Security Dialogue*, Vol. 24, No. 4, (1993), p.359.

sions to adopt a more severe strategy in dealing with the crisis in former Yugoslavia have been more pronounced.

The experiences of the UN in dealing with such intra-state conflicts have raised three key questions. The first relates to whether traditional peacekeeping, which the UN had successfully applied to many inter-state conflicts, can effectively deal with difficult conflict situations within states. The second concerns the will of the international community to respond to conflicts that do not directly serve their national interests. The third is what will constitute the legal bases for operations other than traditional peakeeping, partticularly those conducted outside UN auspices. The conflicts that have occurred in Africa have pushed these questions further to the fore. The demise of the Cold War had profound consequences for Africa. Although the new global strategic landscape had contributed somewhat to the emergence of a democratic government in South Africa and equally eased other conflicts such as that in Western Sahara, it also marked Africa's loss of strategic importance and a drastic reduction in international attention on the continent. This development is significant because it has occurred at a time when the intensity of local conflicts in Africa has sharply increased. For example, the slow response of the UN to the crisis in Rwanda, where the estimated death toll mounted to over half a million, is an indication of how local conflicts can escalate in the absence of a timely and effective international response. The consequences of these conflicts often spread beyond the affected country, into neighbouring states, most of which face the threat of disintegration from the influx of refugees and related strategic fallout from the escalating chaos. The capability of the many poverty-stricken neighbouring states to contain these conflicts has been seriously questioned.

The civil war that erupted in Liberia in December 1989 served as an early test of the capability of the UN to respond to conflicts that do not impinge on the interest of the majority and the most powerful members of the organization. It also questioned the suitability of the traditional methods of intervening in such conflicts. The Liberian war was among the earliest to highlight the challenges that internal conflicts were to pose for the international conflict resolution machinery in the post-Cold War period. This war resulted in about 200,000 deaths, most of which occurred in the first few months of the conflict. Over half a million refugees fled to neighbouring states within the first year, creating other security problems for these countries. The practice of killing civilians indiscriminately, kidnapping foreign nationals and attacking internationally accepted sanctuaries heightened the intensity of the war. This was compounded by the blurred distinction between combatants and non-combatants in this conflict.[4] The problems for Africa in particular were emphasized by the reluctance of the international community, including Liberia's traditional ally, the United States (US), to intervene decisively in the crisis and stop the carnage. When eventually Liberia's neighbours intervened in the conflict under the auspices of the Economic Community of West African States, the global organisation failed to give legal guidance to the regional body. The conceptual void in peace operations and the absence of a clear legal basis for new operations were still apparent when, seven years after the Liberian mission began, the military intervention in Sierra Leone occurred.

The main argument of this book is that any effort aimed at dealing effectively with internal conflicts of this nature cannot avoid strategies that combine peacekeeping principles with those of enforcement to create peace and that the legal basis for such operations must be revisited. This strategy is termed 'Peace Creation'. The method adopted largely by the UN in the Cold War era, of responding to conflict through diplomacy backed by conventional peacekeeping, appears to be inadequate in the resolution of many of these intra-state conflicts. Consequently, it argues that this strategy of peace creation would be more willingly employed by neighbouring states in the regions within which the conflicts have occurred. This invokes the logic that finding lasting peace to these conflicts would be in the direct interest of neighbouring countries. Thus, regional bodies may employ methods different from those of the UN in resolving local conflicts and in doing so, they are treading in new legal paths. This book examines the character of peace creation, the conditions under which it can be effectively applied, and the legal, political and operations issues that confront a force seeking to create peace. It focuses on two case studies: The Liberian one, where both peacekeeping and enforcement strategies were alternated in an effort to create peace in the intractable civil war in that country, and the Nigerian led intervention in Sierra Leone, which was aimed at reinstating a democratically elected regime, which was ousted in a coup d'etat. It examines these experiences from the perspective of theory and practice.

Although a study of the ECOMOG experience in Liberia and Sierra Leone is very important for the resolution of similar conflicts within Africa, there is also a global relevance. The Liberian conflict, for example, was one of many post-Cold War internal conflicts raging around the world. The eruption of violent intra-state conflicts and the escalation of pre-existing ones have been witnessed in Angola, Burundi, Rwanda, Sudan and Somalia but the trend has not been limited to Africa. A wave of national-

---

4   Details of the Liberian crisis are discussed in chapter three.

ism has swept across other parts of the world.[5] The civil war in the former Yugoslavia appears to have been the most vicious of the conflicts in Europe. As in the case of Liberia, many of these conflicts have illustrated the shortcomings of traditional peacekeeping in dealing with internal conflicts. Traditional peacekeeping theories have been found inadequate as a means of containing these conflicts. There is a search for an effective role for military forces in these conflict situations, and for a new peacekeeping doctrine. A study of the ECOMOG experience is therefore vital. It is necessary to understand the workings and effectiveness of the initiative, in order to assess how best to regulate missions of that kind. Furthermore, the lessons of such missions might be learnt to enhance the prospect of resolving other conflicts both within and outside Africa. Studying the ECOMOG experience will serve to underline the possible correlation between existing theory and practice.

This book comprises seven chapters. The first discusses the development of the peacekeeping concept from the Cold War to the post-Cold War period and the need for a refinement of this concept in the light of changes in the international political climate and the fading relevance of the traditional peacekeeping concept. It highlights the significance of peace creation to the conflict situations of the post-Cold War period and to emerging theories of peacekeeping.

In the second chapter, an analysis of the practical application of peacekeeping during the Cold War period is conducted. The chapter compares the approaches of the UN and regional organizations to peacekeeping and the political, legal and social situations that dictated the kind and level of their response.

The third chapter illustrates the nature of the challenges confronting peacemakers in the post-Cold War period through an analysis of the civil war in Liberia. It discusses the roots of the crisis that eventually led to the collapse of the Liberian and Sierra Leonean states, and how the conduct of the war, created particular difficulty for the resolution efforts.

Chapter Four discusses the evolution of peace creation in response to the Liberian crisis. The legal and political circumstances surrounding the creation of the peace force, the ECOWAS Monitoring Group (ECOMOG) are discussed as well as the effects of the adoption of this strategy on the overall peace process.

The fifth chapter conducts an analysis of the military aspects of the ECOMOG operation. It discusses the planning and execution of the opera-

---

[5]   See Malcolm Keir, 'The Strange Survival of Nationalism' in *The Geographical Magazine*, July 1992, pp. 25-29.

tion and the extent to which the force's operational approach affected the situation on the ground in Liberia and its relationship with the UN, in the bid to fulfil its mandate. In particular, the chapter assesses how command, control, logistics, training and doctrine within the force affected ECOMOG's ability to create peace. Much of the analysis in this chapter relies on data obtained largely from ECOMOG, particularly from interviews with officers and other ranks who had served in ECOMOG at various stages in the operation, and from documentary evidence.

Chapter Six focuses on the social organization of ECOMOG and the extent to which the social backgrounds of the different contingents affected the entire force in terms of cohesion, overall effectiveness, respect for rules of war and ability to create peace. Throughout this chapter, the testimonies of the military personnel who served in ECOMOG during 1994 are used to assess the social and psychological factors that are likely to determine the effectiveness of troops who would be required to create peace. Such testimonies include for example, their perception of their mandate, of other soldiers, and of the local community in which they were operating, and their belief in the mission and the factors which impacted on their morale.

In Chapter Seven, the concluding chapter, an overall assessment of peace creation is conducted. Its features are reassessed, the operational and legal conditions under which such a strategy should be employed are analyzed, and the factors which would determine the success of an operation seeking to create peace are discussed.

CHAPTER ONE

The Changing Nature of the Theoretical Premises of Peacekeeping

INTRODUCTION

The assumptions upon which the concept of peacekeeping was based in the 1950s, which guided most, if not all UN operations until around 1990 are no longer applicable to many present day conflict situations. Events of the last few years have dictated the need to develop a new concept based on the operational environment of the post-Cold War era. The concept of peace creation proposed in this book is designed to address specific conflict situations, which are not amenable to conventional peacemaking approaches, including peacekeeping, whether in its traditional or other forms. This chapter explains the peace creation concept, its relationship to other theories and its significance in the overall conflict resolution process. It begins by defining key terms associated with conflict resolution and describing the different stages of a peacemaking process, using a model. Peace creation is analysed within the overall context of this conflict resolution process. The chapter then traces the evolution of traditional peacekeeping from its inception during the Cold War to the post-Cold War period, when changes in the international order have indicated a need for the modification of this concept. It concludes with a discussion of the relationship between peace creation and other proposed alternative strategies to traditional peacekeeping.

THE PEACEMAKING PROCESS AND DEFINITION OF KEY TERMS

Peacekeeping and enforcement (which together constitute peace creation), along with other strategies, are part of an overall peacemaking process, designed to resolve, or at least manage violent conflict. Peace creation can be better understood through an analysis of the role this activity plays in the process designed to address conflict at different levels. 'Conflict avoidance' and 'conflict prevention' are generally considered the best ways to reduce or manage conflict. The former prevents a situation of conflict from arising by identifying potential sources of conflict and addressing them, whilst the latter prevents undesirable 'conflict behaviour' once a conflict situation has occurred. 'Conflict behaviour', which, may include demonstrations, riots and violent confrontation, is defined by Mitchell as 'actions undertaken by one party in any situation of conflict aimed at the opposing party, with the intention of making that opponent abandon or modify its goals'.[1] Indeed, the entire conflict process is sometimes considered an effort to seek a solution to the conflict.[2] Each party to a conflict utilizes conflict behaviour in ways which will either guarantee victory for it and defeat for the other, or, at least enable it to negotiate from a position of strength. However, apart from the fact that this situation rarely occurs, such a solution would merely suppress the conflict rather than achieve lasting peace.

Peacemaking is fundamentally a diplomatic exercise aimed at achieving a settlement or resolution of conflict, and it begins on the bilateral level. This bilateral process is however a very delicate one and it becomes particularly difficult to handle after the onset of disruptive conflict behaviour. It is common for conflicting parties to experience difficulty in reaching agreement to terminate conflict through bilateral negotiations. In particular, conflicting parties tend to encounter communication problems during direct negotiations, which serve to escalate the conflict rather than produce a settlement.[3] It is not unusual for conflicting parties to make threats and counter-threats as they misinterpret information.[4] Zartman argues that even after the onset of what he describes as a 'mutually hurting stalemate', problems of 'entrapment'or 'sunk costs' often prevent parties who have been engaged in a bitter violent struggle from abandoning their unilateral search for solution.[5] The role of third parties becomes very prominent in this regard, although there is a debate over how successful third parties have been in conflict resolution.[6]

---

[1]   C.R. Mitchell, *The Structure of International Conflict,* (London: Macmillan Press, 1981), p. 29.
[2]   Mitchell, *The Structure of International Conflict,* p. 253
[3]   Mitchell, *Structure of International Conflict,* deals with problems involved in bilateral management extensively. See pp. 165-250. The literature on pre-negotiation and negotiation in conflicts is extensive. See, for example, I. William Zartman, *Ripe for Resolution,* (Oxford: Oxford University Press, 1985)
[4]   Morton Deutsch and Robert Krauss, 'Studies of Interpersonal Bargaining', *Journal of Conflict Resolution* 6, (1952) p. 52
[5]   William Zartman, 'Conflict Reduction: Prevention, Management and Resolution' in Francis M. Deng and William Zartman (eds.). *Conflict Resolution in Africa,* (Washington D.C.: Brookings Institution, 1991), p. 315
[6]   See, for example, Jacob Bercovitch, Theodore Anagnoson, and Donnette Willie, 'Some Conceptual Issues and Empirical Trends in the Study of Successful Mediation in International Relations', *Journal of Peace Research,* Vol. 28, No.l, (1991), pp. 7-17; see also A.B. Fetherston, 'Putting the Peace Back into Peacekeeping: Theory Must Inform Practice', in

Peacemaking initiatives frequently include third parties whose task is to alleviate many of the problems encountered with direct negotiations and facilitate settlement of the conflict. Third-party involvement can occur on a number of platforms namely, adjudication, conciliation, arbitration, good offices, inquiry and mediation. There is no controversy as such over the meanings of these terms. Many analysts simply classify all of them under third party activity, which involves non-coercive attempts at resolving conflict.[7] Some commentators agree that a thin line separates many of these third party activities. For example, Assefa argues that good offices and inquiry could indeed pass for components of mediation.[8] The term 'Good offices' is defined as 'a technique of peaceful settlement of conflict whereby a third party acts as a go-between, transmitter of messages, and provider of meeting place, with the aim of bringing about direct negotiation between the parties'.[9] Inquiry is described as 'a formal and impartial determination of the facts underlying a dispute in which the third-party reports his/her findings to the parties with the aim of clarifying the basis for the conflict'.[10] Merrills considers mediation as falling between good offices and conciliation.[11] In conciliation, the third party may '... investigate the dispute and present the parties with a set of formal proposals for its solution'.[12] As a mediator, the third party is ' ... an active participant, authorised, and indeed expected to advance his own proposals and to interpret, as well as to transmit, each party's proposals to the other'.[13]

A series of hypotheses have gradually evolved on the recipe for successful mediation. Two opposing aspects of theory can be identified within the literature on mediation. The first places responsibility for successful mediation on the mediator, outlining the important skills, and the strategies that must be employed by the mediator.[14] The other argues that the influence of the

---

International Peacekeeping Vol. 1, No. 1, (Spring 1994), pp. 3-20; and A.B. Fetherston, Towards a Theory, of United Nations Peacekeeping (Basingstoke: Macmillan, 1994).

[7] For example, Mitchell, *Structure of International Conflict;* Adam Curie, *Tools for Transformation: A Personal Study,* (Stroud: Hawthorne Press, 1990); and Lillian L. Randolph, *Third Party Settlement of Disputes in Theory and Practice,* (New York: Oceana Publications, 1973), which categorizes third parties as mediators.

[8] Hizkias Assefa, *Mediation of Civil Wars: Approaches and Strategies – The Sudan Conflict,* (Boulder: Westview Press, 1987), p. 4.

[9] Jack C. Plano and Ray Olton, *The International Relations Dictionary,* 3rd Ed., (California: ABC-Clio, 1982).

[10] Ibid.

[11] J.G. Merrills, *International Dispute Settlement,* (Cambridge: Grotius Publications, 1991), p. 27.

[12] Ibid.

[13] Ibid.

[14] For details, see Oran R. Young, *The Intermediaries: Third Parties in International Crisis* (Princeton: Princeton University Press, 1967); and Roger Fisher, *International Mediation: A Working Guide,* (Boston: International Peace Academy, 1978).

mediator in some conflicts is extremely limited, thus, many other factors dictate the success of mediation.[15] Some studies have however attempted to blend these two sides into a general theory.[16] Perhaps a more striking approach to the study of mediation is that of Bercovitch, Anagnoson and Wille, which places empirical investigation within a theoretical framework.[17] The findings of this study indicate that the success or failure of mediation is determined by a combination of mediation strategy, the character of the conflicting parties and the issues involved in a given conflict.[18]

The salient factors of this evolving mediation theory are discussed here under three broad areas. These include the nature and characteristics of the conflicting parties, the conflict itself, and the mediator. Concerning the first, the identity of parties to a conflict and their major representatives must be clearly defined.[19] Such parties must be internally united and an intense personality conflict must be absent within the parties, if a lasting settlement is to be achieved. It has also been argued that the parties' dependence on outside sources for support increases the chances for successful mediation.[20] Concerning the conflict itself, a stalemate is seen as an important precondition for successful mediation.[21] Stalemate is also referred to in some sources as 'power parity'.[22] In addition, the issues at stake in the conflict must not be 'zero-sum'. Rather, they must be multiple, allowing for negotiations. Regarding the last category, the mediator must possess a number of skills, amongst which are: ability to analyze the conflict situation, to communicate effectively, to listen actively, to have empathy and a good sense of timing.[23] Furthermore, the mediator must be impartial, independent of the conflicting parties, possess leverage and enjoy international support.[24] There is a degree of controversy about the general applicability of some of these characteristics to internal conflict situations and about the character of the mediator.[25] Whilst many commentators support the idea of impartial outsiders, others argue that

---

[15] For example, Marvin Ott, 'Mediation as a Method of Conflict Resolution: Two Cases', *International Organization,* 26, (1976), pp. 596-618.

[16] Assefa, for example, utilizes the general theory in his study of the Sudanese Civil War.

[17] Bercovitch et al, 'Some Conceptual Issues'.

[18] Ibid.

[19] George Modelski, 'International Settlement of Internal Wars', in James Rosenau (ed.). *International Aspects of Civil Strife,* (Princeton: Princeton University Press, 1964), p. 142.

[20] Assefa, *Mediation of Civil Wars,* p. 15.

[21] See Modelski, 'International Settlement of Internal War' *p.* 143; and Bercovitch et al., 'Some Conceptual Issues', p. 11.

[22] See, for example, Joseph Himes, *Conflict and Conflict Management,* (Athens: University of Georgia Press, 1980). *p.* 240.

[23] See Paul Wehr. *Conflict Resolution* (Boulder: Westview Press, 1979), pp. 51-52.

[24] See Ott, 'Mediation as a method of Conflict Resolution:' p. 599.

[25] See Assefa, *Mediation of Civil Wars,* p. 23.

mediators from within the conflict area, who are strongly associated with the parties may be better suited for the task. The literature on this category identifies these two types of mediators.[26]

A view that threatens to upset this emerging theory is that which argues that cultural differences in negotiating styles are important determinants of the conduct and outcome of a peacemaking effort. Cohen, for example, argues that there is a marked difference in negotiating behaviour in Western and non-western societies:

> When interlocutors attempt to convey messages across linguistic and cultural barriers, meanings are lost or distorted in the process. What one culture takes to be self-evident, another may find bizarre. Strangely enough, international negotiation has implicitly or explicitly, been excluded by many political scientists from this general tendency.[27]

This position is supported by other sources sceptical about the prospects of those alien to the culture successfully 'acting as third parties, facilitators, or mediators of one sort or another'.[28]

It appears however that this inadequacy would affect the tactical aspect of the mediator's activity rather than the overall mediation strategy. For example, mediators are still expected to be good communicators, with the ability to analyse a conflict situation but in addition to these, they must not neglect to take the cultural background of the parties into consideration. Whilst a mediator might be able to overcome the cultural barrier in this way, a bilateral negotiation process (particularly between adversaries from different cultural backgrounds) may not easily overcome the hurdle.[29] Thus, it is still possible to cautiously apply the general framework of mediation theory to conflict at most levels. The role of the mediator and the level of success of the mediation efforts determine the extent to which other third party activities discussed below, will be useful. This link is not often emphasized by commentators.[30]

---

[26] See Louis Kriesberg, 'Formal and Quasi-Mediators in International Disputes: An exploratory analysis' and Paul Wehr and John Paul Lederach: Mediating Conflicts in Central America in *Journal of Peace Research,* Vol. 28, No.1, (1991).

[27] Raymond Cohen, *Negotiating Across Cultures: Communication Obstacles in International Diplomacy.* (United States Institute of Peace Press, 1991), p. 153.

[28] Kevin Avruch, 'Culture and Conflict Resolution', in Kevin Avruch, Peter W. Black, and Joseph A. Scimecca (eds.), *Conflict Resolution: Cross Cultural Perspectives* (Westport: Greenwood Press, 1991), p. 14.

[29] See Cohen's analogies of the Camp David Accords and the Sino-American talks of the 1970s respectively, in Cohen, *Negotiating Across Cultures.*

[30] There are few exceptions. Fetherston, in 'Putting the Peace Back into Peacekeeping', discusses the need to establish a clear relationship between peacekeeping and peacemaking and peace building.

PEACEKEEPING

As the name suggests, peacekeeping is intended to keep a peace that has been arranged, or about to be concluded.[31] It is essentially a third party activity, which plays a limited, but important role in the peacemaking process. Its role complements that of the mediator. Mitchell aptly describes this term when he states that '... [W]hile peacekeeping activities focus on the behavioural component of any conflict, peacemaking concentrates on goals and attitudes'.[32] Even when conflicting parties agree to pursue their conflict via non-violent means, undesired conflict behaviour may persist because troops that have been engaged in bitter violent conflict may find it difficult to abandon their original course of action. Thus, incidents of cease-fire violations may arise, threatening any peace negotiations. The UN sees peacekeeping as performing two tasks:

> ... To stop or contain hostilities and thus help create conditions in which peace-making can prosper; or to supervise the implementation of an interim or final settlement which has been negotiated by the peacemakers.[33]

Peacekeeping cannot, by itself, terminate, or resolve, a conflict. Rather, it is intended to maintain an atmosphere in which a settlement can be achieved, especially in conflicts where destructive conflict behaviour has set in, or is imminent. Cox describes peacekeeping as 'an activity which requires the use of soldiers, not to fight and win, but to maintain cease-fires, and keep law and order while negotiations are being conducted'[34]

Although activities resembling peacekeeping date back to the inter-war years, the term was only conceptualized in the 1950s. Peacekeeping assumed prominence in international security with the inoperativeness of the enforcement powers outlined in Chapter VII of the UN Charter, empowering the Security Council to take 'such action by air, sea and land forces as may be necessary to maintain or restore international peace and security'.[35] The term came into use when the first United Nations Emergency Force (UNEF1) was established during the Suez crisis in 1956. The concept of this force was outlined by Dag Hammarskjold, the then UN Secretary General. It was to be a neutral, impartial force chosen from amongst nations other than the permanent members of the UN Security Council. It was to be despatched only

---

[31] Peacekeeping has however been used as preventive deployment in the post-Cold War period in Macedonia.

[32] Mitchell, *The Structure of International Conflict*, p. 280.

[33] *The Blue Helmets: A Review of United Nations Peacekeeping*, (New York: UN Department of Public Information, 1990), p. 8.

[34] Arthur M. Cox, *Prospects for Peacekeeping*, (Washington D.C.: Brookings Institution, 1968).

[35] Article 42 of the UN Charter.

with the consent of the conflicting parties and use force only in self-defence. Peacekeeping operations mainly entailed the creation of buffer zones and interposition of troops between warring factions.

As peacekeeping was not contemplated by the drafters of the UN Charter, the legal foundation for peacekeeping operations has been widely debated over the years. Some commentators[36] argue that peacekeeping is intended to support the peacemaking functions outlined in Chapter VI of the UN Charter, which provides that

> International disputes likely to endanger the maintenance of international peace and security can be brought to the attention of the Security Council or General Assembly. The Security Council is expressly mandated to call on the parties to settle their disputes by peaceful means, to recommend appropriate procedures or methods of adjustment and, in addition, to recommend actual terms of a settlement.[37]

The suggestion that the Security Council can organize peacekeeping operations through its powers to arrange pacific settlement of disputes has been rejected by some scholars, arguing for example, that:

> ... The use of force is not entirely excluded from the carrying out of the peace-keeping operations here under consideration, and only by a stretch of the imagination could one tentatively suggest that the competence of the Security Council in the peaceful settlement of disputes includes, if necessary, the use of armed force.[38]

Believing that Chapter VI of the UN Charter does not provide the constitutional basis for peacekeeping operations, some commentators argue that part of the provisions in Chapter VII provide such foundation. Article 40, which permits the Security Council to 'call upon the parties concerned to comply with such provisional measures as it deems necessary or desirable ...' appears to be the one widely held to provide the basis for peacekeeping operations. Others even find Article 41 as providing better legal foundation, from the perspective that peacekeeping, could be described as 'measures not involving the use of armed force', despite the provision that peacekeepers may use force in self defence. In defence of this view, one analyst argued that:

> ... the fact that the force may use its weapons in self-defence affects its status as little as does a civilian's exercise of his right of self defence under municipal law.[39]

---

[36] See, for example, Gareth Evans, *Cooperating for Peace: The Global Agenda for the 1990s and Beyond,* (New South Wales: Alien and Unwin, 1993); and Paul F. Diehl, *International Peacekeeping,* (Baltimore & London: The Johns Hopkins University Press), 1993.

[37] *The Blue Helmets,* p. 3.

[38] Dan Ciobanu, 'The Power of the Security Council to Organize Peace-keeping Operations', in A. Cassese (ed.) *United Nations Peace-keeping: Legal Essays,* (Alphen Aan Den Rijn: Sijhoff & Noordhooff, 1978), p. 19.

[39] G. Schwazenberger, 'Report on Problems of a United Nations Force', cited by Ciobanu, 'The Power of the Security Council to Organize Peacekeeping Operations', p. 18.

Another debate surrounds the applicability of any part of Chapter VII, in the absence of the implementation of Article 43 on the provision of armed forces and Article 47, on the establishment of a Military Staff Committee.[40] However, the UN itself admits that peacekeeping operations 'fall short of the provisions of Chapter VII [but] at the same time go beyond purely diplomatic means or those described in Chapter VI'.[41]

The UN makes a clear distinction between peacemaking and peacekeeping. Peacemaking, is primarily a diplomatic activity conducted by a mediator or third party while peacekeeping is essentially conducted by the military, to support the peacemaker's efforts. Peacemaking only transcends this level when diplomacy fails to achieve the settlement of conflict. The use of force is then considered, after all other options have failed.[42] Peacekeeping, however, does not always entail the use of soldiers alone. Sometimes, civilians are used on peacekeeping missions, to accompany military men, as observers.[43] Peace Observation in this regard is often considered as part of peacekeeping, rather than a separate activity.[44]

The changes in the international political system following the end of the Cold War have essentially limited the relevance of the peacekeeping activity described above as a tool for conflict resolution, generating a debate over what the activity should now entail. In a new era where the features of many conflicts have deviated from those where this type of peacekeeping was effectively applied, a certain degree of confusion presently surrounds the meaning of peacekeeping. Peace operations have frequently come to entail mine clearance, election monitoring, delivery of humanitarian aid, amongst other things. This expanded role of peacekeepers in conflicts world wide led to the advent of new terminologies, among them, 'wider peacekeeping', 'second generation peacekeeping operations', 'peace enforcement', 'strategic peacekeeping' and 'peace support operations'. The difference between

---

[40] For a discussion of this, see Rosalyn Higgins, 'A General Assessment of United Nations Peacekeeping' in A. Cassese (ed.), *United Nations Peacekeeping*, pp. 1-12; See also, Rosalyn Higgins, 'The New United Nations and Former Yugoslavia', in *International Affairs*, 69, 3 (1993), pp. 465-68; and in *United Nations Peacekeeping 1946-1967*, Vol. I (Oxford: Oxford University Press for Royal Institute of International Affairs, 1969), pp. 260-73.

[41] *The Blue Helmets*, p. 5.

[42] Ibid.

[43] For detailed discussions of cases where the UN dispatched civilians as part of different commissions to observe cease-fires during the Cold War, see David W. Wainhouse, *International Peace Observation: A History and Forecast*, (Baltimore: Johns Hopkins University Press, 1966), pp. 221-41, 293-323, 357-73.

[44] Whilst David Wainhouse in *International Peace Observation*, dealt largely with Peace Observation as distinct from peacekeeping, he later used the term peacekeeping, '... in the generic sense to cover both peacekeeping forces and peace observation missions ...' in *International Peacekeeping at the Crossroads: National Support Experience and Prospects*, (Baltimore & London: The Johns Hopkins University Press), 1973.

peacekeeping and other military operations has become dangerously blurred in the post-Cold War era. The peacekeeping concept is stretched to include activities that were not previously classified as part of the activity conceptualized during the Cold War, which, is now commonly referred to as traditional peacekeeping or first generation peacekeeping.

There have been a number of attempts to make a clear distinction between traditional and second generation peacekeeping. Many post-Cold War peacekeeping, and indeed, some specific operations during the Cold War, are described by some analysts as second generation peacekeeping. In Ratner's analysis of the major differences between both, the former performs a monitoring and inter-positional role, whilst the latter is concerned with 'operations responsible for overseeing or executing the political solution of an interstate or internal conflict, with the consent of the parties'. Abi-Saab also states that:

> The new peacekeeping is very different in its instrumentalisation as part of a larger strategy. ... it is ideally part and parcel of a peacemaking package where there is an agreement, or at least an agreed framework for the settlement of dispute along certain lines.[45]

However, consent is a strong feature of both types of peacekeeping. Ratner points out that

> '... consent remains the sine qua non of peacekeeping, and any mission that includes warfighting ... is operating under a different set of conceptual and practical assumptions and constraints'[46]

Consent would thus differentiate peacekeeping from peace enforcement or other military operations. The term 'peace support operations' would however envelope peacekeeping, combat operations, and other tasks which may include humanitarian aid.[47]

PEACE CREATION

The strategy of peace creation, which is examined in this book, combines peacekeeping with peace enforcement in the bid to control violent conflict. The specific type of peacekeeping that this would entail is discussed in later

---

[45] Georges Abi-Saab, 'United Nations Peacekeeping Old and New: An Overview of the Issues' in Daniel Warner (ed.) *New Dimensions of Peacekeeping,* (Dordrecht: Martinus Nijhoff Publishers 1995), p. 7.

[46] Steven R. Ratner, *The New UN Peacekeeping: Building Peace in Lands of Conflict After the Cold War,* (London: Macmillan, 1995), p. 18.

[47] For more on peace support operations, See, for example, Dennis J. Quinn, 'Peace Support Operations: Definitions and Implications' in Dennis J. Quinn (ed.). *Peace Support Operations and the U.S. Military,* (Washington DC: National Defense University Press, 1994).

chapters. At this point, it is necessary to focus attention on the definition of peace enforcement. The term is sometimes used interchangeably with enforcement which is described as :

> The use of coercive measures to maintain international peace and security, carried out with the authorization of the Security Council, and based on measures set out in Chapter VII of the UN Charter.[48]

Observers who make a distinction between both terms argue that 'enforcement, even for valid reasons, is not "peaceful".'[49] Such a distinction is irrelevant for the purposes of this book, since both activities may ultimately entail the use of force. However, the above definition would generate the kind of debate surrounding the legal basis for peacekeeping, given its emphasis on Chapter VII of the UN charter. To avoid the sort of confusion that now surrounds the description of peacekeeping, this chapter offers a characterization of peace enforcement, which will provide the framework for the analysis of peace creation. The analysis of peace creation in Liberia in later chapters will further put the term into its proper perspective.

PEACE ENFORCEMENT

Although peacemaking is primarily a diplomatic effort to bring about peace, which is sometimes supported by peacekeeping, when this fails to achieve peace or alleviate human suffering, the means of making peace may be fortified through enforcement. Peace enforcement is the second level of peacemaking, which is employed to bring about peace by literally forcing the adversaries in a conflict to the negotiating table when the diplomatic option has been exhausted. Peace may be enforced via political, economic or military means. Enforcing peace politically may take the form of international condemnation of the actions of the principal aggressors, and economically, it is commonly carried out through trade sanctions. Both options are often ineffective or slow to take the desired effect. This book is more concerned with peace enforcement through the use of military force.

Making peace through peace enforcement is an option of last resort and certain conditions appear to influence its adoption. It would appear that some or all of these conditions have to be met before any peace enforcement action can occur or be granted legitimacy. One is a situation where conflicting parties do not favour peace at all notwithstanding diplomatic pressures. This could be due to the absence of a mutually hurting stalemate or the failure of the

---

[48] Fetherston, 'Putting the Peace Back into Peacekeeping', p. 5.
[49] Ibid., p. 21.

peacemaker to notice the occurrence of such a stalemate prior to the escalation of the conflict. Secondly, the parties may renege on an agreement to pursue the conflict via peaceful means, which is often the case. Another rather important factor that often precipitates peace enforcement as a peacemaking strategy with a measure of legitimacy is the extent of human suffering resulting from a conflict. The human and material costs of a conflict may be so great that the international community might not be able to ignore the conflict or to wait for a mutually hurting stalemate to occur. Peace enforcement is thus embarked upon in order to alleviate the human suffering caused by a violent conflict.

It should however be stressed that the enforcement of peace in this regard is not merely geared to guarantee passage of humanitarian aid, but is essentially conceived as part of an overall peacemaking effort. Humanitarian relief is extremely limited if it is offered outside the context of overall peacemaking. It is not uncommon that enforcement actions are viewed largely in terms of their contribution to disaster relief.[50] Nonetheless, the view that ensuring humanitarian aid should not be seen in isolation of a larger peacemaking effort, is gaining wider acceptance in the aftermath of the UN/US intervention in Somalia. Clarke and Herbst for example, argue that:

> The distinction between humanitarian intervention and nation-building that is central to so many critiques of the Somalia operation and intervention is problematic.[51] ... The international community should discard the illusion that one can intervene in a country beset by widespread civil violence without affecting domestic politics and without including a nation-building component ... .Unless development aid and external assistance address the long-term political and economic implications of an intervention, it is doomed.[52]

Certain elements tend to distinguish peace enforcement from any other strategy of peacemaking. The first is limited consent. The consent of the target-state is not necessarily obtained for an enforcement operation.[53] This factor, coupled with the application of force beyond self-defence, precludes an activity from the traditional, or indeed, second generation peacekeeping category, and helps to differentiate peacekeeping from peace enforcement. Secondly, in employing military force to bring about peace, the impartiality of such a force would need to be ensured. The assumption here is that this can

---

[50] See, for example, Leon Gordenker and Thomas G. Weiss, 'The Use of Soldiers and Peacekeepers in Coping with Disasters', and John Mackinlay, 'The Role of Military Forces in a Humanitarian Crisis', both in Leon Gordenker and Thomas G. Weiss, (eds.) *Soldiers, Peacekeepers and Disasters,* (London: Macmillan, 1991), Chapters 1&2.

[51] Walter Clarke and Jeffrey Herbst, 'Somalia and the Future of Humanitarian Intervention', *Foreign Affairs,* Vol. 75, No.2, March/April 1996, p. 74.

[52] Ibid. p. 78.

[53] The legal issues surrounding this are discussed in Chapter Four.

be done by ensuring that the same rules apply to all sides. For example, in denying access to all ports, such access must be denied to all the parties to a conflict. Such a display of impartiality may serve to highlight the exceptional quality of this activity in relation to other combat operations.

Thirdly, whilst force may be used on warring parties to secure or deny access to routes, and to ensure the flow of humanitarian aid, care should be taken to secure the confidence of the local populace by maintaining a non-threatening outlook. Any force that intimidates the masses may ultimately fail to create peace. This is the one factor distinguishing a force which has been forced to create peace from a force of occupation, which, is intervening for selfish interests. Thus, peace enforcement can be recognized where a force is militarily ensuring humanitarian aid, forcibly disarming combatants to put an end to violence, in order to create a conducive atmosphere for negotiations. This must be done with due consideration of the civilian populace, which the force is seeking to rescue.

Lastly, an operation to enforce peace must be conducted by adequately armed forces and by organizations or states that can wield power greater than the combined ability of the warring factions, and have the resources to back up such a position of strength. Peace enforcement, like peacekeeping, is also dependent on the wishes of the peacemaker, who is continuing with negotiations to move conflicting parties to the negotiating table. Thus, in conducting these operations, the military must take its cue from the politicians, the third parties who are overseeing the peace process. A great limitation of peace enforcement (which is discussed elsewhere in this book), is its inability to generate real peace. Its sole function is the termination of violence.

PEACE CREATION AND THE PEACEMAKING MODEL

The model of the peacemaking process presented in this book is illustrated by Figure 1.1 below. It is based on the premise that if the destructive intra-state conflicts that have become the hallmark of the post-Cold War period are to be resolved or at least controlled then any peacemaking effort must be prepared to combine both strategies of peacekeeping and peace enforcement. The process of combining both strategies is referred to as 'peace creation'. Figure 1.1[54] shows that when third party mediation fails to resolve a conflict situation, the outbreak of violent conflict may not be prevented. Where intense mediation is then successful in bringing about an agreement, peacekeepers are deployed to monitor the peace agreement. The failure of such mediation may

---

[54] The ideas for this figure were obtained from Ken Aldred et al., *European Security: Discussion Document* (The British American Information Council – BASIC), Nov. 1992.

result in continued violence and human suffering. It is at this stage that the mediator employs force to stop the human suffering and related atrocities, and to create a peaceful atmosphere. Success results in the negotiation of a peace agreement and the deployment of peacekeepers, to maintain the peaceful environment. Failure would mean further mediation efforts and the process begins again from level **G**. The process from **F** to **L** describes peace creation. The concept (i.e. peace creation) is highlighted by the ability to cross from the peace enforcement phase in **J**, back to peacekeeping in **H**, after the termination of violence in **K** and peace agreement in **L**. Whether the force which keeps the peace beyond **L** would be the same as that used in **J**, and whether the mediator would enjoy the same credibility it did previously, after **M**, are some of the issues to be examined in the Liberian case.

Peace creation here is not taken to mean the existence of lasting peace or a complete resolution of the conflict. It refers to a situation where violent conflict behaviour has been terminated, human suffering reduced and mediators are actively working with conflicting parties toward the pursuit of conflict through non-violent means, and its eventual settlement. For this situation to exist, this book argues that peacekeeping and peace enforcement cannot individually, or indeed, jointly, achieve this. Both strategies, along with peacemaking must be seen as interdependent. Peacekeeping on its own cannot terminate the violence. Although peace enforcement is capable of terminating the violence and easing human suffering, it can easily be misconstrued as war, and military occupation, thus a switch to peacekeeping would serve to reassure belligerents and the local population that the use of force was intended purely for humanitarian and peaceful reasons.

The interdependent relationship between the political and military components of the peacemaking process (i.e. peacemaking and peace creation) is illustrated in Figure 1.1. Upon the failure of initial diplomatic peacemaking efforts, the mediator is dependent on the military for the creation of an atmosphere in which negotiations can be conducted. Likewise, military operations aimed at keeping the peace, or enforcing it, cannot by themselves bring peace. A lot is dependent on the mediator's ability to obtain the agreement of conflicting parties to pursue their conflict through non-violent means. Effective peacekeeping operations are dependent on a well coordinated diplomatic peacemaking effort, which is itself dependent on a controlled impasse or a mutually hurting stalemate. However, cultural, economic or other societal factors determine whether or not a mutually hurting stalemate should be allowed to occur naturally. Yet, peacemaking cannot be successful without the effective termination of violence. Even when the parties desire peace, violence may persist. The mediator will depend on the military to establish a peaceful environment. If a peace agreement has been reached (after a

Figure 1.1

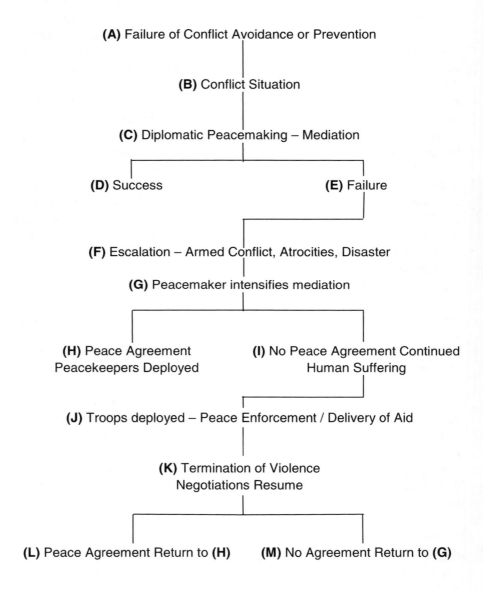

(A) Failure of Conflict Avoidance or Prevention

(B) Conflict Situation

(C) Diplomatic Peacemaking – Mediation

(D) Success   **(E)** Failure

(F) Escalation – Armed Conflict, Atrocities, Disaster

(G) Peacemaker intensifies mediation

(H) Peace Agreement   **(I)** No Peace Agreement Continued
Peacekeepers Deployed   Human Suffering

(J) Troops deployed – Peace Enforcement / Delivery of Aid

(K) Termination of Violence
Negotiations Resume

(L) Peace Agreement Return to **(H)**   **(M)** No Agreement Return to **(G)**

controlled impasse), the military would act as peacekeepers. But if there is no impasse and hence no agreement, then these military forces must of necessity be peace enforcers, who will need to terminate conflict behaviour to create an atmosphere conducive for negotiations. Throughout however, the military branch takes its cue from the political: the mediator, who may be an individual or an organization.

An operation may fulfil all the above conditions, and still fail to achieve the desired goal of either successfully keeping the peace or creating it. Other factors govern the extent to which operations fail or succeed. The discussion in this chapter is aimed at giving adequate description of a peacemaking process and strategies involved in the process. Its aim is not the analysis of the shortcomings of these strategies or the analysis of the conditions under which they can best function. These are issues for subsequent chapters. The rest of this chapter will focus on creating an understanding of the factors that have threatened to render traditional peacekeeping irrelevant and highlighted the need for other strategies such as peace creation.

THE EVOLUTION OF PEACEKEEPING FROM THE COLD WAR ERA

There was a general understanding during the Cold War years, of what the concept of peacekeeping entailed. The concept, as outlined by the UN Secretary-general in 1956 had been somewhat broadened with slight modifications by the late 1980s. James summed up the most striking features of peacekeeping in four distinct categories namely personnel, values, functions and context.[55] Although civilians could perform quasi-military peacekeeping tasks, peacekeeping was (and still is) seen primarily, as a military task.[56] The values that distinguish peacekeeping from any other military activity, according to James, consist of impartiality and light arms for use only in self-defence.[57] Peacekeeping was seen to perform the functions of defusing a crisis and maintaining stability. Peacekeeping operations were found to occur in four contexts. First, a peacekeeping force must be deployed by a qualified authority which may be an international organization, an ad hoc group of states, or 'a single acceptable state'.[58] Second, provision had to be made for men and

---

[55] James, *'Peacekeeping in International politics'* pp. 1-2. Although James' work is one of the most prominent in this aspect of peace keeping, others have covered similar issues. See, for example. Henry Wiseman, 'Peacekeeping and the Management of International Conflict', Background Paper No. 15, Canadian Institute for International Peace and Security, September 1987; Henry Wiseman (ed.). *Peacekeeping, Appraisals and Proposals,* (Pergamon Press, 1983).

[56] James, *Peacekeeping in International Politics,* pp. 1-2.

[57] Ibid. p. 3.

[58] Ibid. p. 6

funds. Third, and very crucial was host-state consent without which a force could not be deployed. Lastly, peacekeeping was to take place with the political co-operation of all the immediate parties to the conflict.[59] This characterization of peacekeeping has, however, been thrown into disarray, following the end of the Cold War as discussed below.

The uniqueness of the peacekeeping concept generated discussion around the political, legal, military and social implications of the activity. Legal and political commentary for example, focused on basic issues such as the Cold War politics and the failure of the collective security system; the legal foundation for peacekeeping operations; preventive diplomacy and the exclusion of the great powers from participation in peacekeeping; the need to obtain the consent of a host state before the deployment of a peacekeeping force and the minimal use of force, which differentiated the activity from standard military operations. Some commentators favoured the establishment of international peacekeeping or police forces and examined the possibility of maintaining such forces on a permanent basis. Cox, for example, analysed this concept and the possibility of conducting peacekeeping operations at the regional level.[60] Frye saw the success of UNEF1 as paving the way for the development of peacekeeping forces. He however considered some of the political and financial problems likely to confront such efforts.[61] Pearson, then Canadian Foreign minister and one of the architects of UNEF, also discussed a machinery, under which the concept of this UN force could be made permanent.[62] Against a background of the failure of the collective security mechanism in the UN Charter and the partial success of the 'Uniting for Peace' resolution. Urquhart discussed 'interim measures', which could be developed to improve the efficiency of the peacekeeping system.[63] In general, peacekeeping was assessed from the point of view of inter-state politics and conflicts.

Comments on the military aspects of peacekeeping centred around organizational, training requirements and logistics issues. Lumsden, for example remarked that

> ... Almost no account is being taken of the fact that to use military force as a third party to a conflict, with the task of producing more suitable conditions for the resolution of that conflict, is a task of infinitely greater subtlety and magnitude than that of traditional military situations. Such a task may therefore require quite different conceptions of strat-

---

[59] Ibid.

[60] Cox, *Prospects for Peacekeeping.*

[61] William R. Frye, *A United Nations Force*, New York: Oceana Press, 1957).

[62] Lester B. Pearson, 'Force for the UN', *Foreign Affairs,* 35, April 1957, pp. 395-404.

[63] Brian E. Urquhart, 'United Nations Peace Forces and the Changing United Nations: An Institutional Perspective', *!nlernaitonal Organization* vol. xvii No. 2, Spring 1963.

egy and tactics; quite different kinds of personnel and training; quite different kinds of activity.[64]

Bowman and Fanning thoroughly analysed the logistics problems of international peacekeeping forces, using the UN experience in UNEF and the Congo as case studies.[65] Rikhye also provided a useful insight on the operational difficulties faced by UN forces. He analysed the impact of a variety of factors such as transportation, training, differences in national policies, rotation patterns, command and control, etc. on UN operations.[66] Using the Suez, Congo and Cyprus crises as case studies, Boyd wrote extensively on the military aspects of peacekeeping operations. These included problems of force creation, composition and organization, command and control, and military readiness.[67] A substantial part of this work also discussed the political and legal basis of these operations. Fabian's work analysed the problems involved in mobilizing the required human and material resources for UN peacekeeping, using the experience of a few countries that had participated in UN operations.[68] Boyd's and Fabian's works were reviewed amongst others, by James Stegenga, who argued that no amount of planning, training and preparedness for UN peacekeeping would remove the inherent political obstacles to such operations.[69] Erskine's work provides first hand account of the operational issues that confronted the UN Interim Force in Lebanon (UNIFIL)[70] Mackinlay's work is significant for its in-depth military assessment of peacekeeping operations in the Middle-east, including the Multinational Force and Observers in Sinai, in which he participated.[71]

The ability of peacekeepers to effectively project the peacekeeping values, which were inconsistent with the traditional military values to which they were accustomed formed an interesting part of the discussion of peacekeeping

---

[64] Malvern Lumsden, 'Research on International Peacekeeping Forces: A Scanning of Institutions', in *Journal of Peace Research*. No. 2 1966, pp. 194-196.

[65] Bowman and James E. Fanning, 'The Logistics Problems of a UN Military Force', *International Organisation,* Vol. XVII, No. 2, 1963, pp. 355-376; Similar issues were also discussed in P. Bloomfield, *international Military Forces*.

[66] Major-General I. J. Rikhye, 'Preparation and Training of United Nations Peace-keeping Forces', *Adelphi Paper* No. 9, IISS, 1964.

[67] James M. Boyd, *United Nations Peace-Keeping Operations: A Military and Political Appraisal'* Praeger Special Studies in International Politics and Public Affairs, (Praeger Publishers, 1971).

[68] Larry Fabian, *Soldiers Without Enemies: Preparing the United Nations for Peacekeeping,* (Washington D.C: The Brookings Institution, 1971).

[69] James A. Stegenga, 'Peacekeeping: Post-Mortems or Preview?' *International Organization,* 27, Summer 1973 see p. 384.

[70] Emmanuel A. Erskine, *Mission with UNIFIL: An African Soldier's Reflections,* (London: Hurst and Company, 1989).

[71] John Mackinlay, *The Peacekeepers: An Assessment of peacekeeping Operations at the Arab-Israel Interface* (London: Unwin Hyman, 1989).

during the Cold War. The peacekeeping values involved the minimum use of force, impartiality, and submission to international command.[72] Of direct relevance to this is Janowitz's concept of the constabulary model of armed forces:[73]

> ... The military establishment becomes a constabulary force when it is continuously prepared to act, committed to the minimum use of force, and seeks viable international relations rather than victory. ... The constabulary force concept encompasses the entire range of military power and organization.[74]

Segal and others also conducted a study examining how American soldiers in a peacekeeping mission and their families perceive the peacekeeping role.[75] Peacekeeping had a commonly accepted characterization and attention was focused on improving this activity to cope with conflict in the international environment of the time. However, peacekeeping has been transformed by events in the international community after the Cold War.

THE POST-COLD WAR DECLINE OF TRADITIONAL PEACEKEEPING

The demise of the Cold War ushered in great optimism that the United Nations would be transformed into an effective tool, for the maintenance of international peace and security. The occurrence of the Gulf War was a clear indication of the new-found strength and unity of the UN Security Council. It was thus envisaged that most regional conflicts would be amenable to mediation supported by peacekeeping, and that new conflicts would be reduced, given the end of bipolar rivalry. Optimism that the UN could now competently handle international security issues was evident even before the Gulf war. The firmness shown by the UN in responding to the Iraqi invasion of Kuwait simply reinforced this optimism, prompting remarks that:

> THE EVENTS OF summer 1990 in the Persian Gulf region, and in particular the August 25 decision of the United Nations Security Council to authorize the use of "minimum force" to put teeth in a blockade of Iraq and Kuwait, dramatize the fact that the United Nations is now politically in a position – for the first time in its 45-year history – to em-

---

[72] These issues are dealt with in a series of articles in J.A. Van Doom (ed.) *Armed Forces and Society,* (The Hague: Mouton, 1968); See also. Henry V. Dicks, 'National Loyalty, Identity and the International Soldier', in Bloomfield, *The Power fo Keep Peace,* pp. 133-51.

[73] Morris Janowitz, *The Professional Soldier* (Glencoe, Ill: Free Press, 1960); also, in Van Doom(ed.), *Armed Forces and Society.*

[74] Janowitz, *The Professional Soldier,* p. 418.

[75] David R. Segal and Mady Wechsler Segal et al., *Peacekeepers and Their Wives: American Participation in the Multinational Force and Observers,* (Westport and London: Greenwood Press, 1993). The experience of US soldiers in the Multinational Force and Observers (MFO) in the Sinai was used as case study.

ploy all of its mandated authority in the advancement of international peace and security.[76]

Much of the immediate post-Cold War commentary reflected this optimism. The UN was seen by many watchers of international politics to have acquired the political capability and institutional resolve to control conflicts worldwide. Analysts suggested wide-ranging scenarios in which the UN could now respond to conflict and the wide variety of operations it may freely conduct. It was suggested that the peacekeeping mandate of the organization be widened to include response to situations requiring disaster relief, drug interdiction, counter-terrorism, amongst others.[77] Emphasis was also placed on conflict prevention roles by the UN. The UN itself, produced a list of plausible new peacekeeping roles for the organization, similar to those described above.[78] Rikhye analysed the potential problems and feasibility of carrying out a variety of such operations.[79]

Some analysts during this period predicted the possibility of the use of force by the UN, or at least a show of force, to deter obstinate parties. Mackinlay, for example, foresaw that UN peacekeeping forces may be deployed to new dangerous territories to render assistance to an interim government, or 'guarantee the delivery of humanitarian support to a disaster area' and that they would have to use force.[80] He asserted that 'in any of these roles, peacekeepers deployed in their familiar reactive mode may face awkward situations which demand more than a turning of the cheek'.[81] Hagglund suggested the use of heavy weapons in peacekeeping operations if only to deter a threatening party. He argued that 'the best weapons in peacekeeping are long-range, direct-fire weapons, such as guns, armoured cars, heavy machine guns, and missiles, with pin-point accuracy to be sure not to miss the target'[82] Hagglund envisaged UN enforcement operations under Chapter VII which should be conducted by great power troops, which should then hand over to the 'less gallant peacekeepers'.[83] Even Urquhart, who previously opposed the use of

---

[76] Blodgett, 'The Future of UN Peacekeeping', p. 207.

[77] A consensus of opinion along these lines was indicated by Brian Urquhart, 'Beyond the Sheriffs Posse', *Survival,* 32. May-June 1990, pp. 25-31; and Aleksandr M. Belonogov' 'Soviet Peacekeeping Proposals', *Survival* 32, May-June 1990, pp. 206-211.

[78] UN *Doc. A/44/301,* 9th June 1989 – Comprehensive Review of the Whole Question of Peacekeeping Operations in All Their Aspects, Report of the Special Committee on Peacekeeping Operations.

[79] Indar Jit Rikhye, *The Future of Peacekeeping,* Occasional Paper No. 2, (New York: International Peace Academy, 1989), pp. 14-27.

[80] John Mackinlay, 'Powerful Peacekeepers', *Survival,* 32, May-June 1990, p. 243.

[81] Ibid.

[82] Gustav Hagglund 'Peacekeeping in a Modern War Zone' *Survival* 32 May-June 1990, p. 239.

[83] Ibid. p. 240.

heavy weapons by the UN[84] had by 1990 modified this position, favouring improvement of the armament and equipment of UN troops and perhaps even including major power units in operations.[85] He however maintained that there is a distinction between 'the show of strength and the use of force'.[86] Nonetheless, some advised that caution should be exercised in widening UN peacekeeping role, stressing that the distinction between peacekeeping and enforcement would become blurred.[87]

With few exceptions, opinions in the immediate aftermath of the Cold War did not reflect the need for any radical change in the traditional peacekeeping concept despite accurately predicting the effects of the political changes. Furthermore, whilst many envisaged a broader scope of UN peacekeeping missions, this was not always accompanied by an in-depth analysis of the concept of these new operations. They were still largely perceived as belonging to the traditional peacekeeping category. James, for example, based his conceptualization of peacekeeping on several case studies, most of which occurred in the Cold War Era.[88] Rikhye et al mostly analysed the lessons of peacekeeping since its inception.[89] The latter work expressed the need to extend the same principles to cases of internal conflict, naval peacekeeping, and the improvement of the operational performance of UN peacekeepers. In particular, it argued that peacekeeping is only a small part of a wide peacemaking effort.[90]

The failure to immediately analyze a new concept was perhaps influenced by the fact that the peacekeeping operations authorized in the immediate post-Cold War period involved traditional peacekeeping principles, and they enjoyed a measure of success. The conditions surrounding these conflicts were very similar to those existing in the Cold War period. These operations included the UN Good Offices Mission in Afghanistan and Pakistan (UNGOMAP), which monitored the withdrawal of Soviet troops from Afghanistan; the UN Iran-Iraq Military Observer Group (UNIIMOG) whose task was to supervise the cease-fire between Iran and Iraq; the UN Angola

---

[84] Brian Urquhart, *A Life in Peace and War.* (New York: Harper and Row, 1987), p. 178.

[85] Urquhart, 'Beyond the Sheriffs Posse', p. 202.

[86] Ibid.

[87] Johan Jurgen Hoist, 'Enhancing Peacekeeping Operations', *Survival* 32 May-June 1990, pp. 264-275.

[88] James, *Peacekeeping in International Politics.*

[89] Indar Jit Rikhye and Kjell Skjelbaek (eds.), *The United Nations and Peacekeeping: Results, Limitations and Prospects: The Lessons of Forty Years of Experience,* (London: Macmillan, 1990).

[90] Ibid. See Chapter 11 on 'The Future of Peacekeeping', by Indar Jit Rikhye; and also Chapter 4 – 'UN Peacekeeping: Expectations, Limitations and Results: Forty Years of Mixed Experience', by Kjell Skjelsbaek.

Verification Mission (UNAVEM)[91] responsible for monitoring Cuban and South African troop withdrawal; and the UN Transitional Assistance Group (UNTAG) deployed to Namibia, to oversee the transfer of power from South Africa to a democratically elected government of Namibia, and to maintain law and order during the elections. All of these early post-Cold War peacekeeping missions were largely observer missions, which hardly deviated from the traditional method of peacekeeping. It was therefore easy to conclude that this would be the trend in the post-Cold War period.

Urquhart and Mackinlay were amongst the analysts who foresaw a conceptual problem and the need to redefine the peacekeeping concept. Urquhart predicted that the increased demand for peacekeeping would require modifications in at least two major areas. One concerned sovereignty, which was likely to become an issue as UN operations may have to conduct operations without the consent of parties. Where the mission is for 'the general good', he argued, 'some curtailment of national sovereign authority' would be required.[92] The question of sovereignty would now gain attention as the UN responds to more intra-state conflicts. Urquhart suggested that this problem could be controlled by negotiating agreements such as the Status of Force Agreement at every stage.[93] The second main area for Urquhart was the use of force and 'whether a greater latitude and capacity to use force is desirable and necessary.'[94] Mackinlay observed that whilst suggestions were being made for enhancing the potential of the peacekeeper, 'there is a disturbing gap in the train of logic so far'.[95] He further stated that:

> ... There is still a lack of thought as to how this enhancement will be put to use by the troops standing in the epicentre of the future conflict scenario. As things stand, there is still at least a balance between the capabilities of the buffer zone peace-keeper and the concept for his operations. Unless an attempt is made to create a similar balance for the enhanced peace force of the future, it is likely that a concept for their operations will be 'hot-drafted' in theatre, and the lessons of military aid to the civil power re-learnt in a messy fashion.[96]

Subsequent events confirmed the need for a critical re-examination of the responses to conflict. The intra-state conflicts to which the UN found itself responding were a marked contrast from the mainly inter-state conflicts it dealt with in the previous era. Parties to these conflicts failed to respect any of the long standing rules of war. The lack of regard for agreements height-

---

[91] The Angolan situation later changed drastically, making it impossible to effectively apply traditional peacekeeping principles.
[92] Urquhart, 'Beyond the Sheriff's Posse', pp. 200-1.
[93] Ibid. p. 201.
[94] Ibid. p. 200.
[95] Mackinlay, 'Powerful Peacekeepers', p. 247.
[96] Ibid. p. 248.

ened indiscriminate killings, creating casualties amongst both civilian populations and peacekeepers. The consent and co-operation of conflicting parties could no longer be guaranteed. Peacekeepers in Cambodia and Somalia for example, were severely punished for carrying light arms and maintaining a small presence.[97] Thus, traditional peacekeeping principles proved inadequate for dealing with these conflicts. The confusion which began to surround peacekeeping operations prompted remarks that the 'apparent early success in dealing with the problems of the post-Cold War era has been largely illusory, although some situations (for example, Cambodia) have been greatly ameliorated.'[98] The chaos generated by many conflicts would perhaps offer a less dramatic view of Van Creveld's work, which predicted new trends in conflict with drastic implications for societies.[99]

Further developments began to reflect the need for a refining of the concept of peacekeeping, to suit the changes in the international community. Traditional peacekeeping became difficult to conduct without addressing the humanitarian disasters resulting from many of these conflicts. Some commentators admitted for example, that '... some situations, like that in Yugoslavia, call for a less strict interpretation of the traditional conditions governing UN operations'.[100] It was also recognized that:

> with the end of the cold war, have come situations of internal conflict – civil wars, regional and ethnic conflicts, failed nation-states – which confront the international community with the need to address simultaneously, a wide range of political, security, humanitarian and even developmental problems. ... So a whole new lexicon is being formulated: A glossary of terms which attempt to define the new and different political and military functions that have emerged in recent years.[101]

The challenges posed by the situations in Cambodia, Somalia, and former Yugoslavia also led to the assertion that '... other recent UN military operations are so different in scope and mandate that they can be characterized as "peacekeeping" only by stretching analytical categories to the breaking

---

[97] UN peacekeepers were killed at random in Somalia, and kidnapped in Cambodia. Michael W. Doyle discusses the initial bleakness of the UN operation in Cambodia and the attacks on UNTAC, in *UN Peacekeeping in Cambodia – UNTAC's Civil Mandate,* (Boulder, Colorado, 1995), p. 13. See also, Janet E. Heininger, *Peacekeeping in Transition,* (New York: Twentieth Century Fund, 1994).

[98] Edward Marks, 'UN Peacekeeping in a Post-Cold War World', in Edward Marks and William Lewis, *Triage for Failing States,* McNair Paper 26, (Washington D.C.: Institute for National Strategic Studies, National Defense University, 1994), p. 6.

[99] Martin Van Creveld, *On Future War* (London: Brassey's UK, 1991), see in particular, Chapter Seven – Future War, pp. 192-223.

[100] Advisory Council on Peace and Security, *What is Peace Worth to Us? : The United Nations after the Cold War,* (The Hague, May 1992), p. 17.

[101] Admiral John Anderson, Address at Peacekeeping Symposium – *Peacekeeping: Norms. Policy and Process,* Centre for International and Strategic Studies, York University, 9-14 May 1993.

point'.[102] Ruggie called for a definition of 'the new domain of collective military activity that lies between peacekeeping and enforcement ...'[103] Implying the need for a new approach, James remarked that: '... there is a clear thread of historical continuity linking the impact of recent excitements on internal peacekeeping activity with the international society's earlier, less busy operational role.'[104]

THE SEARCH FOR A USEFUL CONCEPT

Although there is now a general search for a different approach, few sources have outlined genuinely radical proposals for responding to difficult conflict situations. Generally, attention is focused on issues such as the new range of tasks performed by peacekeeping forces in the field, the shortcomings of the classical peacekeeping approach in dealing with these tasks, and the need to conduct these operations more effectively.[105] The search for ways to improve UN operations has led to greater scrutiny of its command and control, planning, intelligence and other aspects of relevant operations.[106] Some works have rightly envisaged a greater peacekeeping role for the armed forces of the great powers. Some of such works examine the role of the US in new peacekeeping operations.[107]

The multifaceted nature of the tasks performed by peacekeepers has led to the identification of different types of peacekeeping, widening the areas for conceptual analysis.[108] New terms such as Peace Support Operations (PSOs),

---

[102] Thomas Weiss, 'UN Military Operations After the Cold War: Some Conceptual Problems' in *Peacekeeping: Norms, Policy and Process,* p. 44. Thomas Weiss also discusses similar issues in 'New Challenges for UN Military Operations', *The Washington Quarterly,* Vol. 16, Winter 1993, pp. 51-66.

[103] John Gerard Ruggie 'Wandering in the Void: Charting the U.N.'s New Strategic Role', *Foreign Affairs,* Nov./Dec. 1993, p. 27.

[104] Alan James, 'The History of Peacekeeping: An Analytical Perspective', in Centre for International and Strategic Studies, *Peacekeeping: Norms, Policy and Process.*

[105] See, for example, Mats R. Berdal, 'Whither UN Peacekeeping? An Analysis of the Changing Military Requirements of UN Peacekeeping with Proposals for its Enhancement', *Adelphi Paper,* IISS, October 1993.

[106] See, for example, Richard Latter, *Coordinating UN Peace Support Operations;* Hugh Smith, 'Intelligence and UN Peacekeeping', in *Survival,* Autumn 1994.

[107] See, for example, John Mackinlay, 'Problems for U.S. Forces in Operations Beyond Peacekeeping'; and Sir Brian Urquriart, 'Peace Support Operations: Implications for the U.S. Military', in William H. Lewis (ed.), *Peacekeeping: The Way Ahead?,* (Washington D.C.: Institute for National Strategic Studies, November 1993).

[108] See Marrack Goulding, 'The Evolution of United Nations Peacekeeping', *International Affairs* 69, 3 (1993), pp. 451-464; Bernard A. Goetze, 'The Future of Peacekeeping: A Military View', in Alex Morrison (ed.), *Peacekeeping, Peacemaking, or War: International Security*

second generation, and aggravated peacekeeping have been introduced.[109] The attempts, in different sources, to coin new terms and phrases and to find new definitions for the activity are however not matched with a thorough analysis, or prescription, for an effective doctrine. The UN presented one of the early responses to the challenges posed by the new conflict situations, evaluating its role in the new security environment. The Secretary-general's report, the first *Agenda for Peace*, outlined ways in which the UN could meet some of these challenges. The report went beyond the previous UN concept of peacekeeping, proposing the preventive deployment of troops to prevent the escalation of conflict;[110] ending a conflict through peacemaking which begins primarily with diplomacy according to Chapter VI of the Charter, and may include the use of military force as stated in Chapter VII,[111] peacekeeping; and post-conflict peace-building.[112] Whilst the ideas in this report received support in some quarters,[113] they came under sharp criticism in others. Weiss observed for example, that the report:

> ... covers much ground and contains many intriguing suggestions. It also contains a host of conceptual ambiguities that limit its utility as a road map for determining the future directions of UN Military Operations ... [114]

Mackinlay also noted that whilst the report 'energised the search for a new concept, it lacked conceptual detail'.[115] He criticized the report for not providing a generally accepted definition or an in-depth analysis of the concept of peace-enforcement.[116]

The methods devised by different armed forces for dealing with these conflict situations can hardly be described as revolutionary. The British Army for example, adopted ' wider peacekeeping' which is used to indicate:

> ... the doctrinal distinction between today's increasingly multi-faceted peacekeeping op-
> erations and Cold War 'traditional' peacekeeping – whilst at the same time asserting that
> the defining attributes of traditional peacekeeping (the non-use of force other than for

---

Enforcement, (Ontario: Canadian Institute of Strategic Studies, 1994) pp. 29-38; and Sarah Sewall, 'Peace Enforcement and the United Nations, and Dennis J. Quinn, 'Peace Support Operations: Definitions and Implications' in Dennis J. Quinn (ed.), *Peace Support Operations and the US Military*, (Washington D.C.: National Defense University Press, 1994).

[109] See, for example, Sewall, p. 101; and Quinn, p. 18.

[110] Boutros-Ghali, *An Agenda for Peace*, pp. 16-18.

[111] Ibid. pp. 20-27.

[112] Ibid. pp. 32-34.

[113] See, for example, Indar Jit Rikhye, 'The United Nations of the 1990s and International Peacekeeping Operations', *Southampton Papers in International Policy*, No.3, (November 1992).

[114] Thomas Weiss, 'UN Military Operations After the Cold War', p. 43.

[115] John Mackinlay, 'Improving Multifunctional Forces', *Survival*, Autumn 1994, p. 153.

[116] Ibid.

self-defence; the consent of all parties to the dispute; and the impartiality of UN components) apply equally to its 'wider' variant.[117]

Mackinlay's review of the responses of a few other armed forces indicate that although they constitute a good starting point for understanding these new conflicts, 'none , however, is more than a manual for individual and unit survival, explaining how to endure, but not how to succeed.'[118] Overall however, most of the ideas put forward in these writings reflect a purely theoretical perspective, which can hardly be applied successfully in practice.

On the whole, there is no consensus on what a new peacekeeping concept would entail. Generally, new peacekeeping literature reflects a division along two broad perspectives. The first argues that the principles of traditional peacekeeping can still be applied successfully even though the role of peacekeepers has been expanded considerably. One position is that 'peacekeeping needs to be placed on a firm conceptual footing directly congruent with its peaceful third party role'[119] However, a clear line is often drawn between peacekeeping and peace enforcement, with a prescription that the two must never be combined in one operation.[120] Berdal's work for example recognises the problems posed by traditional peacekeeping principles but he still advocates that the line between peacekeeping and peace enforcement must not be crossed in one operation.[121]

Of particular significance within this body of thought, is Dobbie's view. Whilst also arguing that the barrier between peacekeeping and enforcement must not be lowered in an operation, he moves beyond this, to outline a concept for dealing with these new conflicts.[122] For Dobbie, the distinction between peace enforcement and peacekeeping rests solely on the presence or absence of consent.[123] According to him,

> Consent equates more realistically to a general public attitude that tolerates a peacekeeping presence and represents a quorum of cooperation. At its most limited, it might amount to an absence of systematic and concerted armed action against the mission. If such consent is present in a theatre of operations, then wider peacekeeping is likely to be a reasonable option. If it is absent, wider peacekeeping tasks are unlikely to prove relevant to the

---

[117] Richard Latter, *Co-ordinating UN Peace Support Operations,* (Global Security Programme, University of Cambridge, July 1994), pp. 18-19.

[118] Mackinlay, 'Improving Multifunctional Forces' pp. 155-6.

[119] Fetherston, 'Putting the Peace Back into Peacekeeping: Theory Must Inform Practice', p. 3.

[120] Ratner and Abi Saab expressed such views in *The New UN Peacekeeping* and 'United Nations Peacekeeping Old and New' respectively.

[121] Mats R. Berdal, 'Whither UN Peacekeeping?'

[122] Charles Dobbie, A Concept for Post-Cold War Peacekeeping, *Survival,* Vol. 36, no. 3, (Autumn 1994), pp. 121-148.

[123] Ibid. pp. 122-124.

root-causes of the conflict. Without consent, peace enforcement will probably represent the only realistic means of effective outside intervention.[124]

Thus, with consent, it is possible to conduct wider or second generation peacekeeping which include preventive deployment, humanitarian relief, military assistance, demobilisation operations and guarantee and denial of movements.[125] Such consent could, however, be in the form of support from the local population, or the conflicting parties. Dobbie also outlines some principles that must be adhered to in order to uphold consent and maintain a peacekeeping posture. These include impartiality, negotiation and patience, amongst others. Nonetheless, although he acknowledges that where consent is non-existent, peace enforcement may be unavoidable, he does not outline guidelines for dealing with situations where peace enforcement must precede peacekeeping.The need may arise to keep the peace after an enforcement action may have created an atmosphere conducive for negotiations. The British Army's subsequent review of the wider peacekeeping doctrine is an indication of its irrelevance to present day operational environment.

The second viewpoint expresses scepticism about Dobbie's position, recognizing that this could pose serious problems in reality. Whilst keenly aware of the need for more radical, but effective, approaches to handling intercommunal conflicts, Mackinlay argues that the best hope for dealing with these conflicts remains the multifunctional forces, given the lack of political will, particularly in the Third World to support the development of a powerful UN force which may one day act against their interests.[126] He is more flexible in his application of the consent theory, devising the best type of forces for dealing with conflict at different levels of consent.[127] Gow and Dandeker also view the strict application of consent as detrimental to the conduct of these new multifunctional second generation operations.[128] They see 'strategic peacekeeping' as becoming a 'practical necessity' in situations where 'neither the conditions for peace-enforcement nor for peacekeeping had been met'[129] The success of peace support operations, they argue, will not rest solely upon consent, but on legitimation. This legitimation is derived from the support

---

[124] Ibid. p. 124.

[125] Ibid. pp. 124-125.

[126] Mackinlay, Improving Multifunctional Forces; See also, John Mackinlay and Jarat Chopra, *A Draft Concept of Second Generation Multinational Operations,* (Providence, RI: The Thomas J. Watson Institute for International Studies, Brown University, 1993).

[127] Mackinlay, 'Improving Multifunctional Forces'.

[128] James Gow and Christopher Dandeker, 'Peace-support operations: the problem of legitimation'. *The World Today.* Vol. 51, Nos. 8-9, (Aug.-Sept. 1995). See also, Christopher Dandeker and James Gow, The Future of Peace Support Operations: Strategic Peacekeeping and Success, Armed Forces and Society, Volume 23, No. 3, Spring 1997, pp. 327-348.

[129] Ibid. p. 172.

generated from three main sources. First, from 'the bases' on which a mission was established; second, the effectiveness of an operation; and lastly, the local population in the area of operation and the international community at large.[130] In a separate work, Gow, through a discussion of UNPROFOR's experience in Bosnia, argues that there is merit in injecting enforcement measures into peacekeeping 'without resorting to war'- an approach he describes as 'peace assertion'.[131] Although these views reflect the reality of present day conflict situations, they stop short of including peace enforcement operations at the extreme end of the spectrum of these responses to conflict.

Perhaps the best idea, thus far, for dealing with contemporary conflict situations is that (within the second group), which recognizes that situations may arise which would require a switch from peacekeeping to peace enforcement.[132] This view recognizes that military intervention may be an option of last resort if preventive diplomacy, mediation and peacekeeping fail[133]. Intervention appears to be used here interchangeably with peace enforcement, and the conditions for its employment are carefully outlined. Amongst the conditions are that there must be a 'just cause' for intervention, guarantee of non-combatant immunity, and the assurance that intervention would 'do more good or avert more harm than the evil done in the process'.[134]

CONCEPTUAL VOID

A definite concept for new peacekeeping operations has not emerged and despite attempts at reorganization in the UN, its peacekeeping operations have had mixed results. Its failure has been notable for example, in its inability to stop the genocide in Rwanda. No government volunteered its troops despite the request of the UN Secretary-general and the commitment of a few to the stand-by system.[135] This has exposed the organization's inherent political weaknesses. Following the UN's failure at timely intervention in Rwanda, Boutros-Ghali admitted that there was a 'general fatigue' in the international community, to intervene in these conflicts. The Special Representative of Secretary-general (SRSG) in Somalia, noted that 'the UN does not have the

---

[130] Ibid. p. 173.
[131] James Gow, 'Strategic Peacekeeping: UNPROFOR and International Diplomatic Assertion', in Espen Barth Eider (ed.). *Peacekeeping in Europe,* (Norwegian Institute of International Affairs, 1995).
[132] Aldred et al., *European Security: Discussion Document*
[133] Ibid. p. 6.
[134] Ibid. pp. 6-7.
[135] Boutros-Ghali, *Supplement to An Agenda for Peace,* p. 9.

authority to hold individual nations to a fixed contract.'[136] Other commentators have also discussed the loss of UN credibility as a result of its inability to control many of its military operations.[137] Indeed, the UN Secretary-general later seemed to have lost his initial enthusiasm, admitting that the Security Council does not have the capacity to 'deploy' and 'direct' complex operations.[138]

The implication of all of this is that the UN could only muster the political will to handle small, traditional peacekeeping and observation missions, such as preventive deployment or indeed, its 'wider' variant, with the consent of parties. The latter may occur when a conflict has run its course, with one party emerging victorious and the other(s) defeated as was the case in Rwanda after the loss of about half a million lives. In such circumstances, the UN will perhaps find it easier to obtain authorization and support for a second generation mission where the parties have given their consent. The force would mainly be involved in monitoring cease-fire, elections, supporting humanitarian aid, or indeed, act as an interface between peacemaking and peace building, as suggested by Fetherston.[139]

The real question in this case is whether the international community should wait for conflicts to be decided on the battlefield, incurring heavy losses and human suffering, before responding. Even in such cases, an end to violence is not a certainty. A similar issue faced the UN and the US in Bosnia, in respect of which a peace agreement was signed in Dayton Ohio, after the conflict had claimed over 250,000 lives. There were concerns in the US over the safety of troops that will be committed to monitoring the peace agreement. In this situation, political will was still difficult to secure, as some American commentators seemed to question the rationale for sending American troops to Bosnia, arguing that it was not in the wider national interest of the US.[140] Thus, more often than not, such missions and complex operations may be in the interest of neighbouring states in the target territory, particularly those affected by a given conflict.

---

[136] Jonathan Howe , 'The United States and United Nations in Somalia', *The Washington Quarterly,* Summer 1995, p. 54.

[137] Jim Whitman and lan Bartholomew, 'UN Peace Support Operations: Political-Military Considerations' in Don Daniel and Bradd Hayes (eds.), *Beyond Traditional Peacekeeping,* p. 184.

[138] Boutros-Ghali, *Supplement to An Agenda for Peace,* p. 15.

[139] See Fetherston, 'Putting the Peace Back into Peacekeeping'.

[140] ABC News Nightline, 28 November 1995.

THE SIGNIFICANCE OF ECOMOG

Although the central argument in this book has some connection with the views of Mackinlay, Dandeker and Gow, in that they recognize that some use of force may be necessary in peacekeeping operations, it adopts the position ofAldred et al as a useful starting point for any attempt to develop a concept.[141] This view recognizes that an attempt to resolve a violent conflict via diplomatic means has a reasonable chance of failure. Thus, peacemakers may be compelled to intervene militarily in order to halt humanitarian disasters, and to create the chance for a settlement. Such intervention may not be too limited in its application of force. There is a possibility that peacekeeping may be employed after such a force has successfully created a peaceful atmosphere. This is an issue on which most studies have failed to focus. The Liberian conflict demonstrated that employing peacekeeping and peace enforcement in one conflict is sometimes unavoidable. Present day conflict situations often present a difficult choice between waiting for full consent, and responding urgently to humanitarian emergencies. This book aims to contribute to the systematic theorization of a new peacekeeping approach, co-ordinate the fragmentary literature and develop a series of hypotheses that determine the success of efforts to conduct this new class of operations. The West African sub-regional experience is presented here in order to analyse the possible correspondence between existing theory and actual practice.

The experience of the ECOWAS Monitoring Group (ECOMOG) in Liberia has received very little attention in terms of its possible contribution to the development of a new concept. Much of the literature on the Liberian war focuses on the humanitarian and legal aspects of the war; and the politics of the international involvement.[142] Indeed, it is simply dismissed in some sources as an activity that bears no relevance to peacekeeping, nor to any of the attempts to find a new approach discussed above.[143] Few works have focused on the operational aspects of ECOMOG's activities.[144] Another collection of essays discusses several aspects of ECOMOG's role in the Liberian civil war.[145] This constitutes a useful source of data on the origins of

---

[141] Aldred et al., European Security: Discussion Document.

[142] See, for example, Hiram Ruiz, *Uprooted Liberians: Casualties of a Brutal War,* (U.S. Committee for Refugees Report, 1992): Kofi Oteng Kufuor, 'Developments in the Resolution of the Liberian Conflict' *American University Journal of International Law and Policy,* Vol.10, NO.1, 1994; and Abiodun Alao, *The Burden of Collective Goodwill: The International Involvement in the Liberian Civil War,* (Aldershot: Ashgate, 1998).

[143] Weiss, 'UN Military Operations After the Cold War'.

[144] See, for example, C.Y. Iweze, 'Nigeria in Liberia', in M.A. Vogt and A.E. Ekoko (eds.) *Nigeria in International Peace-keeping 1960-1992,* (Lagos, 1993).

[145] M.A. Vogt (ed.), *A Bold Attempt at Regional Peacekeeping: ECOMOG and the Liberian Crisis,* (Lagos: Gabumo Publishing Press, 1992).

ECOMOG and the early parts of the civil war, legal and political problems within ECOWAS following the deployment of the force. This volume however does not cover other aspects of the operation, or the period beyond 1992 for that matter. Other writings on the ECOWAS intervention in Liberia appear to be limited to comments in journals and papers by military personnel who have served in the ECOMOG operations.[146] The latter also constitute useful sources of data on the operational and organizational aspects of the operation.

In seeking to evaluate the relevance of the ECOMOG experience to theory, a number of assumptions are made in this book. The first, upon which all the others rest, is that any peacemaking effort geared toward resolving multiparty internal conflicts would require planning beyond peacekeeping, and include the possibility of peace enforcement. Thus, peacekeeping and peace enforcement are seen as inter-dependent strategies (see Figure 1.1). In making peace in violent internal conflicts, the character of the mediator and the functions he or she performs are important determinants of the success of a military operation. Furthermore, the military requirements for both peacekeeping and enforcement are totally different but not irreconcilable. Peacekeeping and peace enforcement operations perform only one task and not more: to create an atmosphere of non-violence, where negotiations for a settlement can occur.

Having proposed that peacekeeping and peace enforcement may be alternated in these new conflicts, a vital aspect of this study is the analysis of the type of force that will he required to deal with such conflict situations. It examines the relevance of Janowitz's constabulary concept in the search for the type of armed forces best suited to this situation. To what extent can the military be made to understand the political context and implications of the various military operations that they may be required to perform? What attributes are needed to alternate between peacekeeping and peace enforcement? A study of ECOMOG is conducted in an attempt to address some of these issues. In doing so, this study relies on the work of Moskos and the methods he employs in his analysis of UNFICYP.[147] In particular, his method of analysing UNFICYP's organizational features through the 'conflict approach' is adopted in Chapter Six of this book.

The conceptual framework of this book is best summed up by the inter-dependence argument, which is supported by Figure 1.1. Peacemaking is fundamentally a diplomatic activity, which becomes complicated once undesired conflict behaviour (e.g. violence) is introduced into a conflict

---

[146] See, for example, Abiodun Alao, 'ECOMOG in Liberia, The Anaemic Existence of a Mission', *Jane's Intelligence Review,* Vol. 5 No.9, (September 1993); and 'Peacekeeping in Sub-Saharan Africa' *Brassey's Defence Yearbook.* (1993).
[147] Moskos, *Peace Soldiers.*

situation. The peacemaker employs the help of peacekeepers to maintain a peaceful atmosphere during negotiations or to monitor the parties' compliance with the terms of an agreement. Peacekeeping is not aimed at terminating conflict by itself. The job of the peacekeeper here is essentially a non-coercive one. When the diplomatic effort supported by peacekeeping fails to end a conflict, it becomes necessary to enforce peace, especially where the level of human suffering has increased due to disruptive conflict behaviour. The role of the military in such a situation is to restore calm through the use of force. The creation of a calm atmosphere is intended to put an end to human suffering as well as to create an atmosphere where negotiations may be attempted once more. If negotiations succeed, peacekeepers may again be deployed to prevent the outbreak of violence. Thus, the peacemaker or mediator, is dependent on the military, either to prevent the outbreak of violence, or to stop violence by force, if necessary. The success of the military in achieving any of these tasks does not mean resolution of the conflict. It merely paves the way for the peacemaker to negotiate the peace. The military performs essentially different roles under peacekeeping and peace enforcement. Whether the same military personnel can blend both roles as required, and whether the peacemaker can successfully broker peace after employing peace enforcement are issues that will be explored further in subsequent chapters.

CHAPTER TWO

Peacekeeping in Practice

The previous chapter established a conceptual framework for this book, discussed the scope of existing literature and the gap that this work seeks to fill. Having put forward the argument that it may be necessary to create peace in violent internal conflicts, and that this strategy is likely to be employed more by regional arrangements than the UN, this chapter seeks to discuss the background of military operations supporting peacemaking efforts. It conducts an analysis of responses to conflict by both the UN and regional bodies in the Cold War period, and the challenges confronting them in the Post-Cold War era. The chapter suggests that there were indications during the Cold War, that peace creation or a similar strategy would be a more effective response to certain kinds of difficult intra-state conflict. The Cold War politics, however, suppressed the development of this strategy, or at least, its exploration.

The analysis conducted here is done in two parts. The first examines military operations by the UN during the Cold War, and the context in which they were conducted. The second part discusses the pattern of regional operations in the Cold War period, analysing the distinctions in principles employed at both levels. It discusses how major changes in the international community have altered the pattern of responses of the Cold War period. In discussing the role of regional groupings, this section focuses more on Africa largely because the case study under analysis occurred within this region.

I

UNITED NATIONS PEACEKEEPING DURING THE COLD WAR

With the exception of the UN involvement in an internal conflict in the Congo, UN operations generally followed the traditional peacekeeping approach outlined in the previous chapter. This section conducts an analysis of what UN peacekeeping and other peacemaking strategies entailed during this period, and the international political climate that dictated their composition. The UN experience in selected operations are employed in this analysis.

THE UN IN INTER-STATE CONFLICTS:
THE FIRST UN EMERGENCY FORCE (UNEF I)

UNEF I was the First United Nations peacekeeping operation involving the use of peacekeeping forces as opposed to peace observers, and it set precedent for future UN peacekeeping missions. The force was deployed as a result of the crisis that broke out in the Middle East in October 1956 following the invasion of Egyptian territory by Israel, Britain and France. This crisis had a real potential of exploding into a much greater one if care was not taken to halt it. The attacks enraged the international community, particularly the US, which was not consulted by either of her allies. Their actions held the risk of inviting the Soviet Union to gain foothold into the Middle East.[1]

The UN Emergency Force seemed a perfect instrument to control the crisis. It was established 'to secure and supervise the cessation of hostilities' in accordance with resolution 997-ES, which called for an immediate cease-fire and withdrawal of all forces behind the armistice lines, and the reopening of the Suez Canal.[2] The guidelines adopted by the Secretary- general in deploying UNEF I provided the force with its main features, and set the pattern for future forces of its kind.[3] Hammarskjold enumerated some guiding principles for the organization and functioning of the force.

Amongst these guiding principles was first, that the force should be recruited from member states other than the permanent members of the UN Security Council. The reasons for this were to exclude Britain and France, and equally important, to keep Soviet troops out of the Middle East. This formed the basis for Harmmarskjold's doctrine of 'preventive diplomacy' which was to be applied in later conflicts. Second, the force was not intended to influence the military balance in the conflict and thereby the political balance. Third, UNEF was not to be an enforcement organ, but merely an extension of the peaceful settlement function of the United Nations. The force would be a buffer force with policing duties, not a fighting army with military objectives. 'The force would be more than an observer corps, but in no way a military force temporarily controlling the territory in which it was stationed ...'[4] The

---

[1] See James, *Peacekeeping in International Politics,* p. 212.
[2] *The Blue Helmets*, p. 46; and Boyd, *United Nations Peacekeeping Operations: A Political and Military Appraisal,* p. 83.
[3] Frye, *A United Nations Force*, p. 11.
[4] *The Blue Helmets*, p. 48; & Frye, *A United Nations Force,* p. 13.

duty of the force was not to impose peace or the will of the international community on the invaders, but rather, to expedite peace. It was assumed that this would be done with the co-operation of all the governments involved. Thus, the peacekeeping operation was to be a part of a peacemaking exercise on the diplomatic level.

Fourth, was the respect for Egypt's sovereignty.[5] The force would not enter Egyptian territory until a cease-fire had been secured. It was to enter with the consent of the Egyptian Government, to help maintain calm during and after the withdrawal of Israel, France and the United Kingdom, and to secure compliance with all the other terms of the UN resolution. The issue of host-state consent is an important one for which UNEF laid the precedent. Fifth, the force was to be 'as nearly neutral, politically, as possible'.[6] The last was on the issue of financing. The basic rule laid down in Hammarskjold's report was that a country contributing a unit would be responsible for the cost of equipment and salaries, while all other costs were to be financed outside the normal budget of the UN.

Thus, peacekeeping had been conceptualized. Overall, UNEF matched all the prescriptions of its founders – an impartial, non-threatening military force, deployed under a competent authority, with the consent of the host state, and charged with the task of defusing the crisis in the Middle East and stabilizing the situation. The experiences of UNEF set precedent for future forces and its lessons were studied. The operation demonstrated the important role which such a force plays in defusing a crisis. UNEF was formally established on 7 November 1956 when the General Assembly voted in favour of establishing the force. Within eight days from this date (15 November), the first UN troops landed on Egyptian territory.[7] It was instructive on how a force of its kind could act as a face-saving device for some of the parties to a conflict – Britain and France in this case. The stabilizing role that a peacekeeping force can play in a conflict, was emphasized by UNEF. The force occupied positions between Anglo-French and Egyptian forces, thus reducing the likelihood of armed clashes.

UNEF however, revealed a basic limitation of a peacekeeping force – its inability to remain in a territory once the host state wishes it to leave, without taking on the appearance of a force of occupation. Following tensions between Israel and Syria in 1967, Egypt formally requested the complete withdrawal of UNEF. The Secretary-general's acceptance of Egypt's request generated

---

[5] Hammarskjold later commented (to the Advisory Committee) that 'the very basis and starting point' of this effort, was the 'recognition by the General Assembly of the unlimited sovereign rights of Egypt'. Frye, *A United Nations Force*, p15.

[6] Ibid.

[7] Ibid., p. 21.

some controversy, as some believed that it was this action which led to the outbreak of the Six Day War.[8] The alternative line of action, which was to remain on Egyptian soil without its consent, would however have generated similar, if not greater controversy. This UNEF experience further highlights the fact that peacekeeping is dependent upon the desire of the conflicting parties to pursue peace. UNEF was on Egyptian soil for so long, basically because the conflicting parties assented. The mission could no longer be justified as one of peacekeeping, once the circumstances changed.

Undoubtedly, the relative success of this mission meant that future operations of a similar nature would be expected, at the very least, to follow the pattern of UNEF, and build upon its experiences. Most of the operations after UNEF appeared to take a cue from it, and they were utilised for similar purposes. A second United Nations Emergency force (UNEF II) was despatched to the Middle East after the October 1973 war where Egypt in conjunction with Syria, launched a surprise attack on Israel. The features of this force were similar to those of its predecessor.[9]

The type of conflict which dominated the international scene during that period, appeared to determine the purposes of the missions, and their lessons. For example, due to decolonisation, a number of missions played face-saving roles amongst other duties. The transfer of West New Guinea or West Irian from the Netherlands to Indonesia (1962-63) is an example of this.[10] Apart from minor exceptions, most other UN operations were modelled after UNEFI. For example, the UN Force in Cyprus (UNFICYP) which was deployed to defuse tensions between the Greek and Turkish Cypriots[11] was the first UN force to include troops contributed by a permanent UN member.

Many other UN peacekeeping efforts did not involve the use of peacekeeping forces. They were mostly observer missions, composed of a few men. Amongst these were UN India and Pakistan Observer Missions (UNIPOM)[12], UNIIMOG which was deployed to observe the peace in the aftermath of the Iran-Iraq war[13]; UNGOMAP and its monitoring of the withdrawal of Soviet

---

[8]   See James, *Peacekeeping in international Politics,* p. 221; and Wiseman, 'Peacekeeping and the Management of International Conflict', pp. 1-2.

[9]   For more on this conflict and attempts at resolution, see Kurt Waldheim, *In the Eye of the Storm,* (London: Weidenfeld & Nicholson, 1985); Michael Harbottle, 'The October Middle East Wars: Lessons for UN Peacekeeping' *International Affairs,* 50, (4) October (1974); and Henry Kissinger, *Years of Upheaval* (London: Weidenfeld & Nicholson, and Michael Joseph, 1982).

[10] This is discussed in D.W. Bowett, *United Nations Forces* (London: Stevens 1964).

[11] See Glen D. Camp, Greco-Turkish Conflict over Cyprus', *Political Science Quarterly* 95 (1) Spring (1980); and Kurt Waldheim, *In the Eye of the Storm.*

[12] See Robert W. Reford 'UNIPOM : Success of a Mission', *International Journal,* 27 (3) Summer (1972).

[13] See Shahran Chubin, 'The Last Phase of the Iran-Iraq War: From Stalemate to Ceasefire', *Third World Quarterly,* 11 (2) April (1989).

forces from Afghanistan; UN Angola Verification Mission, UNAVEM, and the withdrawal of troops from Angola, and UN Transition Assistance Group, UNTAG.

KEY FEATURES OF UN OPERATIONS IN INTER-STATE CONFLICTS

Political

Although each conflict presented its own unique challenges, most UN peacekeeping missions in inter-state conflicts had similar features. These UN operations were designed to be part of a third party peacemaking or mediation effort. A mediator appointed by the UN, or the UN Secretary-General himself, provided a channel of communication between the conflicting parties, in order to reach a settlement. However, the depth of such mediation exercise and its success are questionable.[14] The existence of the peacekeeping missions in Cyprus, the Middle East and in Kashmir would lead one to conclude that the success of mediation by the UN has been marginal. In the decolonising cases, the operations were relatively easier, since agreements between parties had been concluded. The peacekeeping forces were merely overseeing a process.

Generally, the UN peace operations focused more on conflict control, than addressing the actual issues of the dispute, towards reaching a settlement.[15] Peacekeeping served mainly to contain many of these conflicts, defusing crisis and preventing their escalation. The UN peacekeeping system has come under serious criticisms. It is claimed that the operations 'foster a false sense of security without inspiring the will for settlement'.[16]

Thus, UN operations were characterized by limited mandates. The mandates, although addressed to different undertakings, had common elements. They were based on consent and the objectives were limited. Generally, they were restricted to recognizable and attainable goals. Boyd argues that the pursuit of limited objectives indicates that 'there might be more comprehensive goals which the UN could not reasonably expect to achieve.'[17] In none of these situations was the force designed to take enforcement action. There was

---

[14] Paul F. Diehl discusses the failure of the UN in the area of conflict resolution in *International Peacekeeping*, pp. 37-61.

[15] Fetherston discusses such issues in *'Putting the Peace Back into Peacekeeping'*. James, in *The Politics of Peacekeeping*, p. 337, states that 'the immediate aim [in peacekeeping] is to bundle the issue into cold storage, and so avert an explosion'; See also, Ramesh Thakur, 'From Great Power Collective Security to Middle Power Peacekeeping', in Hugh Smith (ed.), Australia and Peacekeeping, (Australia Defence Studies Centre, 1990), pp. 1-21.

[16] Cox, *Prospects for Peacekeeping*, p. 7.

[17] Boyd, p. 83.

always the risk that if the UN sought to address deeper issues than simply controlling the conflict, then it might have to employ greater means to ensure settlement of a conflict. There was a strong possibility that it would find itself powerless to provide, and effect a stronger mandate given the lack of consensus among the permanent members of the UN Security Council. After all, it was such a situation that led to the creation of peacekeeping.

These operations experienced similar problems of force creation. The forces were created under the pressure of mounting an operation rapidly to prevent a dangerous situation from the possibility of further deterioration. There were similar political and legal factors involved in the creation of these forces. For example, the nature of constitutional provisions governing the use of national defence forces which varies from country to country, had a degree of influence on the deployment of these forces. Generally, parliamentary consent is required to send a national contingent abroad. In Canada, for example, the government must advise parliament and secure approval for participation in an operation.[18] Ireland had legal restrictions on the use of Irish soldiers outside its territory.[19] The effect of this was that a volunteer contingent had to be raised, thus creating its share of problems for the early operations.[20] However, this was revised due to its participation in UN operations. Its forces can now be sent as part of an international force which has been duly created by the UN.[21] Some countries, for example, Canada, had specific prohibitions precluding their armed forces from taking orders from foreign nationals. A compromise was found, whereby Canadian officers served as officers on the force commander's staff.[22]

Organisational and Operational Issues

The organizational patterns of all of these forces were similar. Like all the other features, the command and control arrangements in later operations benefited from UNEF's experience. The responsibility for the operations were placed in the hands of the Secretary General (SG). The line of authority from the SG proceeded directly to the commander of the force, in whose hands the command of the force rested. The force commander under the SG was endowed with full command authority for field operations. As in any military

---

[18] Ibid.

[19] Ibid.; and Major General I.J. Rikhye, Preparation and Training of United Nations Peace-keeping Forces, *Adelphi Paper* No. 9. (1964), p. 5.

[20] Ibid.

[21] See for example, Hidejiro Kotami, "Peace-keeping: Problems for Smaller Countries", *International Journal*, XIX (Summer 1964), pp. 311-312 .

[22] See Boyd.

force, the command and control for these UN forces consisted of institutions and procedures for ensuring that the wishes of the governing authority are fulfilled.[23]

For forces whose task might be considered a simple one when compared to the combat operations for which the military was designed, the execution of these operations was not always as clear-cut and was by no means easy. A lot of challenges were encountered in the conduct of these operations, most especially those involving large forces. With very few exceptions, UN peacekeeping forces during the Cold War observed certain restraints in order to retain their credibility as a neutral, non-coercive force. Peacekeepers carried only light arms which included side arms and armoured personnel carriers, for transportation and self-defence. Heavy artillery and support weapons were deliberately excluded.[24] Aircraft were restricted to those used for transportation and medical evacuation.[25] The use of intelligence capabilities was avoided in order to gain the confidence of conflicting parties.[26]

It was extremely difficult for the UN to develop a fully integrated international force. Some of its experiences demonstrated the problems likely to confront any effort to establish a multinational force, even one with limited objectives. Many of the problems were created by the fact that these operations lacked advance military planning. They were launched in response to international emergencies. Thus, a lot of improvisation went into establishing the operations. The forces often had to contend with problems of logistics, training and doctrine, which compounded command and control problems. UNEFI for example, had to deal with major supply problems like acquisition of rations, a unifying symbol, and surface transport equipment.[27] Individual contingents were required to provide some of their own logistic support (such as rations, sidearms and tents) for the first few days, giving contingents a certain degree of autonomy. In the case of UNEFI, the host country assisted in providing some of these items.[28] The ad hoc nature of the operations sometimes led to shortage of trained logistics personnel.[29] Lack of adequate information on the target territory led some units to arrive with inappropriate clothing. According to Rikhye,

---

[23] For an illustration of the organization of UN peacekeeping operations, see *Blue Helmets*, pp. 409-418.
[24] See Berdal, 'Whither UN Peacekeeping?', pp. 5-6.
[25] Ibid.
[26] Ibid.
[27] Bowman and Fanning, 'The Logistics Problems of a UN Military Force', p. 359.
[28] Ibid. pp. 359-360.
[29] Bowman and Fanning, in Lincoln P. Bloomfield et al, p. 148.

... In some instances contingents have arrived with heavy woollen clothing to operate in tropical conditions and vice versa. Some contingents have arrived without cooking utensils.[30]

Furthermore, troops were not given prior training for the roles they performed in the operations.[31]

In addition to these problems, a few other factors served to complicate these operations, making integration virtually impossible. There was generally, lack of standardization of equipment, such as communication equipment. In addition to this, there were differences in training and disciplinary standards. It is the regulation in most countries that the discipline of their force can be exercised solely by the national force commanders. Thus in these operations, the commanders of the national contingents assumed responsibility for enforcing discipline within their national units.[32] There was also the tendency for home governments to exercise a measure of control on their contingents within UN operations. This element of autonomy, which the contingent commanders enjoyed, added to the deep cultural differences among the units, and made unity of command an unattainable goal in many of these operations.

UN PEACEKEEPING IN INTRA-STATE CONFLICTS

Although intra-state conflict was higher in frequency than inter-state conflict even during the Cold War, the former was often appraised in the context of international politics. Some of the internal conflicts which attracted UN attention, indicated that this type of conflict would pose difficult challenges for any resolution effort. The experience of the UN in the Congo, in particular, emphasized many of the problems. In many respects, the UN operations in the Congo, varied sharply from the traditional approach which had come to be accepted as peacekeeping.

United Nations Operation in the Congo (ONUC)

Within two weeks of Congo's independence (30 June 1960), the Congolese army mutinied against its Belgian officers, Belgium intervened, law and order broke down completely, and the province of Katanga seceded. The coalition government of Joseph Kassavubu and Patrice Lumumba sought UN military assistance to protect their national territory against acts of aggression posed

---

[30] Rikhye, *Preparation and Training*, p. 5.
[31] Ibid.
[32] Boyd.

by Belgian military troops who claimed to have intervened under the Treaty of Friendship and co-operation.[33] This situation was compounded by the fact that Belgian pattern of colonial administration left the new nation with a severe shortage of educated labour, for example, engineers, doctors, and senior staff in any field.

The UN Secretary-general was of the opinion that the doctrine of preventive diplomacy particularly applied in such a circumstance in which the ending of the colonial system had resulted in conflict and anarchy. His aim was to temporarily fill the power vacuum and provide the newly independent states with time to produce solutions to ongoing conflicts and engage in nation-building, while protecting them from becoming breeding grounds for east-west competition.[34] The Secretary-general was able to secure a mandate from the security council, to provide the Congolese with the necessary military assistance. The United Nations Operations in the Congo (ONUC) was established. Thus, the UN was able to provide a 'stop-gap' arrangement as opposed to Belgian troops, until the Congolese national security forces were able to establish order. This removed any justification for the continued presence of Belgian troops as Belgium had earlier given the same explanation for their military presence in the Congo.

ONUC's task was initially limited to assisting the government of Congo in the maintenance of law and order. The same principles of non-exercise of force except in self defence applied. However, Lumumba expected the UN to use more expeditious methods to effect the withdrawal of Belgian troops from Katanga, regardless of the legal implications. Lumumba was concerned that the Katanga secession would be successful with the support of Belgium, which then maintained a military presence only in the province. The internal nature of the problem accounted for Hammarskjold's initial reluctance to assist the Congolese government militarily in Katanga. Lumumba issued an ultimatum that if Belgian troops were not withdrawn from Katanga, the Congolese authorities would 'appeal for assistance elsewhere'[35]

With the realization that the UN Secretary General could not assist him militarily against Katanga, Lumumba launched a military campaign against

---

[33] This was an arrangement which allowed most of the Belgian administrators and technical personnel to remain in the Congo and continue to discharge their duties after independence. However, this treaty was never ratified by the Congo. Furthermore, the treaty did not give Belgium any right of intervention without the express request of the Congolese government – Georges Abi-Saab, *The UN Operations in the Congo, 1960-1964*; p. 6; see also, Durch, 'The UN Operation in the Congo', in William J. Durch (ed.), Chapter 19; and Indar Jit Rikhye, *Military Adviser to the Secretary-General: UN Peacekeeping and the Congo Crisis*, pp. 1-16.
[34] Abi Saab, *UN Operations in the Congo*, p. 5.
[35] Abi-Saab, *UN Operations in the Congo*, p. 25; & Brian Urquhart, *Hammarskjold* (New York: Knopf, 1972), p. 405.

the secessionists, accepting assistance from the Soviet Union, which supplied military equipment and personnel.[36] Dag Hammarskjold saw this as defeating the very essence of the operation, which was meant to circumvent the extension of the Cold War to the Congo through intervention and counter intervention of the superpowers. The nature of the campaign further compli-cated the situation. Inadequate logistic support led the government forces to confiscate food and vehicles from the occupied towns. This resulted in ethnic clashes where killings ensued.[37]

Following the constitutional crisis and the murder of Prime Minister Lumumba,[38] ONUC's mandate was expanded to deal with this new situation. The Security Council in February 1961, passed a resolution which urged the UN to take 'appropriate measures to prevent the occurrence of a civil war in the Congo, including prevention of clashes, and the use of force, if necessary, in the last resort'.[39] In September 1961, on the initiative of the Special Representative, ONUC, which by now had numbered about 20,000 troops, launched an attack on the Katanga secessionists. The Katanganese forces in conjunction with mercenaries, dealt a crushing blow to ONUC, which had to negotiate from this position of weakness. However, ONUC later built a stronger force and eventually over-powered the secessionists, preserving Congo's territorial integrity.

ONUC's success is debatable. While the outbreak of the civil war and the secession of Katanga was prevented, there was massive bloodshed. Further-more, it reaffirmed the importance of both superpowers' support for the successful implementation of any peacekeeping mission. Indeed, the Congo experience highlights the real problems involved in making peace in an internal crisis. However, ONUC is significant. It went beyond the usual UN approach of conflict control, to one which sought to achieve conflict resolu-tion and lasting peace. This operation can be categorized amongst present day peace support, multifunctional operations. It was the only UN peacekeeping operation during the Cold-War period, which combined the strategies of peacekeeping and peace enforcement in one operation. ONUC reinforced the fact that these strategies involve two distinct approaches. The effects of this on the conduct of the operation are discussed below.

---

[36] The soviet Union supplied Congo with 100 trucks and 16 Ilyushin transport planes with their crews. See Brian Urquhart, *Hammarskjold*, p. 436.
[37] This included massacre in a mission school where over 70 civilians including children were killed. Brian Urquhart, *Hammarskjold*, p. 435 & p. 438.
[38] Details of the constitutional crisis and events leading to Lumumba's killing are discussed by Cox; and Abi-Saab, *UN Operations in the Congo* .
[39] Moskos, *Peace Soldiers,* p. 20.

KEY FEATURES OF UN PEACEKEEPING IN INTRA-STATE CONFLICT

ONUC's experience illustrates how a force's mandate can change after an operation has begun. The operation began as one designed to perform basic conflict control functions as in UN peacekeeping operations in inter-state conflict. But in addition, the operation resembled what is now referred to as 'second-generation peacekeeping' from the outset – it had a large civilian component, which was to render technical assistance to the Congolese government.[40] This mandate was later widened to include the use of force when the aim of the authorizing body moved beyond conflict control. This enabled the force to deal decisively with many of the underlying causes of the violent conflict in the Congo. The experience highlighted other problems of force creation: if the mandate changes, contributing states may find it necessary to review their original consent. This was the case in ONUC when some African countries withdrew their forces after the change of mandate.[41]

ONUC's organizational pattern though basically similar to that of UNEF and other inter-state peacekeeping, had minor differences. One was the creation of the position of Special Representative in-between the Secretary-general and the Force Commander. Furthermore, ONUC's command and control problem was more complicated. The size of the force was larger, there were more national contingents,[42] the distances involved were greater, the relationship with the local population was more complex, and the mandate was more difficult to fulfil. In addition to this, the countries that voted to establish ONUC did not all share the same view regarding the terms of the mandate.[43] The Special Representative became an additional link in the chain of command and was responsible for insuring that proper directives were transmitted to the Force Commander.

ONUC began as a peacekeeping mission and it suffered many of the UN readiness and operational problems discussed above. The most severe were transportation and communication. The size of the force served to intensify this problem. The appropriate communication equipments were in short supply at the initial stages of the operation. Language barriers compounded this problem as bilingual operators were unavailable.[44] In addition, there was severe shortage of medical personnel and pilots to operate the aircraft.[45] The change to peace enforcement emphasized many of these problems.

---

[40] This is now considered second generation peacekeeping in some sources. See for example, Ratner, *The New UN Peacekeeping*, pp. 10-16.

[41] Boyd, p. 114.

[42] Thirty-five countries including ten African states contributed troops to ONUC.

[43] Abi-Saab, *UN Operation in the Congo* .

[44] Bowman and Fanning in Lincoln P. Bloomfield (ed.), p. 153.

[45] Ibid. p. 152.

The switch to enforcement meant a complete change of all the peacekeeping principles that had guided the operation. It required the removal of all the restrictions that had previously been self imposed. The use of heavy support weapons became a necessity. Aircraft then included those used for tactical support roles as well as fighter aircraft.[46] The application of the use of force beyond those required for self-defence during the enforcement phase removed any considerations of impartiality and co-operation of at least one of the conflicting parties. Congo portrayed all the problems of intra-state conflict, in particular, that a stronger strategy than peacekeeping is needed, if such conflicts are to be prevented from escalating into an intractable war. However, the political weakness of the UN in handling such conflicts became highlighted by the unmistakable reluctance of the UN to conduct such operations after the Congo experience. This continued at least, until the end of the Cold War.

POST-COLD WAR CHALLENGES FOR UN PEACEKEEPING

The slackening of East-West tensions from the late 1980s provided the UN with the opportunity to resolve many regional conflicts. Thus, the observer missions referred to earlier in Afghanistan, Namibia, Angola and Central America were deployed. Although these operations entailed new tasks such as election monitoring and repatriation of refugees, they were conducted within the framework of traditional peacekeeping. However, it gradually became obvious that many of the operations in which the UN would be involved in the post-Cold War period had changed drastically from those to which the organization was accustomed. The large-scale operations launched by the UN in 1992 in the former Yugoslavia, Cambodia, Somalia and Mozambique revealed the nature of the problems confronting peacemakers in this type of conflicts.

Operational Problems

The operational environment in which these operations have been conducted is in many ways different from many of the UN's previous missions, and the character of belligerents has changed significantly. Duke remarks on some of the problems which this class of conflict poses for the international community:

---

[46] Rikhye, 'Preparation and Training'.

It is often extremely difficult to identify the aggressor from the aggrieved, combatants from civilians, and legitimate authority from despots – the latter makes gaining consent for UN operations problematical. This raises the question of whether and in what circumstances the UN should intervene without the consent of the state, thus challenging the central precepts of state sovereignty.[47]

In addition to this, conflicting parties are often in control of territories that are not-clearly defined, and the control of such areas often switches from one party to another.[48] Unlike inter-state conflicts, many of the parties in internal conflicts hardly abide by any of the accepted rules of war, creating heavy casualties amongst civilian populations and sometimes amongst peacekeepers. Peacekeepers thus have to operate in dangerous environments.

Due to the emergencies created by such conflicts, peacekeeping operations have changed considerably. They are now multifaceted and as such, the tasks of the peacekeepers have increased.[49] Such tasks include humanitarian assistance, mine clearance, disarming paramilitary forces, collection and custody.[50] In addition, there is now the need for the military to co-ordinate its operations with other organizations working in the conflict area. These often include civilian police, human rights observers, electoral officials, relief organizations, amongst others.[51] It has become clear that the traditional peacekeeping doctrine cannot be effectively applied in the conduct of such operations. Better planning and co-ordination, command and control standards and intelligence activities would be required.

The problems that have been encountered in devising more effective methods are aptly summed up by Mats Berdal:

The pace and pressure of events, especially in 1992-93 has meant that the UN Secretariat itself has been unable to identify the military requirements of current and future operations. In addition, much of the academic literature on the UN after the Cold War has been the product of aspiration, focusing largely on what is theoretically desirable rather than on what is politically and practically feasible.[52]

---

[47] Duke, 'The United Nations and Intra-State Conflict', p. 377.
[48] See Berdal,' Whither UN peacekeeping' pp. 10-11.
[49] Ibid.
[50] Ibid. p. 12.
[51] See Hugh Smith, 'The Challenge of Peacekeeping', Hugh Smith (ed.), *Peacekeeping Challenges for the Future*,(Canberra: Australian Defence Studies Centre, 1993), p. 187.
[52] Berdal, p. 9.

Organisational and Political Problems

The demands which intra-state conflicts now place on the UN have exposed the inherent weaknesses of the organization in conducting the complex operations required by the difficult conflict situations, as demonstrated in Somalia and Bosnia-Herzegovina for example. The sheer magnitude of these operations highlighted the need for a reorganization in the UN Secretariat, resulting in the restructuring efforts discussed in Chapter One. Apart from the weaknesses in the machinery for organizing these operations, many organizational problems have been created by the political weaknesses of the UN. There has been a lack of political will amongst UN member-states, particularly the more powerful, to commit men and resources to these dangerous missions. The lack of timely intervention in Rwanda, and the quick departure of the UN/US force in Somalia, emphasized the lack of political will in the UN, to commit men and materiel to involvement in such conflicts. In the cases where decisions were taken to embark upon these more ambitious and complex operations, the reluctance of parts of the force to participate in operations which moved beyond peacekeeping created command and control problems.

II

REGIONAL PEACEKEEPING OPERATIONS

The experiences of regional bodies in responding to conflict within their regions indicate that they possess political will in abundance, to address these conflicts. In addition, they often have a strong peacemaking base, but very often, mediation is not the neutral third party activity that UN peacekeeping suggests. However, regional bodies often lack the capability to back third party diplomatic efforts with the required military operations. This section discusses some of the regional arrangements that existed during the Cold War, but greater attention is given to the African region, for the reason stated at the beginning of this chapter.

ORGANISATION OF AMERICAN STATES (OAS)

The Inter-American Peace Force (IAPF)

The OAS has a long record of settling disputes.[53] Much of this has been achieved through third party techniques of mediation and conciliation.[54] The peacekeeping experience of the organization is limited to that of the IAPF.[55] The force was created after about 19,000 American troops were deployed in the Dominican Republic following the outbreak of fighting in April 1965 between two ideologically opposed groups. The desire to prevent communist groups from infiltrating its 'backyard', most especially after the Cuban experience of 1959, led the US to intervene in the Dominican without the invitation of the host state.[56] Opposition from one of the parties and allegations of partiality, led the UN to despatch observers to the area, known as Representatives of the Secretary-General in the Dominican Republic (DOMREP), much to the irritation of the US. The presence of the force became acceptable only when at the US request, forces from other OAS member-states joined the US forces, to form the IAPF. However, over 90% of the forces belonged to the US. The inclusion of other nationalities on the force did not however prevent some OAS members from interpreting the US action as interference in the internal affairs of the Dominican Republic.[57]

The IAPF experience emphasized the point that third parties within regions are unlikely to be neutral and impartial. They often have vested interest in the conflicts and are therefore likely to show an interest in effecting an outcome. Despite its adverse effects on relations between some OAS member-states, the IAPF is considered a success by some commentators, since the force managed to stabilize the situation.[58]

---

[53] For background information on the OAS, see Jerome Slater, *The OAS and US Foreign Policy*, (Ohio State University Press, 1967).

[54] For details of OAS peacemaking efforts, see Cox, *Prospects for Peacekeeping*.

[55] For accounts of the IAPF experience, see Bruce Palmer, *Intervention in the Caribbean: The Dominican Crisis of 1965*, (Lexington: University of Kentucky Press, 1989); and Vaidyanathan Shiv Kumar, *U.S. Intervention in latin America: Dominican Crisis and the OAS*,(New Delhi: Radiant, 1987).

[56] See James, *The Politics of Peacekeeping,*; and Rikhye, *The Theory and Practice of Peacekeeping*.

[57] See for example, Diehl, *International Peacekeeping*, p. 121.

[58] Ibid.

THE ARAB LEAGUE

This organization also showed an interest, and willingness to resolve conflicts in its region, although it has not always been as cohesive as some other regional bodies. Two situations provided the Arab League with peacekeeping opportunity. The first was the Iraqi threat to Kuwait in 1961, and the second was the Syrian intervention in Lebanon in 1975. In the first case, an Arab force of about three thousand mainly from Saudi Arabia, Egypt and Syria, and small contingents from Jordan, Sudan and Tunisia, replaced British troops which had been deployed in Kuwait, following the threat of Iraqi invasion. The fact that the Arab force was expected to perform the same functions as those assigned to the British troops which it replaced, (i.e. deter Iraqi invasion, using force if necessary), eliminated this force from the peacekeeping category. However, there has been some doubt as to whether the Arab League force would have been able to take up arms against other 'Arab brothers' if this became necessary, thereby limiting its task to a psychological deterrence of Iraqi attack.[59]

The second case where an Arab League force was used was in Lebanon, following Syrian intervention in the country's civil war, much to the embarrassment of other Arab nations. The Arab League hastily set up a force in Lebanon.[60] This force which included all of Syria's intervening force, was transformed into the Arab Deterrent Force (ADF), in 1976. Apart from the Syrian forces, there were small contingents from Libya, Saudi Arabia, Quatar and United Arab Emirates. This force was far from a peacekeeping one, as it appeared the force was only used to legitimize Syria's intervention in Lebanon. On both of these occasions however, members of the Arab League showed an interest in containing conflict in their region.

THE COMMONWEALTH IN ZIMBABWE

This is one of the rare cases where a non-UN body successfully conducted an operation that could be categorized as peacekeeping. When in 1979 an agreement was reached to end the liberation war waged by the Patriotic Front (PF) against the white minority regime in Rhodesia (now Zimbabwe), provision was made for a Monitoring Force (MF) to maintain the cease-fire.

---

[59] James, *Peacekeeping in International Politics.*
[60] Istvan Pogany, *The Arab League and Peacekeeping in Lebanon*, (Aldershot: Averbury, 1987); and Naomi Weinberger, *Syrian Intervention in Lebanon: The 1975-76 Civil War*, (New York: Oxford University Press, 1986).

The force consisted of about 1,500 men, mainly British, with small contributions from some other commonwealth states.[61]

Although the mission was not officially termed peacekeeping by the British, many of the force's activities placed this operation within the classical peacekeeping category. The troops were lightly armed, not carrying more than arms for individual self-defence in the last resort. The force kept a neutral stance and did not pose a threat to any of the conflicting parties. However, the Commonwealth may not possess the political will to move beyond such traditional peacekeeping operations. Its diverse membership may make it difficult to muster the political will to carry out stronger action.

INDIA IN SRI-LANKA

India's experience in Sri-Lanka was that of a country keen to control events in its backyard, rather than that of an impartial third party. The cases involving India were very far from peacekeeping or indeed peace enforcement, and raise questions as to the ability of single nation third parties to conduct classical peacekeeping operations. The outbreak of violence following the demand by Tamils in Sri-Lanka for an autonomous state,[62] led the government to request assistance from India, to quash the Tigers' rebellion. An agreement emerged in which India was to despatch an 'Indian Peacekeeping contingent'. However, the situation on the ground was far from peacekeeping. It took on the appearance of a combat operation against the Tamil irregular forces. Indian troops had numbered 50,000 by 1988, all well armed and heavily engaged in battle with the rebels. India became a party to this internal conflict, and later became an army of occupation when it failed to leave immediately after the Sri-Lankan government requested India's withdrawal by the end of July 1989.

PEACEKEEPING IN AFRICA

This discussion of the African region begins with an assessment of African efforts at peacekeeping, demonstrating that despite the keen interest of African nations to resolve their conflict, they have often fallen short of this goal. This

---

[61] See J.H. Learmont, 'Reflections on Rhodesia', RUSI, *Journal of RUSI for Defence Studies,* 125, 4, (December 1980).

[62] Since Sri-Lanka's independence, the Tamil minority had felt discriminated against by the Sinhalese majority. See Dennis Austin and Anirndha Gupta, *Lions and Tigers: the crisis in Sri Lanka,*(London: Centre for Security and Conflict Studies, 1988).

is followed by an analysis of the factors that account for Africa's failure at conflict resolution, during the Cold War period.

The OAU Force in Chad

The war in Chad furnished Africa with its first major peacekeeping experience and a first real test of its capability to resolve major conflicts. Earlier events had presented opportunities for peacekeeping, albeit in different ways. One was the conflict in the Congo discussed earlier, which provided many African soldiers with valuable peacekeeping experience, as part of ONUC. The other, was the Algerian-Moroccan war of 1963 which provided the chance for a purely African solution.[63] An ad hoc commission established by the OAU in October 1963, arranged for direct mediation by emperor Haile Selassie of Ethiopia and president Modibo Keita of Mali, who succeeded in securing a cease-fire agreement.[64] A demilitarized zone was determined by army officers from each of the four states. The cease-fire and zone were supervised by a cease-fire commission made up of Ethiopian and Malian officers. Although a permanent solution to the conflict was not achieved until almost a decade later through bilateral negotiations, there was some optimism that Africans could solve their own security problems. However, in Chad, many factors stood in the way of the success of the OAU peacekeeping operation.[65] It was a disaster, which led to many burning questions one of which is whether the fundamental principles of peacekeeping could be successfully applied to African conflicts.

Chad, a country with at least twenty different tribes and languages, for many years endured factional fighting and struggle for power.[66] The failure of the first Chadian president, Francois Tombalbaye, to integrate the northern tribes, resulted in the emergence of FROLINAT[67], which took up arms against the government. The French military was recalled to assist in restoring order and improve administration in 1968.[68] The French withdrew their troops in

---

[63] For a discussion of the events leading to the Algerian-Moroccan war, see D.L. Price, The Western Sahara, *Washington Papers*, (1983).

[64] See James, *Peacekeeping in International Politics,*

[65] See Amadu Sesay, 'The Limits of Peace-keeping by Regional Organization: The OAU Peace-keeping Force in Chad' *Conflict Quarterly* 11 (1991), pp. 7-26.

[66] For succinct accounts of Chadian politics and international relations, see Rene Lemarchand, 'The Crisis in Chad' in Gerald J. Bender, James Colemanm, and Richard L. Sklar, eds., *African Crisis Areas and U.S. Foreign Policy* (Berkeley and Los Angeles: University of California Press,1985), pp. 239-256; and William J. Foltz, 'Chad's Third Republic: Strengths, Problems, and Prospects,' *CSIS Africa Notes,* No.77, October 30, (1987).

[67] French acronym for Front de Liberation du Tchad.

[68] See Rikhye, *The Theory and Practice of Peacekeeping,* p. 160.

1975 and General Felix Malloum was President of Chad from then, until 1979 when further internal struggles, involving Hissen Habre[69] and others, brought the country to the verge of disintegration.

The internal power struggle in Chad was compounded by external interference from Libya's Colonel Qaddafi who sought to install a pro-Libyan regime in Chad and a formal annexation of the northern border area of Chad. Peacemaking efforts by Nigeria, led to a cease-fire agreement between some Chadian leaders[70], but the fragile peace soon collapsed. Attempts by Nigeria to deploy troops to Chad unilaterally also failed[71]. It was Libya's actions in Chad that eventually brought about rapid action from the OAU. In May 1980, Libya sent 2,000 troops of Chadian origin to support Goukouni as the fighting extended to other parts of central Chad. In November of the same year, Libya intervened directly in support of the government forces, under cover of the collective defence clause of a dubious treaty of co-operation.[72] Three thousand heavily armed troops were sent to Chad, driving Habre's forces out of the capital. The growing involvement of Libya in Chad generated serious concern amongst other OAU members, most especially after Libya's announcement in January 1981 of an agreement on working to achieve the 'full unity' of Chad and Libya.[73] This was fiercely condemned by the international community, as well as many members of the Chadian coalition.

The Chad issue was considered in the OAU meeting of heads of state in Nairobi in June 1981 and an agreement was reached, to dispatch a peacekeeping force to Chad. The OAU was to accept Chad's choice of troop-contributing nations, which would bear most of the costs themselves. Libya was expected to withdraw its troops without loss of face. The OAU agreed to raise a peacekeeping force of about 5,000 men from Nigeria, Guinea, Benin, Togo, Senegal and Zaire. Negotiations were made for UN assistance and bilateral assistance from friendly western nations. By the start of 1982, OAUF's troops had numbered about 3,000 under a Nigerian commander, Major-General Ejiga.

The force was unsuccessful in implementing its mandate in Chad. It was required to conduct a traditional peacekeeping operation which entailed

---

[69] Habre joined Malloum's government in February 1978 and later became prime minister in this regime. He subsequently fell out with this government.

[70] These include Hissene Habre and Goukini Oueddei, who agreed to form a new government, and Col. Kamougue agreed reluctantly, to participate in the government. See Rihkye, *Theory and Practice of Peacekeeping,* p. 161.

[71] Ibid. p. 161; see also, *Keesings Contemporary Archives* Vol. XXVI, (1980), pp. 30065-7.

[72] See Rykhye, *Theory and Practice of Peacekeeping*, pp. 161-3.

[73] Ibid. p. 163.

... physical occupation of zones through the establishment and manning of Observation Posts, Check Points, Road Blocks, 24-hour patrols, preventing Armed Elements from entering area of operation, cordon and search, etc.[74]

Adhering to the fundamental principles of peacekeeping did not achieve the desired results for this force, which stood by, whilst Habre's forces defeated the GUNT forces. The OAU Force was however not expected to fight. It is doubtful that it would have been able to prevent 'armed elements from entering the area of operation' without the possibility of the use of force.

Serious obstacles stood in the way of the success of this force. First, OAUF was deployed in Chad, without securing a cease-fire thus, there was no peace to keep. Second, poor planning and co-ordination impacted on the operation from the outset. Of all the countries that offered to send troops, only Nigeria, Zaire and Senegal sent contingents. More troops were needed for the force to reach its minimal required capability and this was not forthcoming. This was compounded by the lack of co-operation from Libya. Libya refused to synchronize its troop withdrawal with the deployment of the OAU force, thus departing abruptly.[75] The delay in the arrival of the OAU troops provided Hissen Habre, with about 4,000 troops, the opportunity to defeat the less organized government troops. Thus, the numerical inadequacy of the OAUF was emphasized by this.

Third, the mandate was given different interpretations by the force and the Chadian Government of National Unity (GUNT), headed by Oueddei. The Nairobi Accord of 28 November 1981, originally provided the mandate for the force. Signatories to the Accord included the OAU Chairman, Kenya's President Arap Moi, Edem Kodjo, the OAU Secretary-General, and Goukini Oueddei, President of GUNT. The peacekeeping force was authorized to ensure 'the defence and security of the country whilst awaiting the integration of government forces'.[76] In addition to this, the accord affirmed the OAU support for the GUNT, and urged OAU member-states to support it in its effort to maintain peace and stability in the country. Ouddei however misinterpreted this support as a commitment to assist the GUNT militarily against Habre's forces. Although the OAU provided clarification of the force's mandate, emphasizing its neutral stance,[77] this did not change Oueddei's

---

[74] R. Kupolati, 'The Nigerian Contingent in the Organization of African Unity Peace-keeping Operation in Chad', in M.A. Vogt and A.E. Ekoko (eds.), *Nigeria in International Peacekeeping 1960-1992*, pp. 146-147.

[75] Bukar Bukarambe, 'Conflict and Conflict Management in Africa: The Role and Impact of the OAU in the Management of African Conflicts', *Survival*, (1983).

[76] OAU Resolution AHG/Res 102, 103 (XVIII); Also, Nairobi Accord, signed 28 November 1981.

[77] OAU Resolution AHG/ST/Ctte/Chad/Res. 1(III) of the Standing Committee of Chad, 10-11 February 1982; See also, R.Kupolati, The Nigerian Contingent p. 147.

expectations. The force's task was thus further complicated, as it became increasingly difficult to reach an agreement with Oueddei, who resented the non-combative role of the OAU force.

Operational Problems

Operationally, the capability of Africans to conduct such multinational operations was severely tested in Chad. The force suffered command and control problems, resulting from a number of factors. First was the inadequate troop strength, which made control of Chad's vast territory immensely difficult. According to General Kupolati,[78]

> The failure of troops to honour their pledges created deployment problems and reduced considerably the effectiveness of the force. The strength of the force at its maximum was composed of five manoeuvre battalions. This small force was expected to cover an area of 501,000 square miles, i.e. an average of 100,200 square miles of territory was the size of an area of responsibility of a battalion. In comparison to Lebanon, the United Nations Interim Force in Lebanon (UNIFIL) had about ten battalions to cover a territory of only 3,927 square miles.[79]

Whilst the flow of command from the Force Commander to the rest of the force was relatively smooth, this was not the case between the OAU secretariat in Addis Ababa, and the Force Headquarters in Chad.[80] The Secretary-General's representative in Chad was often unaware of events at the headquarters, due to unreliable communication channels. Officers who served in Chad were especially critical of the OAU secretariat. According to General Kupolati,

> Throughout the duration of OAU peacekeeping mission in Chad (November 1981 – June 1982) there were no substantial military directives to the peacekeeping force by the Secretary-General. Periodical operational reports that should have been regularly given by the secretariat to the Security Council or Council of Ministers were not issued. Little or no funds were made available for collective administration of the force, ... Such a situation could not but lead totally to the collapse of the force and it did.[81]

---

[78] General Kupolati was part of the Chad mission and was later the third Field Commander of the ECOMOG force in Liberia.

[79] Kupolati, pp. 148-149.

[80] James O. C. Jonah, 'The OAU: Peacekeeping and Conflict Resolution', in Yassin El-Ayouty (ed.), The Organization of African Unity after Thirty Years, (Westport: Praeger, 1994), discusses the problem of inadequate procedure for reporting between the Force Commander and the Secretary-General – see pp. 6-7.

[81] Colonel P. B. Adebayo, *'Nigeria's participation in Peace-keeping: Problem Areas in Lebanon and Chad Operations and Modalities for Future participation'*, (Paper for National Institute for Policy and Strategic Studies, October 1984), p. 100.

Kupolati remarked on the extent of the ineffectiveness of the Secretary-General:

> Although the OAU Secretary-General, Edem Kodjo paid a three-day visit to Chad in January 1982, it is doubtful if he had an operations cell at the secretariat to monitor the operations in Chad. He was known to be away to Europe for long periods and was hardly available to give necessary guidance/directives to the force. Consequently, the force commander was to establish direct communication between the Force Headquarters and the current Chairman of the OAU, Daniel Arap Moi of Kenya.[82]

The issue of logistics created perhaps the most difficult problem for command and control. The logistic situation was far from what obtained in a UN peacekeeping operation. Participants agree that the differences were obvious from the start:

> Experiences of Nigerian contingents in UNIFIL and Chad differ. The first contingent [to arrive] often suffered having to make provision for advance party who became the reception party for the main body. In UNIFIL, the Force Logistics Department (French Logistics) had the responsibility of receiving the contingent at Beirut Airport and of moving them to Southern Lebanon (Area of Operation). While in Chad, Nigeria's contingent had no such facility of logistics supporting units of other nationality provided by the OAU Force, to meet and settle the contingent in area of operation.[83]

In addition, the OAU secretariat came under serious criticism for failing to provide a logistic contingency plan for the force.[84] Thus, troop contributing nations were entirely responsible for the logistic requirements of their troops. The '... green berets and cap badges the OAU issued to the force at the tail end of the operation' constituted the exception.[85] Indeed, when Zaire experienced considerable difficulty in supporting its troops, Nigeria assumed part of the responsibility.[86] The scarcity of spare parts and petroleum oil and lubricants in Chad made resupply particularly difficult, given the poor transportation system on the continent.

The difficult terrain in which the force had to operate worsened its logistic problems as it was totally unprepared for the situation it met in Chad. The country's vast territory (largely desert) and extremely poor transport network put enormous strain on the already fragile logistic system of the OAU peacekeeping force. Poor roads and long distances made air transport a necessity for logistic supply, troop movement, casualty evacuation, etc. However, the force had no aircraft and each contingent relied on its home government for logistic support by air. Apart from this, the exceedingly high

---

[82] Kupolati, p. 149.
[83] Adebayo, p. 67 .
[84] Ibid.
[85] Kupolati, p. 150.
[86] Adebayo, p. 101.

temperature in Chad, and the effect of sand meant high maintenance cost for aircraft. As General Kupolati points out,

> The vast land mass, near primitive communication and transport system and the ex-
> tremely harsh climate of Chad would pose great challenge to even the best equipped ar-
> mies of the world. The OAU contingents, therefore, were not expected to fair [sic] well
> in view of their countries limited domestic industrial base.[87]

This first African peacekeeping effort in Chad raised a number of questions. One was whether conventional peacekeeping was workable in internal conflicts, particularly those in Africa. The UN Operations in the Congo (ONUC) and its failure to apply peacekeeping successfully until it enforced peace reinforces this. More significantly however, Africa's ability to success-fully plan and execute a peacekeeping mission on its own came under serious question. The keenness of African states to solve their own problems was emphasized by Chad, but whether they have the capability to do this is another issue.

LOST OPPORTUNITIES

Other serious conflicts had occurred in Africa during the Cold War, which the OAU was unable to handle. The organization not only failed to resolve the conflict in Western Sahara, it was almost torn apart by it.[88] The OAU became burdened with the Western Sahara issue in 1976 but concrete action was not taken until three years later at the Monrovia summit. An ad hoc committee was formed in December 1979, which recommended the withdrawal of Moroccan troops from Rio de Oro and establishment of an OAU peacekeeping force. At the summit meeting in Freetown in 1980, twenty-eight states supported SADR's application for OAU membership and Morocco threatened 'to walk out and take another five states with it'.[89] The OAU could not hold any successful meeting for sometime due to lack of quorum. Resolution of the Western Saharan conflict has been handled mainly by the UN especially since the end of the Cold War. The OAU's failure to resolve this conflict goes beyond the effects of Cold War politics. It reflects some fundamental weaknesses in the structure of the organization, which are discussed below.

The Ogaden war confirmed suspicions that a combination of factors reduced Africans' capacity for resolving conflicts in their region. Following the Western Somalia Liberation Front's (WSLF) decision to step up the

---

[87] Kupolati, p. 150.
[88] The Western Saharan war is discussed in detail in Tony Hodges, *Roots of a Desert War*; and in the *Washington Papers* on Western Sahara, (1983)..
[89] See Rikhye, *Theory and Practice of Peacekeeping*, p. 159; & Bukarambe, p55.

guerrilla campaign in the Ogaden,[90] and evidence of Somali support for WSLF,[91] Somalia and Ethiopia went to war in July 1977. Africa's role was limited to a mere diplomatic one by the OAU, largely because of the roles played by the superpowers in the conflict. In a conflict of its magnitude, the OAU would have been expected to attempt to resolve the conflict earlier through mediation and peacekeeping.

This was one of the many conflicts fuelled by the Cold War, where a peaceful settlement was unattainable without superpower support or change of posture. Some argue that it was the contradictory signals from the US and the Soviet Union to the adversaries, which inspired the war.[92] Ethiopia was originally strongly allied to the US, while Somalia on the other hand was firmly allied with the Soviet Union. However, with the overthrow of Haile Selassie in 1974, the new Ethiopian leader sought Soviet friendship, and gradually, the two African states swapped their super-power allies. Following Somalia's invasion of the Ogaden in 1977, the Soviet Union assisted by Cuba, gave its full support to Ethiopia. Somalia severed all links with the Soviets and turned to the US for support. The Somalian leader, Siad Barre, had been assured that there would be little objection to a Somali invasion of the Ogaden.[93] The readiness of the US to enter a security arrangement with Somalia strengthened this belief.[94] The Somalis, who had expected the US position to be at least that of indifference, were shocked when in the wake of the Somali invasion of the Ogaden, the US suspended all military aid to Somalia.[95] The military assistance from the Soviet Union and Cuba to Ethiopia, decided the outcome of the war.

The extent of superpower involvement in this war which occurred at the height of the Cold War, gave little room for African peacemaking efforts. A peaceful settlement could only have been achieved with the support of the superpowers. The conflict had been escalated beyond the capability of African peacemakers. This is explained further below.

---

[90] See Colin Legum and Bill Lee, *Conflict in the Horn of Africa* (New York: Africana Publishing Company,1977), p. 33.

[91] Robert F Gorman, *Political Conflict in the Horn of Africa*, (New York: Praeger Publishers,1981), p. 62.

[92] C.S. Whitaker, *A New Era of Peacekeeping,*(paper for a conference of commission on Regional Conflict Resolution of the project: Africa-Soviet-U.S. Cooperation.) p. 5.

[93] Edmond J. Keller, 'United States Foreign Policy on the Horn of Africa: Policymaking with Blinders on', in Gerald J. Bender, James S. Coleman, and Richard L. Sklar, (eds) *African Crisis Areas and U.S. Foreign Policy* (Berkeley and Los Angeles: University of California Press, 1985), p. 187 .

[94] Donald K. Patterson, 'Somalia and the U.S., 1977-1983: The New Relationship', in Bender et al, (eds), *African Crisis Areas,* p. 196.

[95] Patterson, 'Somalia and the United States', p. 197.

The Angolan conflict also transcended the peacemaking ability of African peacemakers. This war provided independent Africa with its first experience of direct foreign intervention on a massive scale. Before Angola's independence, there was every indication that a political vacuum would be created as none of the three Liberation movements could muster enough support to control a majority in the country. This situation threatened to erupt into a civil war. These liberation movements included the National Front for the Liberation of Angola (FNLA), Popular Movement for the Liberation of Angola (MPLA), and National Union for the Total Independence of Angola (UNITA).

The rivalry which had been the underlying factor of the US-Soviet relations resurfaced in Angola. Each superpower had its protégé either directly or through surrogates. The US intervened in form of CIA clandestine support to the FNLA despite congressional opposition.[96] By April 1975, about two hundred and thirty Cuban military advisers were participating actively in MPLA's camps.[97] South Africa, seriously threatened by the fall of the Portuguese empire, began to strengthen its position along Angola-Namibia border. Shortly afterwards, Cuba airlifted heavy arms and hundreds of troops to Angola through the Congo, while the Soviet Union increased the supply of arms. By the time South African troops crossed the border and moved near the Angolan capital, they were met by 15,000 Cuban troops.

With this large scale foreign, especially superpower intervention in this conflict, it was virtually impossible for African countries or the OAU to intervene or mediate successfully in Angola. Attempts at personal mediation were almost non-existent, and had little effect. Not only did Africa lack the depth of experience and the resources to mount a high level peacekeeping operation which would have been required in Angola, the adversaries' desire for a peaceful resolution was almost non-existent given the level of external backing received by each side.

The above examples indicate that African experience of diplomatic peacemaking supported by peacekeeping during the Cold War was very scarce. The major effort in Chad was unsuccessful. The OAU was better suited to organizing trilateral and multilateral management through the traditional strategies of conciliation, mediation and arbitration of disputes. African nations appeared to have more success at resolving their disputes at the early stages when the conflicts had not witnessed large scale external involvement, as was the case in Morocco-Algeria. A number of reasons account for Africans' failure (particularly before ECOMOG), to make peace

---

[96] See Lawrence W. Henderson, *Angola: Five Centuries of Conflict,* (Cornell University Press, 1979) p. 255.
[97] See John Marcum, *The Angolan Revolution; Exile Politics and guerilla Warfare 1962-1976,* Vol.2 (Cambridge Ma: MIT Press,1978) p. 273.

in their conflicts. The first set of factors relates to the nature and origin of the charter of the organization. The second is the effect of the Cold War and foreign influence in conflicts.

THE OAU AND ITS ROOTS

One of the main reasons for the lack of effective peacemaking prior to the Liberian war was the divergence of opinion amongst founding members along the lines of the former groupings on the continent, which resulted in loose arrangements in the OAU charter. Any realistic attempt to understand the internal factors that delayed the development of an effective peacemaking structure in Africa must therefore begin with the origins of the OAU. Before the formation of the OAU in 1963, a conflict existed between radical and moderate African countries, which influenced the type of conflict management machinery provided for in the OAU Charter. There were three main political groupings in Africa. First was the Casablanca group which consisted of Ghana, Guinea, Mali, Morocco and the United Arab Republic. Second, was the Monrovia group consisting of twenty regional members. Included in the membership of the Monrovia group were twelve Francophone states who were also members of the Union Africane et Malagache (UAM), known as the Brazaville group.[98]

These groups had different positions and perspectives on African problems.[99] In the discussions which preceded the founding of the OAU, different views along the lines of these divisions, were expressed on how best the continent could be united. These views varied from moderate ones such as the establishment of a single African Charter to prevail over those of the various groups whilst allowing for autonomy; to extreme positions which argued for a Union Government of Africa, possessing an African civil service, an African High Command, a court of justice, and many other institutions. This latter view met with tough opposition from members of other groups on the continent.[100] However, this divergence of views influenced the kind of organization that was formed.

In the 1960s, Kwame Nkrumah's proposal that a collective defence structure be included in the charter of the OAU generated serious debate

---

[98] See Jimi Peters, *The Organization of African Unity and Conflict Management in Africa,* (Unpublished reseach paper for the Nigerian Institute of International affairs, 1992) pp. 14-15; & Indar Jit Rikhye, *Theory and Practice of Peacekeeping*, p. 150.

[99] See Joseph Saye Guannu, *An Introduction to Liberian Government : The First Republic and the People's Redemption Council,* (USA: Exposition Press Inc., 1982) pp. 79-81.

[100] Zdenek Cervenka; *The Organization of African Unity and its Charter*, (London: C. Hurst & Company, 1969), pp. 1-3.

which continued over many years on different levels. Nkrumah proposed the formation of a High Command for the purpose of strengthening and consolidating the political independence of the new African states, protecting them against all forms of imperialist aggression, and to assist in the liberation of African states still under colonial rule. Nkrumah saw the threat to Africa as a complex one, consisting of external interference in African affairs as was the case in the Congo, and the danger posed by South African forces.[101] The strategy advocated by Nkrumah for dealing with these threats, transcended the mobilization of the military forces of the continent. He proposed a political union of Africa under an 'African Union Government'. Within such a union, a common defence plan could be evolved, as well as a common foreign policy and a fully integrated economic programme for the whole continent. Such a political union if achieved, would serve as a deterrent against any foreign intervention. It would also remove the need for African states to seek protection from outside powers through formation of alliances and military pacts.[102]

However, the OAU failed to have this entrenched in its charter at the founding meeting of the organization. The main reasons appear to be the differing views on what constituted a threat to the continent, and the unwillingness among African nations to relinquish their sovereignty to a national body. They argued that the proposal called for a substantial loss of sovereignty.[103] Some were suspicious of Nkrumah's motives, thus attention was focused more on his presumed motives, than on his argument.[104] Many opponents of the African High Command were concerned that it might be used against other African states rather than in relation to extra-African states. Nkrumah condemned these criticisms as 'a lack of understanding of some African leaders who think in terms of a sectionalised Africa, permanently

---

[101] See Kwame Nkrumah, *Africa Must Unite*, (London: Panaf, 1963), pp. 133-149; & pp. 173-193.

[102] Nkrumah's proposals for an African High Command and the rationale behind them are contained in many of his speeches and writings. See for example, Osagyefo Kwame Nkrumah, *Speech at The Hall of Trade Unions*, 9th July 1960; *An Address to the National Assembly On African Affairs*, 8th August 1960; *African Unity*, Speech at the opening of Africa Unity House London, 18 March 1961; *Africa Must Be Free*, Speech on Africa Freedom Day, 15 April 1961; *The Fight on Two Fronts*, 1 May 1961; *Africa's Glorious Past*, Speech at the Opening of the Congress of Africanists, Legon, 12 December 1962; *True Freedom For All*, Speech at Fourth Afro-Asian Solidarity Conference, 10 May 1965; and *Africa Must Unite*, (London: Panaf, 1963). A detailed analysis of Nkrumah's views is also contained in H. Assisi Asobie in *'Nigeria in Dilemma: ECOWAS joint Command or African High Command – the Paradoxes of the theory and practice of Nigeria's Strategic Postures,* (Paper for the Nigerian Institute of International Affairs, Lagos, 23 April 1985).

[103] Assisi Asobie, pp. 8-9.

[104] Ibid.

balkanised and exploited by those who want to keep Africa divided'[105] He stated:

> When I am accused by stooges of interfering in the internal affairs of other African countries, my answer is that every true African nationalist has a duty to concern himself with the present-day problems facing Africa.[106]

The debate on the AHC recommenced following a number of acts of aggression against some African states in the 1970s. The Republic of Guinea was invaded in 1970 by a combined force of Portuguese soldiers, German mercenaries, and Guinea dissidents. In 1975, South Africa, the US (via the CIA), and Cuba intervened in the Angolan civil war. In January 1977, the Republic of Benin was invaded by mercenaries backed and financed by foreign powers in collaboration with some African states. France, Gabon and Morocco were strongly suspected of connivance in this act. In March of the same year, Morocco, Egypt, France, Belgium and the US intervened in Zaire, to rescue the corrupt regime of Mobutu Sese-Seko, from disintegration following rebel attacks. In May 1978, France, again assisted by the US sent in paratroopers to recapture the towns which had fallen to the rebels.[107] In the light of all these occurrences, many did not question the relevance or purpose of an African collective defence system. The debate which now ensued concerned the feasibility of such a command. However, lack of consensus over the security structure to be adopted on the continent resulted in the loose provisions in the OAU charter.

THE CHARTER OF THE OAU

The operational problems of the OAU such as delay and difficulty in reaching decisions, and failure to resolve some conflicts (e.g. those in Western Sahara and Chad) through peacemaking and peacekeeping are mainly attributable to the loose arrangements in the Charter of the organization. The immediate needs and fears of the founding members marked the organization's structure and agenda. For many of the nation-states that had just emerged from colonial rule, there was no desire to submit their sovereignty to a supra-national government. The OAU was formed on the basis of two common assumptions namely, pan-Africanism and the need to protect the sovereignty of individual states. These assumptions were reflected in the objectives of the OAU

---

[105] Nkrumah, *African Unity* Speech.

[106] Ibid.

[107] See Bukar Bukarambe, p. 56; Dominique Moisi, 'Intervention in French Foreign Policy', in Hedley Bull ed., *Intervention in World Politics*, (Oxford: Clarendon Press 1984), p. 74; and James O.C. Jonah, 'The OAU: Peacekeeping and Conflict Resolution'.

specified in Article II of the Charter.[108] Like the UN, the Charter of the OAU made no provisions for peacekeeping, despite the prominence of the activity since the previous decade. Indeed, the Congo experience discouraged many African leaders from peacekeeping at the time. After Lumumba's death, ONUC was considered 'an imperialistic instrument to subvert African independence'.[109]

The OAU Charter, which emerged in 1963 in Addis Ababa, provided for an organization of 'sovereign and juridically equal states'. The Charter is very conservative on the internal affairs of member states. Six of the seven fundamental principles enumerated in Article III reinforce the autonomy of member states from interference or coercion by other member states or by the organization as a whole.[110] These principles are: the sovereign equality of all member states; non-interference in the internal affairs of states; respect for the sovereignty and territorial integrity of each member state and for its inalienable right to independent existence; peaceful settlement of disputes by negotiations, mediation, conciliation and arbitration; unreserved condemnations in all its forms, of political assassinations as well as of subversive activities on the part of neighbouring states or any other states; dedication to the total emancipation of dependent African territories; and affirmation of a policy of non-alignment with regard to all blocs.

The ability of the OAU to act decisively in crisis situations, and to promote its proclaimed goal of pan-Africanism has been greatly curtailed by many of the organization's features. First, the OAU at its inception consisted of weak and equal states, a feature rarely found in most international organizations. Thus, there was no 'powerful' state to bully others into compliance. Over the years however, some states have acquired enough resources to coerce other states. This is especially true within the sub-regions, a factor which made the formation of ECOMOG a possibility (see Chapter Four). However, it has been argued that 'the fundamental norms of the African system have in no situation been clearly and decisively reversed'.[111] In addition, the two-thirds requirement for a quorum when calling special meetings, makes it difficult for a state

---

[108] They are: to promote the unity and solidarity of African states; to co-ordinate and intensify their co-operation, and efforts to achieve a better life for the peoples of Afica; to defend their sovereignty, integrity and independence; to eradicate all forms of colonialism from Africa; and to promote international co-operation having due regard to the Charter of the UN and the Universal Declaration of Human Rights.

[109] James O.C. Jonah, 'The OAU: Peacekeeping and Conflict Resolution', p. 4.

[110] The sixth principle is the exception. It pledges an 'absolute dedication to the total emancipation of the African territories which are still dependent.'

[111] See I. William Zartman, 'The OAU in the African State System', in Yassin El-Ayouty and I. William Zartman (eds.), *The OAU after Twenty Years* (Praeger, 1984), p. 29.

or a faction to control the organization. This has encouraged inaction and delay in the OAU.

Second, the OAU is not equipped with independent executive tools capable of enforcing sanctions against either members or non-members hence Zartman's statement that 'there is no OAU; there are only members, and their interests come first'[112] The importance accorded national options has served to weaken pan-Africanist ideals in the OAU. The organization lacks formal sanctions such as suspension or termination of membership, that could be employed against a difficult state.[113] Its resolutions are only advisory, and not binding. Thus, OAU mediation is based on persuasion, since there is no concrete means of ensuring obedience to its will. It bears some semblance to the UN which has enforcement powers entrenched in its charter, but finds it difficult in reality to enforce peace, which was one of the factors which gave rise to peacekeeping. The settlement of disputes cannot be assured if it is based on persuasion without being accompanied by some form of pressure. Each level of peacemaking requires the application of a certain amount of pressure. At the diplomatic level, mediation is perhaps more successful if the mediator has some clout and can make side payments to the parties. A peacekeeping mission supporting the mediator's effort could also benefit from such clout. African mediators almost always lack a combination of these qualities.

The factor that perhaps creates the greatest problem for the OAU in the post Cold War period is the organization's adherence to the principles of sovereignty and territorial integrity. This has seriously limited the role of the organization in internal conflicts. In Chad, it was not until the Libyan threat that the OAU began to play a more prominent role. The reluctance of the OAU to become involved in internal conflicts was also obvious in Angola and Mozambique. Indeed, its chances of participating in the conflict resolution process were hindered by the OAU support for the recognized governments in those countries, in its bid to uphold these principles.[114] The dominance of this class of conflicts in the post-Cold War period has forced the OAU to reassess its policies. This is discussed further in Chapter four.

---

[112] Zartman, 'Conflict Reduction: Prevention, Management and Resolution'.

[113] The exception is suspension for non-payment of dues, a sanction that has not been invoked despite abundance of opportunities.

[114] See Berhanykun Andemichael, 'OAU-UN Relations in a Changing World', in Yassin El-Ayouty (ed.) *The Organization of African Unity after Thirty Years*, (Westport: Praeger, 1994), p. 123.

EXTERNAL FACTORS

The external factors that account for the absence of an effective peacemaking mechanism in Africa before the Liberian civil war include the Cold War, and the influence of erstwhile colonial masters. The Cold War delayed the establishment of a collective defence organization in a number of ways. First, the Cold War encouraged adversaries in African conflicts to pursue policy objectives through warfare as opposed to seeking diplomatic means. This was clearly the case in the conflict between Somalia and Ethiopia. Expectations of US support in a war against Ethiopia led Somalia to invade the Ogaden. Many conflicting parties played one superpower against the other, taking advantage of the bipolar rivalry.

The involvement of the superpowers or their surrogates often had the effect of discouraging parties to a conflict from seeking peaceful solutions, as well as escalating such conflicts. External intervention often fuelled many of these conflicts and ensured that they became too big for African countries to manage. It was virtually impossible for African countries to muster the resources to mediate in any African conflict which involved the superpowers. Mediation would only be possible if the superpowers expressed a desire for settlement and withdrew their support. Similar considerations resulted in the absence of UN peacekeeping missions in Africa after Congo. Superpower involvement in conflicts on the continent not only made UN peacekeeping difficult, it rendered African efforts and solutions ineffective.

Having discussed the problems posed by the Cold War, it should be added that interference from other African countries may also serve as external involvement. This is true for Libya, whose adventurism has served to escalate some conflicts. However many of the African states which intervened directly or indirectly in other conflicts on the continent were more often than not, intervening on behalf of an extra-African ally. An example was the role of Morocco, etc. in the Shaba crisis. Most African countries could not afford to carry out that level of intervention individually and unaided.

The other external influence that played a noticeable role in preventing a collective security mechanism in Africa concerns the role of France. France's determination to remain a significant middle power in world politics, has been a major motive for its involvement in African conflicts and general intervention in the affairs of African countries, particularly Francophone Africa.[115] A number of humiliating defeats suffered by France, one of which resulted from her involvement in the Suez crisis, played an important role in France's policy

---

[115] Daniel Bach, 'France's Involvement in Sub-Saharan Africa: A necessary condition to Middle Power Status in the International System' in Simon Baynham ed., *Military Power and Politics in Africa*, (London: Croom Helm, 1986), p. 75.

of intervention and claim to independence. This claim was reinforced by France's decision to build an independent nuclear weapon, withdrawal from NATO military command, and her privileged economic, political, military and cultural links with Francophone Africa.[116]

Since the francophone African countries became independent dominions in the 1960s, the French to a large extent have influenced policies in their former territories, through intervention in various forms and at different levels. The annual Franco-African summit, which began in 1973, is itself an indication of the French influence in Africa. French intervention in Africa has been highly personalized. Ad hoc institutions were set up in France, to maintain a permanent personal link between the French President and the Francophone heads of states. This way, it has been possible for France to maintain direct influence on these countries.[117] French military interventions in Africa have been grouped under two legal umbrellas. One is under bilateral defence agreements, which allowed for French military intervention conditional upon the request of the host state and at the approval of the French authorities. The other is the military technical assistance agreement which provides for French assistance in the organization, equipping and training of the national armies and police forces of the new states of Africa.[118]

However, factors other than France's ambition and its cultural links have made such level of intervention possible. These include the weakness of African states and their apparent call for outside intervention as discussed in the previous section. In the face of OAU failure to device a collective security procedure, African countries turned to foreign powers. In Francophone Africa, this weakness coincided with France's volition and ambition to remain a power on the world scene.

France made several attempts to thwart efforts to form an effective ECOWAS (The Economic Community of West African States). At the prompting of France, a rival West African Economic Community, CEAO, was created, consisting of the former French territories.[119] France was also instrumental in the formation of Agreement on Non-agression and Assistance in Defence, ANAD, which many anglophone states believe was done to thwart ongoing efforts then to reach a similar collective security arrangement within

---

[116] See Moisi, in Hedley Bull, (ed.), p. 69.

[117] Moisi explains that under the Fifth Republic, the decisions have been made by the President himself assisted by two ad hoc committees, whose role is to maintain a permanent personal link between the French President and the Francophone African leaders. See Moisi, p. 72.

[118] Ibid.

[119] It is believed that ANAD developed from the fourth Franco-African summit conference in Dakar, 1977. Peters, *The OAU and Collective Security in Africa,* p. 8.

ECOWAS.[120] This further widened the Anglophone-Francophone divide. Such moves by France encouraged Cote D'ivoire to assume a rival position to Nigeria in the sub-region thus preventing rapid progress from being made on regional security. The strong French presence in her former colonies has always given Nigeria cause for concern.[121] Thus, in Nigeria, there is the realization that good relations between Nigeria and France is crucial to the success of ECOWAS as Nigeria cannot readily usurp France's influence in her ex-colonies. The French are also of the belief that 'no French policy in Africa can be effective without the inclusion of Nigeria'[122]

CONCLUSION

Even in the Cold War period, there was some indication that the character of internal conflicts was markedly different from the inter-state ones with which the UN was preoccupied. The UN has been more successful than other peacemakers, in conducting effective operations which fall under the traditional peacekeeping category. The objectives of the UN operations were often limited to controlling the conflicts, to stabilize the international political environment. Peacekeeping was just sufficient for this. Most of the operations conducted by non-UN bodies were largely responses to internal conflicts and they often fell outside the classical peacekeeping category. This raises serious questions about the applicability of classical peacekeeping to internal conflicts. This is given more weight by the UN's own performance in the Congo, which initially began as a peacekeeping mission, but was later transformed into one of peace enforcement. It was clear even then that peacekeeping alone could not control this difficult internal conflict.

Some reasons can be attributed to the greater success enjoyed by the UN in peacekeeping over non-UN bodies. Apart from the Congo (ONUC) and perhaps Cyprus, UN involvement in conflicts in the Cold War era was largely restricted to conflict situations involving two states. These conflicts were generally easier for the mediator/peacemaker and peacekeeper to handle when compared to internal conflicts. In inter-state conflicts, peacekeepers are interposed between two professional armies, who have a clear understanding

---

[120] President Houphouet-Boigny of Ivory Coast made no secret of French influence when after the Franco-African summit in 1978, he declared: '... We are counting on French support. We have no complexes about it, since the European members of NATO call on the US in case of attack, and the Eastern European nations call on Russia'.

[121] See Bassey Eyo Ate, 'The Presence of France in West Africa as a Fundamental Problem to Nigeria', *Millennium*, Vol.12, No. 2, Summer (1983); and 'France in Central Africa: The NATO Dimension and Implications for Nigeria', *Nigerian Forum*, August 1981.

[122] *The Times* (London), 5 May 1989, p. 8.

of, and respect for ethics of war. With a long record of making peace in inter-state conflicts, the UN has had a higher rate of success than other peacemakers.

Furthermore, the UN could afford to be selective in the type of conflicts it responded to, while it was more difficult for regional peacemakers to do this. Regional or local actors were sometimes forced to bring about peace in conflicts within their region, given the security and political implications that this could have on their countries and the entire region. The Organization of American States presents a good example of this. In the Cold War milieu, the US preferred to handle any conflicts within its region outside a UN framework, so as not to create an opportunity for the Soviet Union to infiltrate American backyard.[123] These types of interests often took regional peacemaking initiatives beyond the realms of peacemaking, and peacekeeping efforts often fell outside the identified category. The UN, however, did not have this type of urgency, about intra-state conflicts, not unless there was a situation that threatened to result in superpower competition and eventual confrontation. Even this was avoided altogether after ONUC.

In addition, the UN had more success in conducting peacekeeping operations because the organization was seen as a more credible peacemaker. UN peacekeepers were often more acceptable to conflicting parties than local actors. In the case of Cyprus for example, the UN was given preference over NATO (by ArchBishop Makarios) as peacekeepers.[124] This acceptability in itself enabled conflicting parties to co-operate more readily with the UN than other peacemakers.

Generally however, the UN during the Cold War tended to respond to conflicts under the following situations. First, in circumstances where the conflict threatened to develop into a superpower clash if an escalation was not prevented, as was the case in most of the Middle East conflicts. Secondly, where the conflict was likely to attract the interest of the superpowers, and turn the conflict area into a competition ground. This was the case for example, in the early stages of UN peacekeeping in the Suez and Congo. Indeed, the need to prevent superpower competition in these areas led to the guiding principle that precluded a permanent member of the UN from partaking in peacekeeping operations. Lastly, the UN was involved in conflicts where one or more of the major powers had sought UN support in resolving the conflict. This was the case in Cyprus, where Britain, not wishing to be saddled with the problem indefinitely, preferred a UN presence. The case of the UN Interim Force in Lebanon (UNIFIL), is another example, where the US was keen to send UN peacekeepers as quickly as possible.

---

[123] This became an even stronger objective after Fidel Castro's rise to power in Cuba.
[124] Cox, p. 55.

There were areas of low interest that neither attracted enormous superpower interest nor threatened any serious clash between them. The Cold War had a paradoxical effect on these conflicts, escalating them beyond the level which local peacemakers could handle, but not serious enough to threaten a show-down between the superpowers. These conflicts did not attract UN peacekeeping and the local actors were not adequately equipped to handle them. This was the case with many African conflicts. In cases where against all the odds, local peacemakers embarked on peacekeeping, these operations often fell short of that identified as peacekeeping, as many activities removed them from this category.

The end of the Cold War has now clearly revealed new challenges. The UN cannot successfully employ traditional peacekeeping in dealing with difficult and complex conflict situations. Its members are unable to muster the political will to move beyond traditional peacekeeping and sustain such a strategy. Yet, the organization appears to possess both human and material resources to conduct operations beyond peacekeeping, at least in comparison to some regional organizations.[125] The concept of such operations has not however been clearly outlined. Regional organizations on the other hand, particularly Africa, have the political will, but inadequate machinery (operationally) for effecting the required operations for peace. The real challenges of the situation are illustrated in Liberia. Perhaps regions can develop their own concept for responding to conflict. Can they muster the resources to effect such a concept? Is there always a 'way' where there is a 'will'? What such a concept would entail and how it could be successfully implemented are issues for the next chapters.

---

[125] Although there have been reports of shortage of funds for UN peacekeeping, the UN still appears to be better placed than many regional organizations to obtain resources needed for peacekeeping operations.

CHAPTER THREE

State Collapse in Liberia and the Fate of Sierra Leone

INTRODUCTION

In Africa, there were expectations that the end of the Cold War would reduce the vicious conflicts that had become the region's trademark. The Liberian civil war was one of the first cases to dash such hopes. The war that later occurred in Sierra Leone is seen to have resulted in part, from the Liberian imbroglio. It however, provided the opportunity to find 'African solutions to African problems.' Having established in Chapter Two that successful peacemaking and peacekeeping were scarce in Africa during the Cold War, this chapter examines the original circumstances that brought into being a peacemaking approach that achieved a measure of success. It explains how the Liberian civil war resulted in the formation of ECOMOG, by tracing the roots of the war and examining the events which led to the ECOWAS effort to resolve the crisis. It also provides an account of the circumstances that led to the war in Sierra Leone and the Nigerian-led ECOMOG intervention.

HISTORICAL BACKGROUND OF THE LIBERIAN CONFLICT

The Liberian civil war and its implications for conflict resolution in Africa cannot be thoroughly analysed without a discussion of the country's historical origin. The civil war, which began in Liberia in December 1989 (until 1997 when elections were successfully held in Liberia) had its roots in the separatist policies of the founding and early regimes. Liberia is located on the West Coast of Africa. It is bordered on the West by Republic of Sierra Leone, on the North by Republic of Guinea, on the East by Republic of Ivory Coast, and on the South by the Atlantic Ocean.

The state of Liberia emerged with the signing of the 'Dukor contract' on 15 December 1821, between the American Colonization Society and some African Kings, with the acquisition of a piece of land for free slaves from America.[1] An agreement, the 'Elizabeth Compact' relating to the governing

---

[1]   The ACS agents were aware of the existence of native Africans on the Liberian soil before the arrangement was made to buy land for the settlers. It was expected that the settlers would integrate these native people. Sixteen ethnic groups inhabited Liberia prior to the arrival of the

of the new settlement was drawn between the settlers and their American agents on their way from America on board the ship 'Elizabeth'.[2] The free Africans arrived in Cape Montserrado on 25 April 1822. The first settlers dispatched to Africa in 1820 did not reach the 'promised land'. They arrived and took temporary shelter in Sherbo Island in Sierra Leone in March 1920, but many died from severe climate conditions and diseases. The survivors left the island and proceeded to settle in Fourah Bay Freetown, where many slaves from England had been brought to settle in the previous century. It was the second batch of free blacks despatched in December 1821, who finally settled in Cape Montserrado in 1822.[3]

Liberian history has spanned three distinct periods. The colonial period was between 1822 and 1847, within which the commonwealth period existed from 1839 to 1847; the 133 year period between 1847 and 1980 known as the era of the first Republic; and the post-First Republic era. There is a common perception that every major political change in the history of the state of Liberia has been brought about largely as a result of a deep sense of injustice. In particular, the view that the Liberian coup that brought Samuel Doe to power in 1980, and the civil war of 1989 to 1997 resulted from injustice has been widespread among the Liberian people.

When the free Africans arrived in Cape Montserrado in 1822, they did not play any significant role in the process of their own governance. The Government of this settlement between 1822 and 1839 was headed by an Agent, the highest official in Liberia. He was appointed by the ACS, to whom he was accountable. This agent also served as the United States agent for recaptured Africans, known as Congroes,[4] and was accountable to the secretary of the US Navy on their condition.[5] From 1822 until 1839, the settlers demanded a greater voice in the administration of their government from the American Colonization Society. These demands eventually led to a plan in 1839, to unite the settlements of Montserrado and Bassa Cove into a commonwealth, and to grant the settlers greater participation in government. In 1842, Mississippi in

---

settlers and they include the Bassa, Belle, Dan (known as Gio), Dei, Gbandi, Kissi, Gola, Grebo, Kpelle, Krahn, Kru, Lorma (Buzzi), Mano (Mah), Mandingo, Mende, and Vai tribes. See Joseph Saye Guannu, *Liberian History up to 1847* (New York: Exposition Press, 1983).

[2]   The only evidence of the 'Elizabeth Compact' has been Agent Samuel Bacon's record in his journal. No copy of the Compact has been found. See Joseph Saye Guannu, *An Introduction to Liberian Government* (New York: Exposition Press, 1982) p. 14.

[3]   See Shicks, *Behold, The Promised Land*; and Gershoni, *Black Colonialism,* pp. 9-10.

[4]   The Congroes were slaves captured from the slave ships while being transported to America. They originated from the Congo Basin area, Nigeria and Dahomey, now Republic of Benin. They were rescued on the high seas by American and British vessels. See S. Henry Cordor, *Facing the Realities of the Liberian Nation*, p. 28.

[5]   Guannu discusses the government of the colony of Liberia in both *Liberian History up to 1847*, and *An Introduction to Liberian Government*.

Africa, which was found by settlers from the state of Mississippi in the US joined the Commonwealth and became Sinoe County. This arrangement lasted only eight years. The Commonwealth ceased to exist on 26 July 1847, when Liberia became a republic.

The lack of complete political autonomy was not the only reason that compelled the Commonwealth of Liberia to declare independence from the ACS. Another important reason was that the colonial powers, particularly Britain and France, frequently violated Liberia's customs laws. The settlers protests were often ignored as Liberia was not considered by the trespassers to be a sovereign and independent state.[6] In 1847, they issued a Declaration of Independence which contained a long list of injustices which they suffered in America.[7]

AMERICO-LIBERIAN SUBJUGATION OF INDIGENOUS LIBERIANS

From 1847 when independence was proclaimed until about 1964, two opposing social classes existed in Liberia. The settlers, known as the Americo-Liberians, assumed the position of the upper class, which controlled political power. Two groups existed within this class and they competed for control of government – the light (mulattos) and dark Americo-Liberians. The second class, which was the lower class, consisted of aboriginal Liberians. In between the upper and the lower class, were the recaptured Africans, the Congroes.

Despite internal divisions within the Americo-Liberian class, this group dominated indigenous Liberians in all spheres of activity. Mulatto settlers, who were also victims of segregation in the south of America where free blacks were considered 'ignorant and criminal and degraded people', discriminated against the indegenous Africans, as well as their dark coloured contemporaries.[8] Mulattos occupied all the key positions in the Liberian government, until 1870, when Roye, a dark coloured Americo Liberian became President. However, both groups were united by their common interest to suppress aboriginal Liberians. Influenced by the belief in Europe and America then that those who adopted christianity and western ways were themselves superior,[9] the non-mulatto settlers discriminated against the native

---

[6] See Guannu, *Liberian History Up to 1847 pp. 57-58; An Introduction to Liberian Government p. 20*; and Umodem, pp. 15-16.

[7] For the text of the Declaration, see Guannu, *Introduction to Liberian Government*, p. 19 and *Liberian History up to 1847*, p. 58.

[8] Beyan, pp. 3-4.

[9] The leaders of the ACS espoused the view that blacks were inferior and that christianity and western practices conferred superiority on the whites in the Western world. For example, many were of the opinion that 'the christian profession would enlighten dark minds ...' Quoted from

Africans. Most of the black Americans had adopted christianity and western lifestyles during slavery in America and thus considered themselves superior to aboriginal Liberians. They coined several derogatory names for the natives who were neither christian nor western in outlook.[10]

The Congroes received better treatment from the upper class basically because they had adopted Americo-Liberian beliefs and practices. However, this group also received their share of maltreatment from the settlers initially. After they were recaptured, they were used as 'menials'. According to Boley,

> ... some 127 recaptured Africans who returned to Liberia were forcibly indentured and apprenticed to Liberian subjects, the adults for seven years, and the children till the age of twenty-one.[11]

The Americo-Liberians dominated indegenous Liberians in different ways. They created a colonial situation in which native Liberians were subjects and not citizens. They became citizens after embracing the habits and beliefs of Americo-Liberians which were judged to be civilized practices. Many did this until 1904 when citizenship was collectively conferred on all Negroes in Liberia. Liberia was divided into five counties, which were situated on the sea coast, and three provinces, which were in the hinterland. The provinces were governed in ways, which resembled the colonizing state and a colonized territory. The Liberian local government system during this period provided for two government units within the same township or city: one for 'modern Liberians', and the other for 'traditional' Liberians. Under this arrangement, more public funds went to the modern or Westernized areas while less funds were expended on the areas where traditional Liberians resided.[12] The Americo-Liberian discrimination of native Liberians extended to social circles. They were reluctant to sit next to the indigenous people in the churches. Christian Africans were required to enter the homes of Americo-Liberians through the back door, whilst they treated African culture and customs with contempt.[13]

The fundamental weaknesses in the laws of Liberia and in its political institutions made it possible for the settlers to maintain their dominance over the natives. These included flaws in the electoral and party systems, and resentment over the emblem and motto of the First Republic, confirming the deep-seated nature of the injustice felt by the natives. The seal of Liberia

---

'The African Repository', the main journal of the ACS, by Beyan, p. 5. See also Guannu, pp. 95-96.

[10] They were often refered to as 'heathen savages'. See Gus Liebenow, *Liberia: The Quest for Democracy,* (Bloomington: Indiana University Press, 1987), pp. 48-49.

[11] G.E. Saigbe Boley, *Liberia: The Rise and Fall of the First Republic,* (London: Macmillan, 1984), p. 24.

[12] See Gershoni, p. 25.

[13] Ibid. p. 22.

displayed a palm tree, a plow and a spade, a dove and a scroll, the emerging sun, a ship in the distance, and lastly, the motto: 'The Love of Liberty Brought us Here'. Many indigenous Liberians have rejected this motto, arguing that it applied to only a few Liberians, whose ancestors migrated from America.[14]

Up until 1964, the interior was under-represented in the National Legislature, and its residents paid taxes but were not adequately represented in government. Prior to 1964,

> ... indigenous Liberians interested in observing proceedings of the National legislature could do so only upon depositing with Government in Monrovia the sum of $100. As an observer, a tribal delegate had no voting rights.[15]

The property clause was also a serious weakness of the electoral system. According to the constitution, only those citizens who owned property were eligible to vote. Yet the government's policy on land ownership led to the displacement of many poor people, particularly in the rural areas. Their traditional farming lands were bought and taken away by the comparatively affluent settlers. In some cases the meagre amounts the settlers offered for land were not paid.[16] In addition, before an African could be elected to public office, he had to prove beyond any doubt that he had become a 'civilized' person. He must have owned, cultivated his own land, renounced paganism, traditional customs, and accepted christianity and western lifestyle, for at least three years.[17] Only a negligible number of aboriginal Liberians, who had the advantage of Western education occupied any significant posts in government.

Originally known as the Anti-Administration Party, The True Whig Party (TWP) emerged ostensibly in response to social and political factors such as discrimination in the Liberian society and dissatisfaction with aspects of the constitution, but it failed to bridge the wide gaps between the social classes. The True Whig Party won every election between 1877 and 1975. But throughout its ninety-eight years in power, the party did not replace the country's social, economic and political systems with any new and radical ones. The TWP is aptly described by Sesay as

> ... representing a club of individuals, who were prepared to uphold and advance the privileges enjoyed by the minority Americo-Liberians in the country. All those who were not prepared to "play the game" according to the rules of the party were fenced out of the political, economic and social privileges that the elaborate patronage system could confer.[18]

---

[14] See Guannu, *Introduction to Liberian Government*, p. 36.
[15] Sesay, *Historical Background to the Liberian Crisis*, p. 34.
[16] See Liebenow, *Liberia: The Quest for Democracy*, p. 47.
[17] See Gershoni, pp. 22-23.
[18] Sesay, 'Historical Background to the Liberian Crisis', p. 31.

Efforts to create an opposition party which would challenge the TWP were unsuccessful until 1975, when the Progressive Alliance of Liberia (PAL) was established, under the leadership of Baccus Mathews.[19]

Apart from these institutional weaknesses, the Americo-Liberians maintained control over the indigenous people through other methods. First, the elite reproduced itself through marriages within this group. Intermarriages with indigenous people were frowned upon. The Liberian elite from about 1950 to 1980 consisted of about three hundred families, which constituted only about two percent of a population of nearly two million.[20] It was this small group of people that occupied important positions in government, the church and other socializing institutions, and commerce. The powerful Masonic lodges served as a strong socializing channel and served to maintain the group's cohesion. Thus, all the prominent positions, including channels for registering dissent were often occupied by the President, his family and friends. For example, President Tubman's son headed the Liberian Confederation of Trade Unions.

Americo-Liberian stranglehold on indigenous Liberians was complete with economic exploitation, which included the 'contract' or forced labour on the natives.[21] The League of Nations investigated allegations of 'slave labour' in 1929.[22] In their bid to suppress the indigenes, the settlers adopted what has been described as a 'divide and rule strategy', which sowed the seeds of ethnic rivalry in an indigenous population, which was not completely homogeneous. Ofuatey-Kodjoe describes how this strategy was employed:

> the benefits of economic growth were distributed unevenly among the indigenes, so that over time, correlations began to develop between ethnicity, class and social mobility. Also, the pattern of repression was carried out by a policy of recruiting armed forces along ethic lines and deploying them to brutalize other ethnic groups.[23]

A number of factors prolonged this situation. One was the physical distance between the sixteen native tribes, which made it difficult for them to collectively oppose.[24] They were not in close contact with one another given the underdevelopment of the hinterland. This was mainly in the form of bad roads,

---

[19] Accounts of failed attempts are discussed in Gus Liebenow, *Liberia: The Evolution of Priviledge*, (Evanston: Northwestern University Press, 1966).

[20] Sesay, 'Historical Background to the Liberian Crisis' p. 30.

[21] The events leading to the adoption of forced labour or 'contract' and the effects of this policy are discussed in detail in Boley, *The Rise and Fall of the First Republic*; and in Liebenow, *Liberia: A Quest for Democracy*.

[22] For details, see Liebenow, *Liberia: A Quest for Democracy.*

[23] W. Ofuatey-Kodjoe, 'Regional Organizations and the Resolution of Internal Conflict: The ECOWAS Intervention in Liberia', *International Peacekeeping*, Vol.1, No.3, 1994, p. 265.

[24] Guannu, *An Introduction to Liberian Government*, p. 64.

lack of transportation and communication.[25] There was no workable program to achieve unity and development amongst these culturally diverse ethnic groups. Attempts at unification in the early part of the century were blocked by the growing suspicion amongst the natives and their repression by the settlers who were fearful of the possibility that the natives might gain access to positions of power.[26]

Having discussed the various injustices, which existed in the First Republic, it must be stressed however, that some efforts were made to redress this situation in Liberia, at different stages although such efforts were limited. What can perhaps be described as the most effective effort to integrate indigenous Liberians occurred under the Tolbert regime, as discussed below. Many of these efforts manifested themselves through constitutional amendments. Amongst these were the constitutional amendment of 1904, which conferred citizenship on all aboriginal Liberians; that of 1945 which provided for representation of the hinterland in the House; the 1948 amendment, which gave women the right to vote and that of 1975, which lowered the voting age from twenty-one to eighteen years and the repeal of the act which divided the country into county and hinterland jurisdictions in 1964.

THE END OF THE FIRST REPUBLIC

The First Republic was eventually brought to an end after one hundred and thirty-three years, by Master Sergeant Samuel Doe's revolutionary coup of 1980. The long period before a major change of regime occurred raises a significant question. What factors eventually brought about this change? Political change eventually occurred in Liberia largely as a result of President Tubman's 'approach to unity and development'.[27] He took major steps to unite the people through the building of roads, schools, hospitals and clinics, particularly in the coastal towns and cities. He promised the natives increased representation in the National Legislature. It appeared that political motivations surrounded Tubman's actions. His advances into the hinterland occurred because his political base on the coast was no longer strong. The interior thus provided him with a major avenue for support. Dixon sees Tubman's real motives as the need to prevent a crisis, remarking that

---

[25] Ibid.

[26] The issue of unification and development is analysed in detail in S.Henry Cordor, *Facing the Realities of the Liberian Nation: Problems and Prospects of a West african Society* (Books for Africa Press, 1980), Chapter Two.

[27] Guannu discusses Tubman's 'approach to unity and development' in An Introduction to Liberian Government, Chapter Five; Tuah Wreh provides a detailed analysis of 'Tubman and the econonmy' in Chapter Thirteen.

> Keenly aware of this injustice, and the potential danger it posed to security of
> the nation, the Tubman administration tried to involve the native people into the
> mainstream of the political and economic life of the nation.[28]

Other factors that resulted in a change included the decrease of the ruling class
through inter-marriage, and criticism from the US over the settler suppression
of native Liberians.

Tubman attempted to integrate the 'indigenes' in two major ways. The first
was through education. The other was his 'Open Door Policy', in which
foreign investors were attracted to invest in Liberia, with few preconditions.
Tapping of Liberia's natural resources effectively began in 1934 with
Firestone's first tapping of Liberian rubber.[29] Tubman granted concessions for
the extensive mining of iron ore and rubber. By 1960, Firestone and the
Liberia Mining Company had generated average annual pre-tax profit of more
than $32 million.[30] Compared to about $1 million national revenue inherited
from his predecessor, Tubman's regime experienced a major economic boom.
However, whilst this policy resulted in advantages like building of roads,
bridges, airport, schools and hospitals, there were serious pitfalls. For
example, the 'Christie concession', which provided mining rights for the
Liberia Mining Company for all minerals within certain locations for eighty
years from 1945, was found to be worth only '20 cents per ton of ore ex-
ported'.[31]

The Tubman administration however, failed to tackle the problem at its
roots. The social barriers between the aboriginal and settler Liberians, and
many of the weaknesses in the laws of the country and in the political
institutions remained. The majority of Liberians hardly felt the effect of the
economic boom.[32] By 1971 when William Tolbert became president, 4% of
all Liberians controlled 60% of the income.[33] Tubman resisted all opposition
to his government. He encountered serious opposition to the very poor terms
he negotiated with foreign companies under the open door policy. Opponents
of this agreement were harassed and jailed by Tubman's government.[34]
According to Dixon,

---

[28] Dixon, p. 9.

[29] Tuan Wreh, *The Love of Liberty ... The Rule of President William V.S. Tubman in Liberia
1944-1971*, (London: C. Hurst & Company and Monrovia: Wreh News Agency, 1976), p. 113.

[30] Clower, Dalton, Harwitz and Walters, *Growth Without Development*,(Evanston: Northwestern University Press, 1966), p. 133.

[31] Wreh, p. 114.

[32] Clower et al. discussed the negative impact of the open door policy and Tubman's policies
on Liberia.

[33] See Guannu, *Introduction to Liberian Government*,p. 99 .

[34] Wreh, p. 114.

... the welfare of the settlers from America ... who spearheaded the founding of the nation and their descendants was the overriding concern of the government. This element of our society held all the political and economic powers in the country and maintained a single party rule that tolerated no opposition ... The merit system, thus, had no place in the society.[35]

Ironically, it was President Tubman's educational policies that acted as the real catalyst for political change. His foreign scholarship program provided the opportunity for many Liberians to study abroad. This broadened their knowledge and understanding of the situation at home. These effects were perhaps unforeseen by Tubman. Both within and outside Liberia, students began to question the laws which governed their country, and criticized the ineffectual political institutions. Many groups later brought serious pressure to bear on the Liberian government. Amongst them were the Movement for Justice in Africa (MOJA), founded in 1973; The Union of Liberian Associations in the Americas, founded in the US in 1974; and Progressive Alliance of Liberia (PAL), founded in the US in 1975.

When President Tolbert assumed political office in 1971, he promised both to continue the economic progress that was begun under the previous regime, and also to work toward the unity of the Liberian people. But Tolbert who had served for many years in government, neglected to appreciate the political realities of his time. When he took over the reins of power in 1971, there was widespread consciousness amongst the Liberian people, about the poor management of their economy and the denial of their political and civil rights. There was no change to those clauses in the constitution, which prohibited the masses from enjoying their political and civil liberty. The property qualification for example was still a constitutional provision, while slogans like 'The Love of Liberty Brought Us Here', that indigenous Liberians found offensive were still in use.

Pressure mounted from all the groups, both at home and abroad, from MOJA, Union of Liberia Associations in the Americas, and PAL, which transformed into an opposition party and was later banned by the government. A number of incidents such as the 'rice riots', paved the way for the military coup.[36] Tolbert's government was overthrown on 12 April 1980 by Master Sergeant Samuel Kanyon Doe (an aboriginal Liberian), and sixteen other enlisted men, bringing the First Republic to a long awaited end, but it led to the assassination of President Tolbert and many others.[37]

The precise intentions of Samuel Doe will perhaps always remain obscure. In the immediate aftermath of the coup, his intentions appeared altruistic. The

---

[35] Bishop W. Nah Dixon, Great Lessons of the Liberian Civil War, Liberia: 1992), p. 8.
[36] Boley, *Liberia: The Rise and Fall of the First Republic*, p. 173.
[37] For details of the events immediately preceding the coup, see Sesay, 'Historical Background to the Liberian Crisis'; and Boley, *The Rise and Fall* .

composition of his cabinet reflected a desire to truly unite the peoples of Liberia. Appointment of government officials was not tribally based initially. The members of the elite who had advocated a change to the unjust system of the Americo-Liberians were given roles to play within this government irrespective of ethnicity.[38] The native peoples expectations of the Doe regime are finely captured by Dixon:

> ... the native population of this country felt that the day had finally arrived for them to enjoy the full right of citizenship in their own country. They thought that their needs and interests which had been long overlooked would now claim the full attention of their government.[39]

However, subsequent events (discussed below), only reveal Doe as one who utilized the existence of an unpopular government, and the organized outcry for an end to its injustices, to create not only an acceptable motive, but also an opportunity to stage his coup and secure legitimacy for his selfish ends. It was the unpopular policies of the governments of the First Republic which created the events that produced Samuel Doe as the country's first native African leader, paving the way for a civil war.

PRELUDE TO THE LIBERIAN CIVIL WAR

The civil war which occurred after almost ten years of Doe's rule, was the result of dissatisfaction with Doe's regime, for its ruthlessness, corruption, abuse of human rights, and determination to remain in power at all costs. His determination to resist pressure for moves toward meaningful democracy was compounded by growing tribal tensions largely created by his policies, an ailing economy, and the determination of his opponents to remove him from power by force. On his assumption of power, Doe not only assassinated President William Tolbert, he ruthlessly executed any likely opponents. For example, shortly after the coup, thirteen top government officials and civil servants were executed by firing squad on a Monrovia beach.

Doe's initial popularity quickly eroded as his regime bred deep ethnic divisions amongst indigenous Liberians. The deep resentment of the indigenes toward the settlers and their desire to purge Liberia of Americo-Liberian domination largely accounted for their wide support of the coup despite all the brutality.[40] The euphoria was short-lived by unfolding events which revealed the insensitive policies of Samuel Doe's government. Doe gradually sur-

---

[38] Sesay, 'Historical Background' pp. 43-44.
[39] Dixon, pp. 9-10.
[40] Elwood Dunn and S. Byron Tarr, *Liberia: A National Polity in Transition*, (Metuchen, NJ: The Scarecrow Press, 1988), p. 84.

rounded himself with mainly members of his Krahn ethnic group.[41] Most of his advisers, government officials, officer corp in the AFL, were now drawn from his Krahn tribe, and their allies, the Mandingos.[42] In addition to this, corruption was rife in Doe's regime, as misuse of resources of the state compounded the country's economic problems.[43] This caused great dissatisfaction amongst members of other ethnic groups. The united front which had been forged by the discriminatory policies of the Americo-Liberians began to crumble. The cracks in this unity which had been created by Americo-Liberian 'divide and rule tactics' were wide open with Doe's ethnic policies. Thus, ethnicity became a strong element of Liberian politics.[44] However, whilst some commentators simply place 'tribalism' at the root of the Liberian conflict, this factor emerged mainly as a means of attaining political ends.[45]

HUMAN RIGHTS ABUSES UNDER THE DOE REGIME

Elections

Doe's reign was characterized by gross abuses of human rights.[46] The Doe regime is remembered for its atrocities against Liberian citizens which included AFL looting, rape, arson, flogging, arbitrary arrests and summary executions.[47] Furthermore, Liberians were denied free press and free and fair elections. The government of the True Whig Party was replaced by a military government, the People's Redemption Council (PRC). The constitution was suspended and all political parties were banned. Doe ruled by decree through the PRC. A new constitution was approved by the PRC in 1983 and by national referendum in 1984. Political parties were once again permitted, provided they were registered with the Special Electoral Commission

---

[41] See Sesay, 'Historical Background', p. 44.

[42] The importance of this and other factors and their effects are discussed in Henry G. Andrews, *Cry, Liberia, Cry* (New York: Vantage Press Inc., 1993) and Amos Sawyer, *The Emergence of Autocracy in Liberia: The Tragedy and Challenge*, (San Francisco, Institute of Contemporary Studies), 1992.

[43] Sesay, 'Historical Background ...', pp. 44-5; and *West Africa*, 9-15 July, 1990, p. 2066.

[44] See Larry Diamond, 'Ethnicity and Ethnic Conflict', *The Journal of Modern African Studies*, Vol.25, No.1, 1987, p. 120.

[45] See for example, E. Conteh-Morgan and S. Kadivar, 'Ethno-political Violence in the Liberian Civil War', *Journal of Conflict Studies*, Vol. 15 No.1, 1995.

[46] For accounts of gross human rights abuses and atrocities committed by the Doe regime, see *Report of US Lawyers Committee for Human Rights*, (New York, November 1986); and Michael Massing, *Best Friends: Violations of Human Rights in Liberia, America's Closest Ally in Africa*, (1986).

[47] *US Lawyers' Committee for Human Rights*, p. 1.

(SECOM). Doe, who was now the Commander-in-Chief of the Armed Forces of Liberia and had promoted himself to the rank of a General, in 1984, found the National Democratic Party of Liberia (NDPL) and announced his intention to stand for the presidency, much to the shock of the Liberian people.[48] He increased his age by two years in order to meet the minimum age requirement of thirty-five years. By then, there was already growing dissatisfaction with Samuel Doe's regime.

In 1985, general elections were organized, which were won by Doe's party, the NDPL, despite allegations of election fraud. He was pronounced president with 50.9% of the vote. The disappearance of several ballot boxes and their eventual discovery outside Monrovia confirmed suspicions over electoral malpractice by Doe.[49] There were eleven political parties, but they complained about the difficulties of the registration process and only three registered in time for the elections. Amongst the exhausting registration requirements imposed on these political parties was the payment of a fee of $150,000 (US Dollars[50]), when Liberia's per capita income was $400. This registration requirement became the least of the problems that faced political parties other than the NDPL. These parties suffered at the hands of Doe's government which tormented, coerced and assaulted them.

The Liberian People's Party for example, which enjoyed large following amongst students and professionals, and was led by a popular university professor (Amos Sawyer[51]) was banned by Doe's government after enormous molestation. Doe ordered the arrest of Amos Sawyer and fifteen other members of his party on the charge that they were 'plotting to burn down Monrovia and install a socialist government'.[52] This led to protests and demonstrations by thousands of students. Liberian troops opened fire on these demonstrators, killing and injuring several hundreds, many of whom were beaten and raped.[53] Sawyer was imprisoned for seven weeks without being charged, and at the end of which he was released and 'banned' from politics. Protests from other party officials only earned them arrest and eventually, the party itself was banned.[54]

---

[48] Ibid. See also Massing, pp. 10-12.

[49] The *Washington Post*, 22 October 1985.

[50] The US dollar has been Liberia's legal currency since its founding although in recent times the Liberian one dollar coin and a five dollar bill have been minted.

[51] Amos Sawyer was the chairman of the commission which drafted Liberia's constitution. As the next chapter will show, he would later become the Leader of Liberia's Interim Government of National Unity (IGNU), following an effort by ECOWAS to resolve the Liberian crisis.

[52] Massing, p. 13.

[53] Ibid.

[54] *West Africa*, 16-22 April 1990, p. 612.

With one opponent out of the way, Doe's government proceeded to launch its assault on the United People's Party (UPP). The UPP was the largest political party and its leader Baccus Matthews was considered to be the country's most popular political figure. Matthews was foreign minister from when Doe seized power until 1983, when he resigned. However both Matthews and the UPP were banned by the Liberian government on the grounds that the party advocated socialism.[55]

With both the LPP and UPP excluded, the party which posed the greatest threat to Doe was the Liberia Action Party (LAP). Doe ordered the arrest of Ellen Johnson-Sirleaf a LAP official, and it was this that eventually attracted international condemnation of the Doe regime. She was accused of 'sedition' following a speech she made in Philadelphia, criticising the government.[56] She was initially placed under house arrest and later sent to a military stockade. Angry reactions to this came from some West African countries and from the US. Many members of the US Congress protested and this eventually led to the passing of a resolution calling for the suspension of US aid to Liberia.[57] An unrelenting Doe proceeded to sentence Ellen Johnson-Sirleaf (through a military tribunal) to ten years of hard labour at a maximum security prison. However, the government soon began to feel the effect of the US embargo on financial aid to Liberia. Sirleaf Johnson was released along with about twenty-four other political prisoners. Thus only three parties (including LAP) were left to contest elections with Doe's party-NDPL.

Coup Attempts

Two of the most serious coups d'etat were attempted in 1985 by General Thomas Quinwonkpa, and in 1988, by General Nicolas Podier. The two officers were killed, and bloody reprisals were wreaked upon the Nimba region, from where most of the coup plotters originated. Nimba is home to the Gio tribe and their Mano allies, who appear to have suffered the worst of Doe's tribalistic policies. The 1985 coup attempt was launched on November 12.[58] Quiwonkpa, who had assisted Doe in staging the 1980 revolutionary coup was commanding general of the Liberian army until 1983 when he fell out with Samuel Doe over his repressive rule. He left the country after orders were issued for his arrest. He returned to Liberia two years later to stage a coup against Samuel Doe's government. They announced the overthrow of

---

[55] Ibid.
[56] Massing, pp. 17-19.
[57] Ibid.
[58] See *US Lawyers Committee on Human Rights*, and Massing, pp. 23-25.

government through two key radio stations which they had taken control of and Liberians took to the streets in their thousands, jubilating over Doe's fall.

However, the joyous crowds did not know that the coup had failed. The government forces had succeeded in regrouping, regained control of the radio stations and proceeded to viciously attack the jubilating crowds. Hundreds of civilians were killed including a substantial number of members Mano and Gio tribe where most of the coup plotters belonged. The overall death toll in connection to this coup attempt is not known. The US embassy estimated the death toll at between 400 to 500, while the members of the opposition put this figure at 2,000 and above.[59] It is reported that General Quiwonkpa was captured, and killed by government troops who mutilated his body.[60] General Podier's unsuccessful coup of 1988 faced similar fate as Doe's forces went on rampage, killing several members of the Gio and Mano tribes. Podier belonged to the former, but reprisals were unleashed not only on the Gio, but on their Mano allies. Many members of the Gio tribe, which is the principal tribe in Nimba were convinced that Doe's government was determined to eliminate Nimba's Gio majority.[61]

Intimidation of the Press

In January 1986, Samuel K. Doe was sworn in as president of the second Liberian Republic but hopes and expectations that the change from military rule to constitutional government would produce justice and grant civil liberties to Liberians soon faded. The immediate indicators were the continued existence of repressive decrees, including the notorious decree 88A[62], and the bans of LPP and UPP. Furthermore, five leading organizations which had been banned after the coup attempt, remained banned.[63] Ellen Johnson had been arrested again after the coup attempt, accused of treason, but not charged until after five months in prison. However, the strongest indication of the government's insincerity about its claim to practising democracy was its continued intimidation of the press.

---

[59] See *West Africa*, April 16-22, 1990, p. 612.

[60] Massing, wrote this in *Best Friends*, before Charles Taylor made the claim in 1991, that Doe's men mutilated and ate Quinwonkpa's body, in *Patriotic Special Issue Freedom Pangs*, (Gbarnga, Liberia: NPRA Press Centre, May-June 1991), pp. 26-29.

[61] See *Africa Research Bulletin* 15 Feb. 1990; and Max Amadu Sesay, *Bringing Peace to Liberia*, (1996).

[62] This decree (88A) prohibited 'rumours, lies and disinformation', a clear attempt to grant government officials immunity to criticisms, See Massing, *Best Friends*; and *West Africa*, 16-22 April 1990, p. 612.

[63] These included the Press Union, Business Caucus, Teachers' Union and two student groups.

Attempts by some previously banned newspapers to resume circulation after the return to constitutional rule, met with hostility by the new 'civilian' government of Doe. The Daily Observer, for example, was forced by the government to shut down in January 1985 due to the government's displeasure with the paper's pattern of reporting. Many other members of the press incurred the wrath of the government. Journalists were imprisoned arbitrarily. The publisher and editor of another paper – 'Footprints Today' – were arrested and imprisoned by Doe for seven weeks for publishing a story about an official enquiry into corruption in a government ministry which was based upon confidential official documents. Charles Gbenyon, editor-in-chief of the Liberian Broadcasting Service (LBS) was seized by government troops for continuing to broadcast throughout the coup attempt and he later died in their custody. Doe's government refused to release Gbenyon's body to his family.[64]

THE CIVIL WAR

The first shots of the Liberian civil war were fired in December 1989, when Charles Taylor, a former Liberian government official, invaded Liberia's Nimba county from Cote d' Ivoire, with a group of armed dissidents and exiles known as the National Patriotic Front of Liberia (hereafter NPFL). The rebellion, which was started in North Eastern Liberia by Charles Taylor and his men was not a forgone conclusion. Local support from Nimba county was not as great as the rebels had expected, as the people were weary of failed coups which normally generated untold consequences from Doe's forces. Furthermore, Taylor's reputation did not inspire great confidence amongst the people. Taylor, an Americo-Liberian, was Director of the General Services Agency in Samuel Doe's government, until 1983 when he fled to the US after accusations of corruption.[65] He escaped from Boston while awaiting extradition charges. It was the aimless actions of the government forces which breathed life into the rebellion and escalated the conflict. Following the invasion of Northern Liberia by this small and ill-equipped band of rebels pledging to overthrow the government, Samuel Doe dispatched two battalions of government soldiers (who were not only better equipped, but outnumbered the rebels), ostensibly to 'nip the rebellion in the bud'. But his soldiers launched a campaign of terror against the people of the area who responded

---

[64] For details of harassment, see Massing, pp. 35-41.
[65] *Africa Research Bulletin*, 15 Feb. 1990, p. 9557 & 15 April 1990, p. 9633; See also, *Africa Report*, March/April 1990.

by rallying to the rebels in their thousands, against the already unpopular regime.[66]

Attempts to crush this rebellion by the government troops failed and this rebel group remained a thorn in the side of Doe and his troops. The rebellion spread around the country side and gradually advanced toward the country's capital, Monrovia. President Doe issued a shoot-to-kill policy after claiming that rebel forces killed two hundred people including sixteen government officials in Kahnple and Boutuo.[67] The rebellion had by then shown signs of developing into a full blown war and its magnitude was one that was not imagined or expected by many including Doe and perhaps Charles Taylor himself. It turned out to be one of the bloodiest armed conflicts in the sub-region since the independence of West African states.[68] The events of the following months would give an indication of the scale on which the war was waged and its magnitude, particularly the rapid growth of refugees and the fierce ethnic killings.[69]

The Liberian civil war was fought ostensibly to redress the grievances many had against Samuel Doe's regime. Charles Taylor was not alone in his desire to put an end to the injustice suffered at the hands of Doe. Members of the Liberian elite whose support Doe initially sought, and who were later alienated by him were part of a plan to remove him from power. All were agreed on one thing – that Samuel Doe must be stopped. But how he should be stopped was the issue of contention. Claims by the NPFL indicated that other prominent Liberians along with Taylor planned to oust Doe from power. Discord between Charles Taylor and the rest however resulted from lack of consensus over the method to employ in removing Doe from power.[70] United in their bid to remove Doe from power, they sought support for the mission from external sources, obtaining finances, weapons, training of recruits, and asylum from different sources. The problem arose over implementation. Whilst Taylor believed that the only way to dislodge a military regime was through an uprising by the people, others thought this was adventurist, preferring a coup d'etat type of take-over or similar arrangement.[71] Given the division over how to remove doe from power and indeed what Charles Taylor

---

[66] Africa Research Bulletin, 15 Feb. 1990, p. 9557.

[67] *Africa Research Bulletin,* Sept. 1990, p. 9841.

[68] The Nigerian civil war has been the other major war in the sub-region. But this war did not have major spill-over effects.

[69] For a discussion of the deterioration to ethnic killings and the effects of this, see Hiram Ruiz, *Uprooted Liberians: Casualties of a Brutal War* (Washington DC: US Committee for Refugees, 1992).

[70] Personal interview with a senior spokesperson for the NPFL, London, November 1993.

[71] Ibid.

perceived as fear on the part of the others,[72] Taylor embarked on the mission alone.

THE CONFLICTING PARTIES

The Liberian civil war marked the first time in the region that civilians had taken up arms against a military ruler. Although one could argue that Samuel Doe was not a military ruler, having civilianized himself, in many respects, he was still a military leader. He ruled by decree until 1986 when he was sworn in as a civilian president. However, as a civilian leader, his pattern of government hardly differed from his days in uniform. He still retained some of the laws decreed under his military rule. A number of the atrocities committed by his regime were carried out when he was a civilian leader. Furthermore, in the opinion of the people and particularly his counterparts in the sub-region, Doe was regarded as a military ruler. As will be discussed later, amongst the reasons expressed by West African leaders for the ECOMOG intervention, was that Taylor's activities (a civilian attempting to oust a military leader), must not be encouraged in the region.[73]

Thus, on the one side was the government force, the Armed Forces of Liberia (AFL). On the other was Charles Taylor with an army of about two hundred men formed in exile, consisting of other exiles and dissidents, trained in military camps outside Liberia. Libya is believed to have been one of the major bases, of the NPFL.[74] The AFL was thus initially fighting against an NPFL, which was dismissed by Doe and his aides as an illegal force, a small uprising which ought to be put down with relative ease. It was, however, assumed that the two battalions dispatched to quell the rebellion would finish the job quickly. Indeed, few expected the rebellion to fare better than the numerous coups which were ruthlessly crushed by Doe, earning him the description, the 'cat with nine lives'. In February 1990, Doe and his men were dismissing the occurrence in Nimba County as just a 'small house trouble'.

A factor common to all the members of Charles Taylor's camp was their deep hatred for Samuel Doe's regime. However, Taylor himself did not expect or realize the magnitude of the war he was about to unleash in Liberia.[75] He merely believed that a rebellion was the best way to unseat Samuel Doe, and

---

[72]Ibid.

[73] Guinean President, Lansana Conte is thought to have been a strong supporter of this view. See *African Concord*, 27 August 1990.

[74] This was confirmed during my interview with the Senior NPFL spokesperson. He argued that while Libya rendered assistance to the NPFL in the form of training, weapons and other forms of assistance were not received from Libya. This is contrary to popular belief.

[75] The NPFL spokesperson interview.

thought this could easily be achieved given the deep animosity which the people of Liberia felt against Doe.[76] This was particularly true for the inhabitants of Nimba County, the area where Taylor began the rebellion. The county is home to the Gio and Mano tribesmen, who have been the traditional enemies of the Krahn tribe. Apart from this, the Gio and Mano suffered the most at the hands of Samuel Doe's regime and had by now begun to harbour the belief that Doe intended to wipe them out as a nation. The decision to start the rebellion from Nimba County has been interpreted by some commentators as Taylor's exploitation of the region's ethnic grievances to reinstate his Americo-Liberian group in power.[77]

At the outset, it was the militarily weak NPFL with little or no combat experience which sought to confront a professional, superior AFL. The NPFL troops could not wear uniforms both in their bid not to become easy targets, and for lack of resources.[78] At the outset, the NPFL and Doe's AFL were the only parties to the conflict. However, after months of fighting, the parties to the Liberian war had numbered as many as four. By mid-1995, this number had increased to eight, serving to complicate and frustrate peace efforts.[79]

The first contending group to emerge in addition to the existing ones was the Independent National Patriotic Front of Liberia (INPFL) led by Prince Yomie Johnson. This group broke away from Charles Taylor's NPFL, after accusing Taylor of committing atrocities within his own camp.[80] The INPFL leader accused Charles Taylor of ordering the executions of members of his camp at will. He claimed that in some cases, Taylor set members of the same camp against themselves.[81] He reported several incidents at the battle front, where soldiers were hit from bullets fired from within the camp, and were passed off by colleagues as enemy attack.[82] In addition to this, Johnson and Taylor differed on their future roles in post-war Liberia. Whilst Taylor was aiming to control the reigns of power, Johnson argued that 'the gun that liberates should not rule'.[83]

The other group emerged after almost eighteen months of the conflict. The United Liberation Movement for Democracy in Liberia (ULIMO) led by Alhaji Kromah was a coalition of different Liberian groups, many of which were supporters of the late President Doe, reinforcing the ethnic dimension

---

[76] Ibid.
[77] For example, Conteh-Morgan and Kadivar.
[78] Ibid.
[79] See Chapter Four for details.
[80] Personal interview with Prince Yomie Johnson, leader of the INPFL, Nigeria, April 1993.
[81] Ibid.
[82] Ibid.
[83] For details, see P. Johnson, *The Gun That Liberates Should Not Rule*, (Lagos, Pax Cornwell Publishers Ltd, 1991).

which the conflict had assumed.[84] ULIMO members claimed that the group was borne out of the desire of displaced Liberians to return home.[85] They therefore promised to mount an attack on the NPFL unless it co-operated with the peace process. Another faction was to later emerge, breaking from ULIMO to form the Liberian Peoples Council (LPC), led by George Boley. The Lofa Defence Force would later emerge, whilst ULIMO would be split along ethnic lines, into ULIMO-K under Alhaji Kromah and ULIMO-J led by Roosevelt Johnson. By 1995, the NPFL would suffer a further split with the emergence of NPFL Central Revolutionary Council (NPFL-CRC). The entry of these groups into the conflict at the different stages, had profound implications for not only the course of the war, but also for the peace efforts. The effects of this proliferation of factions are discussed in the next chapter.

THE CONDUCT OF WAR

The manner in which the Liberian Civil War was prosecuted revealed the character of violent intra-state conflict and the challenges they pose in the post-Cold War milieu. This conflict, which initially appeared to be more of an outcry against the unpopular regime of Doe, quickly turned into an ethnic conflict. The NPFL's hit and run attacks on army barracks and local government officials in Nimba County attracted heavy AFL retaliation against residents of Nimba county.[86] Thus, the Gio and Mano people were targeted by the AFL from the outset. The AFL was dreaded more than the rebel force because of the tactics it employed. Within the AFL itself, an ethnic conflict was reported to have broken out, which involved Krahn soldiers carrying out vendettas against members of other tribes fighting within the armed forces.[87]

The net effect of the AFL tactics was that the NPFL which previously had limited grassroots support now enjoyed immense support from the entire county. This served to escalate the conflict and provide the NPFL with enormous strength to wage an all out war against Doe. The NPFL, strengthened with a voluntary force throughout, was able to advance rapidly toward Monrovia, waging total war against Doe. Why the AFL adopted such tactics in their bid to crush the rebellion is not hard to comprehend. It is generally difficult to recognize guerrilla forces due to their lack of uniform and their employment of hit and run tactics. In explaining their atrocities against the

---

[84] *Africa Research Bulletin*, 1-30 June 1991.
[85] Ibid.
[86] See *Africa Report*, July-August (1990) p. 47; and *Africa Research Bulletin,* 15 Feb. 1990, p. 9557.
[87] See Mark Huband, 'Doe's last stand', *Africa Report* , July-August 1990, p. 48.

people for example, top AFL men explained that it was difficult to identify the rebels.[88] However, apart from this obvious problem, the AFL did not particularly have a good image prior to the crisis. Outbreaks of indiscipline were regular and the army was constantly used to suppress the people.

One feature that was noticeable almost immediately, was the absolute lack of regard shown for the rules of war by all parties. Terror against civilians was one of the most prominent weapons of this war and it was used effectively by all sides. The AFL however set the scene for its use. For example, in their bid to flush out the rebels, government troops set fire to a number of villages – for example, Siathon and Kpueton. Civilians, including women and children were killed indiscriminately by the AFL who accused them of assisting the rebels.[89] Survivors' accounts indicate that government forces pursued inhabitants as they fled their homes, shooting and killing civilians including several children. In one of the villages for example, decaying bodies of massacred people were left in a heap to rot.[90] In many cases, it was the arrival of the rebel forces at the scene which lessened the sufferings of the masses, as the rebels managed to drive government forces south. The NPFL soon began to terrorize innocent civilians as the conflict spread to other parts of the country, targeting the Krahn people and their Mandingo allies.

Indeed, the atrocities committed by the AFL not only served to strengthen the NPFL, but contributed to the development of another prominent feature of the war – the use of children as fighters in the campaign of terror. The initial surge of child soldiers emerged from the casualties suffered as a result of AFL atrocities. Several thousands who had lost their homes and families in the massacre by government troops joined the NPFL to take up arms against Samuel Doe. The composition of the NPFL was thus rapidly widened to include children as young as twelve years old.[91] Every member of the rebel group thus sought to unleash reprisals against Doe, his forces (AFL), his tribesmen (the Krahn people), and their families. In the midst of the counter-terror unleashed by the NPFL, hundreds of children were forced by the rebels to join the war. In other cases, many boys joined voluntarily following scarcity of food in the country. The little food available was often controlled by the rebels.[92] The use of child soldiers was accompanied by superstitious practices with

---

[88] *Africa Research Bulletin*, 15 March 1990.
[89] Ibid.
[90] *Africa Report*, July-August 1990.
[91] Ibid. Also, Special Report by Sky News on 7 February 1994 featured NPFL soldiers as young as nine years.
[92] In my interviews with a cross section of Liberian women in Oru – Ijebu (Nigeria) and Monrovia (Liberia), many discussed the plight of boy soldiers and problems of reintegration in society.

masked fighters often clad in pyjamas, dressed as transvestites and adorned with "juju" (black magic) supposed to render them invisible, invincible or immune from the harm of bullets.[93]

Another distinct feature of the civil war in Liberia was that with very few exceptions prisoners were hardly taken by any of the sides. Rather, a shoot to kill policy prevailed in every camp. For both rebels and government troops, every individual, not just soldiers, was a legitimate target as long as they belonged to a rival group or supported an opponent. Opponents and their families were butchered without mercy. In some cases, pregnant women were not only killed, but special attention was given to the foetus, which was carved out and shot separately. Such savagery was commonplace in the Liberian conflict.[94] The claim that there were hardly any wounded civilians in Nimba's hospitals (at least initially), confirmed the shoot to kill policies of the parties[95].

Apart from the ready acceptance of civilians, including women and children as legitimate targets, no immunity was granted to foreign nationals, nor were buildings belonging to foreign missions or institutions which would normally be recognized as sanctuaries treated as such. All people or establishments were attacked so long as they were in the way. In May 1990, Doe's troops attacked a UN refugee compound, killing four refugees, and abducting forty. This led to a UN decision to pull out its personnel.[96] Prior to this period (March 1990), as Bahn, a major trading town in Northeast Liberia fell to the rebels, two foreign nationals (British and American) including a missionary, were found dead in the town.[97] In July of the same year, government troops massacred at least six hundred people taking refuge on the grounds of a Lutheran Church in Monrovia.[98] In August, the leader of a breakaway faction of the NPFL (Prince Johnson) took foreigners hostage.[99] Two foreign (Nigerian) journalists also died at the hands of the NPFL.[100] Atrocities in various forms continued throughout the conflict. The most serious after the

---

[93] Max Amadu Sesay, p. 3. For more on this, see also, S.P. Riley, 'Intervention in Liberia: Too Little, Too Partisan', *The World Today*, Vol.49, No.3, March 1993, pp. 42-3.

[94] This was confirmed in several sources including personal interview with ECOMOG's Press Secretary under General Bakut; interview with Gabriel Umoden, who visited Liberia during earlier phases of the crisis; and accounts of survivors in refugee camps in Nigeria, and in Liberia. This and other human rights violations are also discussed in S. Ellis, 'Liberia 1989-1994: A Study of Ethnic and Spiritual Violence', *African Affairs*, Vol. 94 No.375, pp. 165-197; 'Liberia: A Human Rights Disaster', *Africa Watch*, 1990; and 'Liberia: The Cycle of Abuse', *Africa Watch*, 1991.

[95] See *Africa Research Bulletin*, 15 February 1990, p. 9558.

[96] See *Africa Research Bulletin*, Sept 1-30 1990, p. 9841. Also, Report by BBC Focus On Africa.

[97] *Africa Research Bulletin*, 1-30 Sep. 1990.

[98] Ibid.

[99] Ibid.

[100] *African Concord*, 27 August 1990.

initial heat of the war, was the Harbel massacre in 1993, where over three hundred women and children were slaughtered.[101]

Being an irregular army, it would perhaps have been out of character for the NPFL force to adhere to the rules of war. It was the conduct of the AFL that was somewhat more surprising. For a regular army trained to observe the rules of war, the AFL displayed very little of this. Although it could be argued that regular armies employ strategies different from the norm when dealing with irregular forces, the AFL's approach was vicious right from the start, reflecting the level of indiscipline which had been characteristic of the armed forces since Doe's assumption of office. The army had been used by Doe to unleash his reign of terror, inflicting reprisals on his political opponents and other 'offenders'. Furthermore, the AFL had no experience in dealing with the type of war being waged by the NPFL guerrillas. This army was trained mainly, by the US and Israeli Forces who paid greater attention to training required for a conventional war.

TAYLOR'S EARLY SUCCESSES

Despite the widespread atrocities committed by the warring factions, Taylor, with his relatively small and inexperienced force was able to defeat government troops, taking virtually every major town within six months, and was poised to move on Monrovia, the country's capital and the seat of government. Taylor was determined to seek a unilateral solution to the conflict through the defeat of Samuel Doe's troops on the battlefield. A number of factors were instrumental in this level of success. First, Taylor had correctly anticipated the support of the Liberian people, especially those who had been victim to the abuses and prejudices of Doe and his ethnic group. This support, which initially did not appear to be forthcoming, was strongly secured after the AFL's brutality was unleashed on innocent citizens. Many were keen to avenge the evil done to their families by Doe's forces. There was an element of luck here for the NPFL, in the sense that the AFL's viciousness which was not anticipated on that level, generated the high level of support from the masses.

Second, many of the tactics employed by Taylor in waging this war achieved tremendous success at the initial stages. Taylor had read widely on revolutionary warfare and there is some indication that he read Mao's works

---

[101] A UN report found AFL soldiers guilty of this atrocity. *BBC Focus on Afica* Report, 18 Sept. 1993.

and his experiences in Mainland China.[102] Taylor began to wage his war from the rural base areas in the remote and difficult countryside. This secure base protected his forces from defeat by government forces when they were most vulnerable. Had Taylor begun the incursion from Monrovia with his small inexperienced force, the NPFL would almost certainly have faced extinction in the first few days. Their base at the countryside was made more secure by the fact that the government troops were not too familiar with the terrain. As already indicated, earlier generations of Liberian elite concentrated largely on Monrovia, the state capital. The countryside had been largely ignored for many decades and thus it was hardly developed. Routes to the rural areas were inconvenient and as a result, not many travelled to the interior. This factor worked in favour of Taylor and his men.

Weaknesses of the NPFL force such as small numbers, poor equipment and vulnerability, concealed their inherent strengths such as mobility, secrecy, and speed. The force advanced more rapidly to the capital. The problem of low morale commonplace with conscript armies, was minimized as almost every NPFL soldier had a common goal – the elimination of Doe. The Liberian army, though not a conscript army, suffered from low morale and was not cohesive, given the tribal divisions. There were reports that Doe recruited as many as 2,000 troops to flesh out his army of 5,000.[103] Although these troops were supposedly volunteers – mostly from Doe's tribe, there were frequent reports of desertion in the AFL. Thus Taylor's strategy, coupled with sheer luck created huge military successes for the NPFL. Taylor's success was reflected not only in terms of physical control of areas of land, but in terms of the effects on Samuel Doe who was still at the seat of power and whose troops were still in control of the capital, Monrovia.

By the middle of 1990, the rebels had gained extensive ground as fighting intensified. Reporters confirmed that the rebels controlled Nimba and Bassa counties including Yekepa, Liberia's second largest city.[104] The port city of Buchanan also fell to the rebels. As Taylor's rebels captured the country's third largest town, Gbarnga, 100 miles north-east of Monrovia, President Doe began to adopt a policy of appeasement and deception, promising not to run for re-election, indicating the first signs of panic in the government camp.[105] The government was to later announce that it had accepted an invitation from religious leaders to participate in peace talks. The peace talks broke down

---

[102] The senior NPFL spokesperson stated during interview that Charles Taylor had read on a wide range of twentieth century revolutionary wars.
[103] *Africa Research Bulletin,* 15 April 1990, p. 9633.
[104] *Africa Research Bulletin*, 1-30 September 1990, p. 9841.
[105] Ibid. Indeed, Doe later went as far as declaring amnesty for political exiles, lifted ban on three political parties, and promised to restructure his cabinet.

within days, without any agreement.[106] The pressure on Doe was obvious as this time, he offered to step down, if he and the Krahn people were guaranteed immunity. This did not have any positive effect on the rebels who were determined to remove Doe by force. The advancing insurgents shut down Robertsfield International Airport, and captured the US managed Japanese-owned Firestone Rubber Plantation killing hundreds from Doe's ethnic group.[107] Having gained control of the countryside, Taylor's strategy for the conquest of Monrovia was to isolate the capital which was the only place under the control of Doe's government troops.

One factor that served to compound the situation in Liberia and seriously reduced Taylor's chances of victory was the break up of Taylor's NPFL. A rival rebel group, INPFL was formed by Yomie Johnson. Thus, three different factions were struggling for the control of power. A stalemate emerged as no party was able to gain control of the capital, where civil order had totally collapsed. Essential services including water, electricity, transportation, telecommunications amongst others were shut down. Bodies of hundreds of civilians killed were left to rot on the streets of Monrovia. Taylor would later establish a rival government in Gbarnga, known as the National Patriotic Reconstruction Assembly Government (NPRAG). Apart from the above strategies and the element of luck for the NPFL, two other factors however strengthened Taylor's chances of success at that stage – a strong economic base and external support.

ECONOMIC FACTORS

Charles Taylor's success, in terms of maintaining his hold on most of the major towns and cities captured, and his ability to keep up the military pressure on Doe's forces were largely determined by economic factors. The rebels grew into a serious military force as they were able to re-equip, adding many heavy weapons to their armoury. The financing of Taylor's army was largely dependent on the NPFL's control of the port of Buchanan, as well as territory rich in natural resources.[108] Taylor is reported to have freely exploited the mineral resources in the territory under his control, trading with foreign establishments and accumulating substantial funds in banks abroad.[109] Export of timber from the port of Buchanan was supervised by an economic commit-

---

[106] Ibid.
[107] Ibid.
[108] *Africa Confidential*, May 1991.
[109] For details, see W. Reno, 'Foreign Firms and the Financing of Charles Taylor's NPFL', *Liberian Studies Journal*, Vol.18, No.2, 1993.

tee headed by a military Commander. With control over much of Liberia's natural resources, Taylor reaped immense benefits from running the region as private enterprise, without any opposition.[110] He established a rival government, based in Gbarnga – the National Patriotic Reconstruction Assembly Government (NPRAG). In Kakata, about forty miles from Monrovia, the NPFL sold equipment and cars from the German-owned Bong mines company, where Liberia's iron ore deposits are mined.[111] This economic base strengthened Taylor's position militarily and hardened his resolve to pursue victory, seeking a unilateral solution to the conflict. However, this only served to raise the cost of the war, leading to more destruction of lives and property.

ARMS TRANSFER AND EXTERNAL SUPPORT

External support was vital to the initial success of Taylor's rebellion. There were reports of links with Libya, but the NPFL's strongest external supporter was Blaise Compaore of Burkina Faso. The training of his troops were carried out in Burkina Faso which for a long time constituted the supply route for Taylor's ammunition. Such support enabled Taylor to secure the control of the key towns within a few months of fighting. But with a strong economic base, Taylor was not totally dependent on outside sources for funding, but the supply route was still important. His buoyant economic base allowed him to re-equip and acquire heavier weapons. Acquisition of weapons achievable from a strong financial base and a supply route, strengthened the NPFL's position militarily against Doe's army. Thus, like many other African conflicts, arms transfer (to all sides) led to increased militarization of the Liberian civil war which in turn raised the cost of the war and prolonged the conflict, pushing any peaceful resolution further beyond reach.

With all these factors riding in Taylor's favour, and from all indications, Taylor was poised to take over Monrovia after invading the town centre, but he did not. A number of factors that were largely unforeseen, accounted for Taylor's failure to conclude the task and attain his goal. The first, was the introduction into the conflict, of a rebel faction as discussed earlier, which broke away from the NPFL. Led by Prince Yomie Johnson, the force known as Independent National Patriotic Front of Liberia (INPFL), mounted an assault on the centre of Monrovia, wrestling control from government troops.[112] This added a new dimension to the conflict. The second factor

---

[110] See W. Reno, 'Reinvention of an African Patrimonial State: Charles Taylor's Liberia', *Third World Quarterly*, Vol.16, No.1, 1995.
[111] *Africa Confidential*, May 1991.
[112] Interview with the INPFL leader revealed the reasons for the split from the NPFL.

concerned the question of American interference. According to the NPFL, Charles Taylor halted the rebel advance on Monrovia and the executive mansion because he was persuaded by the US (via Herman Cohen) to withhold any attack while efforts were made to get Doe out of Liberia.[113] The NPFL argument is that Cohen negotiated and agreed to the despatch of ECOMOG rather than keep his promise to the NPFL.[114]

The third factor, which in many ways put an end to Charles Taylor's ability to achieve a unilateral resolution to the Liberian war through victory on the battlefield, was the dispatch of ECOMOG to Liberia, and ECOWAS mediation in the conflict. This is discussed in greater detail in Chapter Five. Charles Taylor saw ECOMOG as an obstacle in his path, a deliberate attempt to rescue Doe from the onslaught he would have suffered at the hands of the NPFL. This was not necessarily the case, as the existence of another rebel faction meant that the conflict was degenerating into anarchy. Thus, Taylor was faced with the task of removing two opponents, Doe and Johnson. This threatened to prolong the war and the human suffering. Lastly, the NPFL needed to change from guerrilla to conventional tactics in order to have any chances of overpowering the AFL in the city. This created serious problems for the NPFL, which was unable to transform itself to a conventional army.

This war has demonstrated the vicious nature of African conflicts, and the determination of warring parties to endure and inflict high levels of human suffering while stubbornly pursuing their goals. The high level of suffering only hardened the resolve of the rebels to achieve victory on the battlefield. This factor made any attempt to make peace an extremely difficult task. Mutually damaging stalemates were hardly created throughout the battle. Even when one seemed to exist, it was not matched by the desire in all sectors, to pursue a peaceful solution to the conflict.

ATTEMPTS AT PEACEMAKING

The magnitude and nature of the Liberian civil war made it extremely difficult for Liberia's West African neighbours to ignore the conflict. The domestic efforts to resolve the war collapsed rapidly. Religious leaders inside Liberia invited both sides to participate in peace talks in June 1990. Doe, who by now was convinced of his opponents' determination to drive him from power, announced his acceptance of the invitation in the same month. He seemed ready to welcome any move that would rescue him from the impending rebel

---

[113] The NPFL spokesperson interview. See also, interview with Charles Taylor in the *New African*, Oct. 1992.
[114] Ibid.

onslaught on the Executive Mansion. However, the peace talks broke up without any agreement, dashing any hopes of an end to the conflict.

It was difficult for Liberia's West African neighbours to ignore the fast escalating conflict in the country. Within the first month of fighting between government and rebel forces, Liberians had fled to neighbouring countries in large numbers. Amnesty International estimated that 20,000 refugees were in Cote D'ivoire and Guinea by the end of January 1990. As the fighting intensified, the war weary Liberians continued to flock into neighbouring countries by their thousands. By October 1990, Liberian refugees in Guinea, Cote D'ivoire and Sierra Leone had numbered 600,000.[115] This influx of refugees into neighbouring countries threatened to paralyse the already weak economies of these states. It is estimated that over 200,000 lives were lost in the war. In the wake of the failed peace talks, in August 1990, a mediation committee established by the Economic Community of West African States (ECOWAS) intensified its efforts to find a peaceful solution to the crisis. It adopted a framework for a cease-fire and the establishment of an interim government in Liberia. The ECOWAS Cease-fire Monitoring Group (ECOMOG), was established to monitor the cease-fire.

ECOWAS and ECOMOG's intervention in the Liberian conflict was an unusual development. The historical past shared by the US and Liberia, and the very close ties between both countries up until the beginning of the civil war, made the US a more natural intervener in this conflict than any other country or organization. Liberia had always been the closest ally of the US and her traditional ally on the African continent. The US commanded enormous influence in Liberia and was her staunchest supporter, rendering substantial and other assistance to the country. The US played an important role in changing some of the repressive laws of the Americo-Liberians. Active criticism from the US contributed to the changes in the laws and a degree of change in the attitude of the settlers toward the native Liberians.[116]

Liberia was strategically important to the US. The US had an Omega navigation station in Liberia, which transmitted communications to submarines in the South Atlantic. Furthermore, there was a Voice of America transmitter in the country, which broadcasted to all of sub-Saharan Africa; and US diplomatic messages to and from West Africa passed through Liberia. Liberia's Robertsfield airport was (until the war) readied as a refuelling and landing site for rapid deployment forces. The US also had a 500-strong

---

[115] Figures from United Nations High Commission for Refugees (UNHCR), Cote d'Ivoire, reported in *Africa Research Bulletin*, (October 1st-31st 1990), p. 9873.

[116] For example, the law which changed the townships/ territories into counties, putting an end at least in theory, to the colonial way in which the settlers ruled the natives. see Guannu, *An Introduction to Liberian government*.

embassy which collected intelligence information for the CIA from the region. Firestone, the world's largest rubber plantation, was operated in Liberia, by US interests. Prior to the civil war, almost five thousand Americans resided in Liberia, including businessmen, diplomats, missionaries, and 160 members of the Peace Corps.[117]

Relations between Samuel Kanyon Doe's regime and the US were particularly cordial. US aid to Liberia at the time of Doe's coup, was less than 20 million US dollars, but it began to soar after the coup and by 1985, it was close to $500 million. There were different areas of support. One consisted of 'economic support funds' aimed basically at enabling Liberia to meet interest payments on its foreign debt. There were also supplies of food i.e. rice, and significant military aid. Doe's troops were trained by the US who also built new barracks, and supplied uniforms, rifles, and trucks.[118] Relations between both countries were sealed in 1982 during Samuel Doe's visit to the US, where he promised to return Liberia to civil rule. He further impressed the US government by closing the Libyan mission in Monrovia and terminating diplomatic relations with the Soviet Union, while establishing relations with the state of Israel.[119] Thus, it was only natural to expect that the US would step in to restore order in Liberia, but this did not happen.

Indeed, until the occurrence of the Liberian war when many Liberians were traumatised by the apparent lack of US interest, they identified more with Americans than with their African neighbours.[120] Enoanyi's remarks drive home the extent of Liberians' disappointment at America's failure to intervene in the conflict:

> Liberians – including even the factions involved in the war – continued to hope for the moment when America would step in and blow the only whistle that could not be ignored by anyone or group, for an end to the deadly game. ... The country which President Grover Cleveland urged Americans to consider as "an offshoot of our system", emphasizing the "moral right and duty of the United States in all proper ways the maintenance of its integrity" was evaporating and America did nothing.[121]

---

[117] US ties with, and interest in Liberia are discussed in Michael Massing, *Best Friends*; *Africa Report*, September-October 1990, p. 6; Holly Burkhalter and Rakiya Omaar, 'Failures of State' *Africa Report*, November-December 1990, pp. 27-28; and R.F. Zimmerman, *Dollars, Diplomacy and Dependency: Dilemmas of US Economic Aid*, (Boulder: Lynne Rienner Publishers, 1993).

[118] Massing, p. 10.

[119] Ibid; and see also, *Africa Report*, September-October 1990, p. 6.

[120] Personal interviews with Liberian refugees at the refugee camp in Oru-Ijebu, Nigeria in June 1994 for example, confirmed the shock of many Liberians that the US did not 'jump' to their rescue. Many admitted that knew very little about their African neighbours before the war.

[121] Bill Frank Enoanyi, *Behold Uncle Sam's Step-Child*,(Sacramento: SanMar Publications, 1991), p. 3.

Many reasons can be advanced for US non-intervention in Liberia. Some commentators have argued that the Gulf crisis coincided with the war in Liberia thereby diverting US and international attention from the latter and confirming that the end of the Cold War had eroded Africa's importance to the superpowers.[122] This argument suggests that in the absence of the Gulf war, the US would have intervened in the Liberian crisis. But the situation was not so clear-cut. At the outbreak of the Liberian crisis, and the first few months, the Gulf War had not become imminent and thus it appears the US chose between a number of options in Liberia. The considerations behind its non-intervention strategy in Liberia had military and political aspects.

The initial US reaction appeared to be a pro-Doe one especially given the involvement of Libya on the side of the rebels. The US sent two advisors who were thought to be counter-insurgency advisers, but quickly withdrew them after the atrocities and human rights abuses of Doe's troops became apparent.[123] Indeed, Doe's poor human rights record made it difficult for the US to continue its support for his government. The US senate (in 1985/86) had suspended further aid to Liberia, although political support appeared to continue from the executive branch of government.[124] A US team of financial experts failed in 1988, to remedy the financial crisis which resulted from the incompetence and corruption of Doe's regime.[125]

A US decision to intervene militarily in Liberia may have generated some political problems, mainly in the West African sub-region. ECOWAS member states especially Nigeria may have frowned seriously at the military presence of a foreign power in the sub-region and regarded US actions as blatant interference in Liberia's internal affairs. The fact that this war occurred in the backyard of Nigeria, Africa's largest nation which also carries some political weight within the OAU, suggests that any US intervention would have been a difficult one. Such foreign presence would only emphasize the already obvious weakness of the region and the inability of these states to handle their own affairs – an impression which African states have for long been eager to rectify. Indeed, for fear of setting a precedence which may come to haunt them

---

[122] This view is expressed in a number of sources, amongst which are M.A. Vogt (ed.), *The Liberia Crisis and ECOMOG*; *West Africa*; and *Africa Research Bulletin*.

[123] *Africa Report*, July-August 1990, p. 49; Also, *Africa Report* of November-December 1990 reported that until Doe's army massacred hundreds of civillian in a Lutheran church in July, the US government with 2,000 marines stationed just off the coast of Liberia, was in fact still considering a face saving invasion in support of Doe, but the US was quick to recoil after this unfortunate incident. p. 16; see also pp. 27-28.

[124] *Africa Report*, November-December 1990, pp. 27-28.

[125] Ibid.

in the future, the African members on the UN Security Council delayed the possibility of an early meeting to resolve the crisis.[126]

In addition to this, it would have been difficult for the US to maintain a neutral image, given its long standing support for Samuel Doe's regime. Furthermore, domestic support for a military intervention in Liberia, may not have been forthcoming at home. After the Vietnam experience, subsequent US governments have tended to approach matters regarding military intervention with caution, especially where quick success could not have been guaranteed. While its recent involvement in Somalia is a sharp departure from this, as at the time the war in Liberia began, the new post-Cold War scene which made the coalition against Iraq possible was not well defined.

In Liberia, a US intervention would not have been a guaranteed success, although in a small country like Liberia it would seem that the US, with military superiority in every regard, could go in quickly to restore order. But the situation was uncertain. First, the US could easily have been perceived by the rebels as partial, given the initial presence of US advisers on the side of Doe. In any case, US action would not have been geared towards ousting Doe from power, hence any other line of action may have been unfavourable to the rebels. Thus, US troops might have found themselves fighting hostile rebel forces in good guerrilla terrain, facing a real possibility of becoming embroiled in a guerrilla war. A swift and successful operation was not a guarantee since there were chances that the US could become entangled in Liberia's internal political situation. Thus, although the US may have succeeded eventually in restoring order in Liberia (especially at an early stage in the conflict), the costs of such unilateral military intervention might have been high.

Another option, which was open to the US but was not utilised, was that of mediation or diplomatic peacemaking. This stood a greater chance of success, given the enormous influence of the US in Liberia, and its ability to make side payments to the different parties. Prince Yomie Johnson at some stage displayed eagerness for international or US mediation, when he kidnapped foreign nationals to draw international attention. Also, Taylor revealed in an interview that he was persuaded by the US to delay his impending invasion of the capital.[127] In addition to this, Enoanyi's statement above would support the view that the warring parties would have immediately yielded to American calls for peace at the start of the crisis.

---

[126] See D. Wippman, 'Enforcing the Peace: ECOWAS and the Liberian Civil War', in L.F. Damrosch (ed.), *Enforcing Restraint: Collective Intervention in Internal Conflicts*, (New York: Council of Foreign Relations Press, 1993); *West Africa*, 16-22 Mar. 1992, also reported that some African members of the UN Security Council prevented UN Secretary-General Perez de Cuellar from taking the Liberian crisis to the attention of the UNSC in May 1990 – see p. 449.
[127] *The New African*, October 1992.

There is however some evidence that the US attempted mediation of a different sort – an effort to persuade Doe to leave power and an offer of safe passage to a country of his choice. Doe's eventual refusal of this offer is an indication that peacemaking may not have been all too easy for the US. However, the US could have succeeded in exerting enough pressure on Doe to leave if it was determined to do so, as it possessed the political weight to achieve this in Liberia. Actual realization of this goal was only a matter of national interest or political will.

THE EXPERIENCE OF SIERRA LEONE

The crisis in Sierra Leone was shaped largely by the developments in the country between 1968 and 1991, in particular, from 1978, under the one-party rule[128] of the All-People's Congress (APC), which was characterised by patrimonial rule. During the same period, the regime had to contend with economic decline and various attempted *coups d'etat*. Other political parties such as the Sierra Leone Peoples Party (SLPP) and the United Democratic Party (UDP) had been suppressed and their members forced into exile, with opposition left largely in the hands of students. The military became gradually prominent in the regime's bid to maintain control over the opposition. The continued decline of the economy and the implementation of structural adjustment programmes (SAP) and IMF conditionalities increased the agitation of the opposition for multi-party democracy. The prominent role of the Sierra Leone Military Forces became even more apparent when President Siaka Stevens left office in 1984 and handed over control of the machinery of government to the army commander, General Momoh. SAP was implemented to the fullest in the country and the demand for plural democracy intensified. In a bid to clamp down on the opposition, Momoh's regime threatened to charge those seeking multi-party democracy with treason. It was in this atmosphere that the civil war in neighbouring Liberia began.

Sierra Leone was invaded in March 1991 by rebels known as the Revolutionary United Front, led by Fodah Sankoh, who sought to remove the regime of Momoh.[129] This marked the beginning of a civil war, which continued until 1996, when elections were hastily organised by the international community.

---

[128] One party rule was instituted under the one party constitution of 1977 and was in the process of being reviewed after a referendum in 1991.

[129] Ibrahim Abdullah provides a thorough analysis of the character and composition of the RUF in 'Bush Path to Destruction: The Origin and Character of the Revolutionary United Front', *Africa Development*, Vol. XXII, Nos. 3/4, 1997, pp. 45-76. See also Paul Richards, *Fighting for the Rain Forest, War Youth and Resources in Sierra Leone*, Oxford: James Currey, 1996, for a discussion of the RUF's campaign between 1991 and 1996.

The Sierra Leone war is often seen as an offshoot of the war in Liberia, given the involvement of members of Charles Taylor's National Patriotic Front of Liberia (NPFL) alongside Sierra Leoneans (and Bukinabes) from the beginning óf the war. However, this should not remove the political and economic reality in Sierra Leone at this point. ECOMOG troops were dispatched to Sierra Leone's border with Liberia following the NPFL supported incursions and a small force remained in the country henceforth. In the five years of civil war, the military attempted to gain control over the rebels and the country gradually slid into anarchy. President Momoh was overthrown in 1992 following a mutiny by a group of junior officers. They criticised the regime for not acting decisively to bring the war to an end. An international effort to resolve the Sierra Leone crisis resulted in elections in 1996, which brought Ahmed Tejan Kabbah to power. This was despite continued fighting in parts of the country.

Interestingly, the near total collapse of the Sierra Leone state occurred after the elections. In May 1997, just over a year after President Kabbah's assumption of office, he was ousted in a military coup. This was followed by a coalition of a segment of the Sierra Leone military (the Armed Forces Revolutionary Council – AFRC – led by Johnny Paul Koroma) with the RUF rebels, whom they had previously fought against. The chaos which followed the *coup* led to the intervention of Nigerian troops (ostensibly under the ECOWAS umbrella), in a bid to reverse the coup. Following the initial failure to reverse the coup, large segments of the civilian population in Sierra Leone engaged in civil disobedience, making it extremely difficult for the military to govern. The relationship between the military and the populace had reached the lowest ebb. Following unsuccessful attempts at implementing a negotiated settlement, Nigerian-led ECOMOG troops overwhelmed the troops of the Armed Forces Revolutionary Council in February 1998 and President Kabbah was reinstated in March 1998. His regime has since been confronted with the task of rebuilding the state. In particular, creating a military institution that will be trusted by civil society is one of the main challenges of the reconstruction process in that country.

CONCLUSION

The Liberian experience demonstrates how international, and in particular western, interest in Africa evaporated in the aftermath of the Cold War. The failure of the US to intervene militarily in Liberia, which was clearly its closest African ally, drove home the political realities of the post-Cold War era for Africans. Thus, many agree that there is a strong possibility that the West will stay out of future African conflicts. Liberia represents one of the many Third World countries where corrupt regimes survived because of east-west ideological rivalry.

With the failure of domestic peacemaking in Liberia, and absence of overt US involvement, the ECOWAS peace force went into Liberia. Nigeria's President Babangida in a press briefing, summed up Nigeria's and, indeed, the ECOWAS rationale for sending the force – ECOMOG – to Liberia:

> We are in Liberia because events in that country have led to the massive destruction of property, the massacre by all parties of thousands of innocent children some of whom had sought sanctuary in the churches, mosques, diplomatic missions, hospitals and under the protection of the Red Cross, contrary to all recognized standards of civilized behaviour and international ethics and decorum.[130]

The Liberian operation set a sub-regional precedent and paved the way for the Nigerian-led intervention in Sierra Leone. It now remains to be seen the extent to which ECOWAS and its creation, ECOMOG, were able to restore peace in Liberia.

---

[130] *The Imperative Features of Nigerian Foreign Policy and the Crisis in Liberia*, (Press Briefing by President Babangida), Lagos, 31 October 1990, p. 12.

CHAPTER FOUR

The Course of the ECOMOG Operation

INTRODUCTION

The last chapter traced the roots, and conduct of the civil war in Liberia, which only its neighbours took concrete steps to control. This chapter examines the obstacles encountered in the process of creating peace. An analysis of the ECOWAS Cease-fire Monitoring Group (ECOMOG) is conducted. The political, legal and financial circumstances involved in the creation of the force are discussed, and the success and limitations of the force in following its mandate are assessed. This analysis is conducted in two sections. The first examines the events surrounding the creation of the force and its mandate; and the political and legal issues relating to ECOMOG's establishment. It discusses the objectives of ECOWAS in creating ECOMOG, the force's mandate, and how these objectives determined the type of force that was created. The section argues that although the force was originally intended to perform peacekeeping tasks and was later presented as one, ECOMOG was not initially a peacekeeping force. Rather, it was one of peace enforcement, which later attempted to switch to a peacekeeping role. The second section examines the extent to which the force accomplished its mission, and the factors that influenced the fulfilment of ECOMOG's mandate. This section appraises ECOMOG's effectiveness under four different phases, which are classified according to significant developments in the peace process – phase one was that of unsuccessful peacekeeping; phase two marked the change to enforcement strategy; phase three was one of stagnation; and phase four was the return to peace enforcement.

I

ECOMOG: FORMATION AND MANDATE

At the 13th summit of ECOWAS Heads of State in the Gambia in May 1990 the Community adopted a proposal from Nigerian President Ibrahim Babangida for the setting up of an ECOWAS Standing Mediation Committee.[1] It was agreed that the Standing Mediation Committee (SMC) would be made up of four members, appointed by the Authority of Heads of State and Government (referred to as 'the Authority') and was to be chaired by the current Chairman of the Authority. Membership of the Committee was to be reviewed every three years.[2] The ECOWAS member states on the SMC included The Gambia (as chair nation), Ghana, Mali, Nigeria and Togo. An emergency meeting of the foreign ministers of the SMC was held on July 5th 1990, to work out modalities of a cease-fire.[3] At that 13th summit of Heads of State, reference was made to the ECOWAS Protocol on Non-aggression,[4] the provisions of which were considered to be applicable to the situation that existed in Liberia.

The Liberian conflict became the first issue on the sub-region's list of crisis situations. For the first time since the Liberian crisis began, the organization discussed Liberia's political turmoil and proposed an immediate end to the conflict. This was followed by a resolution that the factions should accept an early holding of free and fair elections with the participation of all shades of political expressions in the country. The expectation of the ECOWAS leaders was that the arrangement would be accepted by both Doe and Taylor. ECOWAS sources confirmed Charles Taylor signed a document supporting ECOWAS mediation in the conflict.[5]

ECOWAS' agenda for peace included amongst other things, the acceptance of ECOWAS mediation by the conflicting parties, cease-fire agreement, release of political prisoners, obtaining President Doe's resignation and the appointment of an interim government with preparations for general elections.[6] Prior to this meeting, the ECOWAS executive Secretary, Abass Bundu was delegated by the SMC to make a fact-finding mission to Liberia. This was

---

[1] These amongst other points were approved in *Decision A/DEC.9/5/90* – referring to the documented decision of ECOWAS members, relating to the establishment of the Standing Mediation Committee.

[2] Ibid; see also, *Official Journal of the ECOWAS*, Vol.17, (June 1990), p.24.

[3] Apart from the five members of the SMC, Guinea and Sierra Leone were invited to this meeting, as these countries harboured the largest number of Liberian refugees. See *West Africa*, 16-22 July 1990, p.2126; and *Africa Research Bulletin*, August 15 1990, p.9772. The meeting was also attended by representatives of Doe, the NPFL, and other Liberian interest groups. See O.B.C. Nwolise, 'Implementation of Yamoussoukro and Geneva Agreements', in M.A. Vogt (ed.), p.273.

[4] The ECOWAS *Protocol on Non-Aggression* signed in Lagos on 22nd April 1978, was an agreement of member states not to use force as a means of settling their disputes, amongst other things. The organization's *Protocol Relating to Mutual Defence* was signed in Freetown on May 29th 1981. Under this Protocol, amongst other things, member states resolved to give mutual aid and assistance for defence against any armed threat or aggression.

[5] *Official Journal of ECOWAS*, (Special Supplement), Vol. 21, 1992.

[6] Nwolise, p.273.

backed up by delicate diplomacy in which Bundu travelled between Liberia, Sierra Leone, Cote D'ivoire and Guinea. He was eventually able to secure the personal agreement of both President Doe and rebel leader Charles Taylor. Each accepted an ECOWAS formula to resolve the conflict.[7] A five-man delegation of the NPFL travelled to Freetown at the invitation of the SMC.

The SMC plans thus far indicated that the duties of the proposed force would be of a peacekeeping nature. The move to create a force for the purpose of keeping the peace at this stage was made with the expectation that the parties would agree to the peace plan and consent to the despatch of a peace force. It would be the first attempt by an economic organization to initiate a peacekeeping mission. Doe's representatives and the NPFL accepted ECOWAS mediation, establishment of an interim government and electoral commission as well as monitoring of the elections by ECOWAS. However, the leadership of the proposed interim administration was a subject of dispute. Both Doe and Taylor desired this position[8]. It was thus decided that neither of them would occupy the position. Indeed, an important part of the peace plan was that members of such an interim administration would be ineligible to stand for general elections.

FROM PEACEKEEPING TO PEACE ENFORCEMENT

The ECOWAS mediation committee could not achieve a negotiated settlement in Freetown, Sierra Leone as planned. The National Patriotic Front of Liberia (NPFL), reneged on its word, as Charles Taylor had previously signed a document supporting an ECOWAS settlement. Charles Taylor refused the ECOWAS proposal for a cease-fire and a peacekeeping force. NPFL delegates withdrew from peace talks, rejecting proposals for a cease-fire and peacekeeping force.[9] The NPFL made it clear that it intended to fight on to resolve the conflict on the battlefield. Taylor and his men expressed their determination to fight any intervening force unless it was a force to which they consented.[10] One of the main reasons advanced for the NPFL's rejection of the peace plan was that the rebel group did not believe that ECOWAS would have the political will to effect Samuel Doe's resignation.[11] The NPFL declared that

---

[7] See *West Africa*, 16-22 July 1990 p.2126; and *Official Journal of ECOWAS*, (Special Supplement), Vol.21, (1992) p.5.
[8] *The Guardian* (Nigeria), 11 July 1990, pp.1-2.
[9] *The Guardian*, (Nigeria) 21 July 1990, p.1.
[10] *The Guardian* (UK), 9th July, 1990; *The Guadian* (Nigeria), 13 August 1990; See also *Nigerian Journal of International Affairs*, Volume 17, No.1, (1991), p.106.
[11] *Nigerian Journal of International Affairs*, Vol. 17, No.1, p.106.

'there will be no cease-fire in Liberia as long as Doe is in the country'[12] Taylor and his men wanted a military solution especially since they were only a few miles away from seizing the presidential mansion and taking control of Monrovia when the ECOWAS peace moves began. The NPFL thus believed that the deployment of ECOMOG would rob them of the political victory that they would secure through victory on the battlefield. This victory was however not a forgone conclusion given the existence of a third contending faction – the INPFL.

It has already been established that the traditional concept of peacekeeping presupposes that a cease-fire already exists or that, at the very least, the parties to a conflict have shown willingness to agree to a cease-fire or to pursue a solution via peaceful means. But in the Liberian situation, one of the parties (the NPFL) rejected a peaceful solution, reneging on its earlier agreement to pursue a negotiated settlement. Consent was thus not unanimous from the warring parties – the AFL and INPFL welcomed the idea of a peace force, whilst the NPFL was totally opposed to it. Confusion over what constituted host-state consent under circumstances of internal wars was demonstrated by events in Liberia. Thus, it became difficult for ECOWAS to embark on peacekeeping in the traditional sense. The organization was then left with a choice between imposing peace upon the warring factions, or allowing the total disintegration of Liberia to occur. The situation in Liberia deteriorated rapidly, as all[13] the parties continued to commit atrocities, leaving ECOWAS with little choice.[14] The evacuation of innocent civilians, including citizens of other West African countries as well as Liberians, all trapped in Liberia, became an unavoidable mission.

In spite of failed efforts by the SMC to secure an agreement from the conflicting parties, it proceeded with plans to deploy the force. The committee agreed in August 1990, on the deployment of a 'peacekeeping force' as part of a peace plan, with the brief of monitoring an immediate cease-fire.[15] This was a move which many believed was underway long before the time of the announcement of the force.[16] It is interesting to note that although there was no agreement between the parties and thus no peace to keep, the force which was to be despatched to Liberia was still referred to as a 'peacekeeping' one. This indicates the preference of politicians (both civilian and military rulers),

---

[12] *Guardian* (Nigeria), 21 July 1990.
[13] 'all' here refers to the Armed Forces of Liberia (AFL – Doe's government troops), the NPFL (rebel faction led by Charles Taylor), and the Independent National Patriotic Front of Liberia (INPFL, led by Prince Johnson the rebel faction which broke away from the NPFL). At this stage in the conflict, ULIMO and others had not become parties to the conflict.
[14] *West Africa*, 6-12 August 1990, p.2236.
[15] *National Concord* (Nigeria) 10 August 1990, pp.1-2.
[16] *West Africa*, 13-19 August 1990.

for the term peacekeeping, which has a more favourable ring and can help pacify the public, giving the mission a degree of legitimacy.

The SMC thus adopted a peace plan on 7 August 1990 at their meeting in the Gambia, which called for the following: an immediate cease-fire to enable the restoration and maintenance of peace and security throughout Liberia; ECOWAS monitoring of the cease-fire and the surrender of all arms and ammunition to the custody of ECOWAS Monitoring Group – ECOMOG (which was also established at the same meeting); full co-operation with the SMC, ECOWAS Executive Secretary, and ECOMOG for the effective maintenance of the cease-fire and the restoration of law and order; the establishment of a broad-based interim government acceptable to Liberians; holding of general elections within twelve months, and the observation of the elections by ECOWAS and other international bodies.[17] ECOMOG was given the mandate to 'conduct military operations for the purpose of monitoring the cease-fire, restoring law and order to create the necessary conditions for free and fair elections to be held in Liberia'.[18] Thus ECOMOG was initially deployed under humanitarian considerations, and on the assumption that it would also monitor a cease-fire which would be successfully brokered by the SMC.

Not only were the objectives set out by the SMC very ambitious given the lack of agreement and the intransigence of at least one of the warring factions (i.e. NPFL), the task set for ECOMOG was a daunting one, if it was expected to adhere to peacekeeping principles. There was every indication that this rebel faction would mount opposition to any intervening force and that its threats to declare war on ECOMOG could not be dismissed as empty ones. It would therefore be impossible for ECOMOG to keep a peace, which was non-existent, especially since it was expected that the force would monitor a cease-fire, which would have been successfully negotiated by the mediation committee.[19]

Thus, the intractable civil war in Liberia was beginning to expose the challenges, which such internal wars pose for peacemaking efforts. Going to the target-state without any consent, no agreement, and severe opposition from one of the parties, would preclude the activity from the traditional peacekeeping category. It would be difficult to convince the NPFL who opposed this intervention, that the force was neutral and impartial. Furthermore, going to

---

[17] Article 1 of *Decision A/DEC. 1/8/90* on the Cease-fire and the establishment of an ECOWAS Cease-fire Monitoring Group for Liberia; Final Communiqué, First session of ECOWAS Standing Mediation Committee, held in Banjul, The Gambia, 6-7 August, 1990; and see also M.A Vogt, The Problems and Challenges of Peacekeeping, in M.A. Vogt (ed.), p. 152, and *Official Journal of ECOWAS*, Vol. 21.

[18] *Official Journal of ECOWAS*, Vol. 21, 1992 p.7.

[19] See Chike Akabogu, 'ECOWAS Takes the Initiative', in M.A. Vogt (ed.), p. 84.

Liberia to rescue innocent civilians trapped between different warring factions would require much more than light ammunition and they would almost certainly have to be used. It was the situation on the ground that dictated the type of force that ECOMOG would be. Under those conditions, the force would not be a peacekeeping one.

CHANGING MANDATE

Notwithstanding these difficulties, the ECOMOG force was initially deployed in a non-threatening manner in the hope of persuading Taylor and his men that this was not a force of occupation, or a force assembled in support of Doe. It was the circumstances on the ground in Liberia, which dictated the type and level of ECOMOG's involvement. The initial task force consisted mainly of naval personnel from Nigeria and Ghana, and additional forces from Guinea, The Gambia and Sierra Leone. Its initial task was the evacuation of ECOWAS and other nationals from Monrovia.[20] The force consisted of ships from the merchant navy, smaller boats designed to facilitate sea-lift and other logistical support.

The hostile climate in Liberia prevented this force from achieving the initial mission of evacuation of innocent civilians. Heavy fighting in Monrovia and the free port area resulted in the diversion of the force to Freetown while negotiations were conducted to persuade the parties – especially the NPFL.[21] It soon became clear that the objectives could not be attained by the token force, and it was expanded to include army units. Eventually, a force of about 3,500 was landed in Monrovia on 24 August 1990. This force came under heavy attack as soon as it arrived in Monrovia, as the NPFL declared war on ECOMOG in line with its earlier promise.[22] A Guinean ship transporting senior officers of the Ghanaian army on inspection tour of the situation in Liberia was attacked by NPFL forces.[23] Another of the many occurrences was the rebel attack on a ship-load of refugees in Monrovia free port, which led to 27 casualties including three deaths.[24] It was thus clear that there was no peace

---

[20] Capt. F.I. Biambo, *Nigeria Navy in Its Peacekeeping Roles*, (paper presented during the Navy Week Seminar '92, at the NNS Quorra, May 1992), p.6; M.A. Vogt, 'The Problems and Challenges of Peacemaking: From Peacekeeping to Peace Enforcement', in M.A. Vogt (ed.), p.153; and Chike Akabogu, pp.83-4.

[21] *West Africa*, 27 Aug.-2 Sept. 1990; For a complete account of the Navy's experience during this period, see Olatunde A. Oladimeji, 'Nigerian Navy's Contribution to International Peace-Keeping' M.A. Vogt and A.E. Ekoko (eds.), *Nigeria in International Peacekeeping 1960-1992*, (Oxford: Malthouse Publishing UK Ltd, 1993).

[22] *Nigeria and the ECOWAS Since 1985*, p.124 and *The Punch* (Nigeria), 27 August 1990.

[23] *Nigerian Journal of International Affairs*, Vol.17, No.1 1991, p.106.

[24] M.A. vogt, 'The problems and Challenges of Peacekeeping', in M.A. Vogt (ed.) p.154.

to be kept and that if the humanitarian objective was to be achieved in Liberia, there was a need to protect the force against NPFL's aggression. Diplomatic pressure was stepped up to secure a cease-fire agreement from the parties to the conflict. For example, the US was able to bring some of its influence to bear, and obtained a cease-fire.[25] But within a few days, this cease-fire collapsed. In the midst of these violent ongoings, Prince Johnson's rebel faction kidnapped Samuel Doe at the ECOMOG base and he (Doe) was later killed by this group. The difficulty of ECOMOG's task in Liberia was further demonstrated by the peculiar character of the rebel forces between which it had to keep peace and the viciousness with which they waged their war. This was elaborated upon in the previous chapter.

The Mediation Committee later readjusted ECOMOG's mandate[26]. The force was given instructions to enforce a cease-fire, clear the Liberian capital of all threats of attack, and establish and maintain an effective buffer.[27] The force was also instructed to prevent further acquisition of arms and ammunition by the rebels.[28] This strategic change to one of 'limited offensive' meant that ECOMOG would now attempt to neutralize the NPFL's capacity to attack it. The ECOMOG troops at this stage numbered about six thousand men. This alteration of ECOMOG's mandate, as in the UN operation in the Congo, demonstrates that a force's mandate can sometimes change after an operation has begun. Thus, the force moved away from its previous grey area, and was now clearly one of peace enforcement.

This strategy of 'limited offensive' enabled ECOMOG to carry out its mandate in Liberia. It was only after the adoption of this strategy that the evacuation of trapped civilians was possible. The employment of this strategy can also be understood from the absolute collapse of social order in Liberia. Water supply, electricity and other social services had been cut off, leaving the streets of the capital with decomposing bodies and severe food shortage for those surviving. Enforcement was pursued until some measure of normalcy was restored in Monrovia. For example, ECOMOG took over control of the central power plant and the main water works from the rebel forces.[29] In addition, ECOMOG was able to drive the NPFL out of mainland Monrovia thereby preventing them from gaining control of strategic facilities such as water works and the electric plant amongst others.[30]

---

[25] Ibid.

[26] Lt. Col. A. Olaiya, 'ECOMOG Mission & Mandate', in *The Peacemaker*, Vol.1, No.1, Sept.91-Mar.92 p.11. See also, *The Guardian* (Nigeria), 14 Sept. 1990 and 20 Sept. 1990.

[27] *African Guardian*, 29 October 1990, p.31; & *The G Guardian* (Nigeria), 20 September 1990.

[28] *African Research Bulletin*, Vol.27, No.10, 1-31 Oct. 1990, pp. 9872-73.

[29] M.A. Vogt, 'The Problems and Challenges of Peacemaking', p.155.

[30] Ibid. p.156.

ECOMOG activities at this stage raised an important question. At what point was this strategy of limited offensive expected to end? Should ECOMOG have applied principles of peacekeeping in dealing with a rebel force like the NPFL which did not operate by any standard codes of warfare, or should it have completely neutralized the rebel forces, thus denying them any means to resort to further violence? The problem confronting a peace force which has to deal with irregular armies are great. The experience of ECOMOG under similar circumstances in Liberia demonstrated the difficulty involved in utilizing both peacekeeping and enforcement in resolving the same conflict. However, the ultimate decision on how ECOMOG should deal with the situation rested with the politicians who authorized the mission. Their immediate objectives determined ECOMOG's response. The force's mandate did not include neutralizing the military capability of the NPFL. It was to utilize only sufficient force to return a semblance of order to Liberia. This is discussed further later in this chapter.

ISSUES OF FORCE CREATION

Under the decision that established the force, ECOMOG was placed under the command of a Force Commander, appointed by the Standing Mediation Committee (SMC). The Force Commander was entrusted with powers to conduct military operations for the purpose of monitoring the cease-fire, restoring law and order to create the necessary conditions for free and fair elections to be held in Liberia.[31] The Executive Secretary of ECOWAS was given the authority to appoint a Special Representative and other supporting staff for the operations in Liberia. The Special Representative was to work in close collaboration with the Forces Commander and assist in carrying out the ECOWAS operations in Liberia.[32]

There are usually complications involved in providing units to an international force. These complications vary from country to country and from one operation to another although as explained in Chapter Two, some factors are common to most operations. In creating ECOMOG, there were some positive factors, which helped to ease the task. First, the armies of some ECOWAS member states had participated in a number of peacekeeping operations and were therefore familiar with the requirements of such operations. Ghana, Nigeria and Senegal had participated under a number of UN operations dating from ONUC. However, at the time the force was being created, it was not known if the soldiers were expected to go beyond peacekeeping to peace

---

[31] *The Official Journal of ECOWAS*, Vol.21.
[32] Ibid.

enforcement. The skills required for peace enforcement vary from those for peacekeeping in a number of respects. These are focused upon in the next chapter.

The second factor was perhaps a positive one from the view point of ECOMOG's creators. Those complications brought about by constitutional provisions and parliamentary constraints in many democratic countries (discussed in Chapter Two), did not apply in this case, at least not at the beginning of the mission. This is because most of the West African countries including Nigeria, which was to provide the bulk of the finance and troops, were governed by military dictators or civilian authoritarians.[33] The decisions relating to the creation of the force were taken by only a few men who were not accountable to any electorate for their actions. This factor in itself accounts for the peculiarity of ECOMOG in the sense that it made the enforcement of peace a possibility, and decisions regarding the functions of the force very easy to reach.

The selection of a force commander is one of the most important considerations in establishing an international force. It was no different in the creation of ECOMOG. The capacity of the force commander more than any other individual factor is crucial not only for the effectiveness of the command and control system (that of ECOMOG is discussed in Chapter Five), but the ultimate success of the operation. Ghana's Lieutenant General Arnold Quainoo was chosen as the first ECOMOG Force Commander largely for political reasons.[34] A Nigerian Force Commander did not seem a wise choice for a number of reasons. The fact that Nigeria was the prime initiator of the peace mission coupled with the initial reluctance of the Francophone countries to participate in the mission (most visibly displayed by Mali and Togo's decision not to contribute troops), gave the mission an Anglophone outlook, opening up speculations of old Anglo and Francophone divisions. Furthermore, since Nigeria was providing majority of the troops and funding, taking responsibility for the military leadership would portray the mission as an attempt by Nigeria to manipulate the sub-regional organization for the its own interests.

Guinea, which was the only Francophone country with a contingent in ECOMOG would have made an ideal choice, erasing any political misgivings. Guinea was, however, unable to provide a suitable candidate but was given the choice of Deputy Force Commander. Thus Sierra Leone, The Gambia, and

---

[33] With few exceptions e.g., Benin, where President Kerekou had bowed to pressures to adopt multi-party democracies after about two decades in power, most West African states were either governed by the military, or civilian dictators.

[34] Jinmi Adisa provides a detailed analysis of the political considerations behind General Quanoo's selection in 'ECOMOG Force Commanders', M.A. Vogt (ed.), pp.237-67; see also, *West Africa*, 13-19 August 1990 & 20-26 August 1990.

Ghana were the other options left for a Force Commander. Sierra Leone was not considered a workable option mainly due to the politicisation of her army. Siaka Stevens, Sierra Leone's former president, in his bid to maintain stability and prevent military coups, had politicised the top echelons of the country's armed forces. This, coupled with the lack of a credible combat tradition raised serious questions about the professionalism of the Sierra Leone Army.

Gambia was also ruled out as a viable option as its army was a relatively young one made up of only about 1,000 men as at then (1990). It was established in 1984 after the abortive coup of 1981, backed by Libya, but put down by British Special Air Services (SAS) and intervention by Senegalese Army. Thus Ghana was left as the only feasible contestant. Ghana's commitment to ECOMOG was strong, and its army had soldiers with peacekeeping experience dating back to the Congo. Retired Lt. General Erskines, the former UNIFIL Commander was a particularly attractive choice but Quainoo was selected since he was the personal choice of the Ghanaian leader, Jerry Rawlings. Nigeria secured for herself, the role of political adviser, a choice which was seen to protect the country's interest and military investment. Nigerians also occupied the positions of Chief of Staff, Head of Intelligence, Chief of Logistics and Chief of Communications. ECOMOG Force Commanders were later changed periodically after Quanoo was removed following the death of Samuel Doe.

Thus by 20 August 1990, a 2,500-man ECOWAS peacekeeping force, ECOMOG, had been airlifted to Freetown, Sierra Leone, in readiness to move into Liberia. The Nigerian contingent was the largest, with 756 troops (720 men and 36 officers).[35] Other troop contributing countries included Ghana (with the second largest contingent), Sierra Leone, Guinea, and the Gambia. Within a month, the troops had numbered 6,000 with more contributions from Ghana and Nigeria. The force rapidly expanded to suit the dictates of the situation in Liberia. Nigeria contributed 70% of the troops, and 80% of the funding for this mission.

FUNDING OF ECOMOG

In establishing ECOMOG, consideration was given to how the operation would be financed although the seriousness of such considerations are hard to determine. It was decided that 'all expenses relating to the operations of ECOMOG shall be drawn from the Special Emergency Fund' created by the SMC.[36] In practice however, the financial burden for the operation from the

---

[35] *African Concord*, 27 November 1990; and *The Guardian* (Nigeria), 15 Aug. 1990.
[36] *Decision A/DEC 3/8/90* of the ECOWAS Standing Mediation Committee..

start was shouldered mainly by Nigeria. Given Nigeria's own dire financial situation, this guarantee promised to be a difficult one for her to honour. Apart from the realities of the country's financial state, domestic opposition was immense. The existence of a military regime in Nigeria, made it easy for what was left of Nigerian funds to flow freely to ECOMOG.[37] However, pledges of financial support from the US was a source of encouragement for troop contributing nations.[38]

Legal Questions

ECOMOG's peculiar situation made it an easy target for those who opposed its intervention in Liberia, for reasons other than the legal ones that they professed. It was the first peace enforcement mission sponsored by a regional economic organization, a radical departure from normal (traditional) peacekeeping missions. This, coupled with divisions and display of partiality amongst some ECOWAS members, and domestic opposition to the mission in some countries, inflated the legal criticisms against the ECOMOG intervention. This and latter sections of this chapter will attempt to support this argument.

The legitimacy of ECOMOG was questioned on a number of grounds. One was the acceptability of an economic organization playing a political or military role. ECOWAS was seen as a regional organization formed for economic integration and thus did not possess the capacity to assume responsibility for mutual security. Second, ECOMOG's legitimacy was challenged on the ground that the Standing Mediation Committee did not have the mandate from a full summit of ECOWAS members, to send a force to Liberia. The NPFL and the Burkinabe leader, Captain Blaise Compaore, were firm supporters of this position.[39] Those who levelled this criticism argued that the only aspect of the ECOWAS constitutional framework which could give justification to the deployment of a force is the Protocol Relating to Mutual Assistance on Defence. Article 18 of the Protocol, which allows for military intervention and assistance where internal conflict in a member state is actively maintained and sustained by outsiders is the part considered to be applicable to the Liberian situation. This implies a situation of third party intervention, but opponents of the ECOMOG mission in Liberia claimed that

---

[37] It is estimated that Nigeria provided about 70% of ECOMOG's funding.

[38] The US was said to have contributed an average of US $10 million a year, to the ECOMOG operation and donated an estimated US$440 million to humanitarian relief in Liberia. See *West Africa*, 6 Nov. 1995; and Max Amadu Sesay, *Bringing Peace to Liberia* (Unpublished research paper, 1996), p.8.

[39] *The Guardian* (Nigeria), 15 August 1990, pp.1-2.

this was not the case in Liberia. This supported the argument of critics that the more powerful state(s) in the sub-region manipulated the organization to satisfy their own interests. Thus the SMC procedure for deploying ECOMOG was questioned by both the NPFL and their backer states in the sub-region.[40]

The last criticism and a very important one, was the claim that the ECOWAS action in Liberia contradicts Article 3 (2) of the OAU Charter and Article 2(4) of the UN, which forbid interference in the domestic affairs of member states.[41] Furthermore, it was claimed that ECOWAS also violated the 1978 ECOWAS protocol on Non Aggression, particularly Article 2, which states that 'each member state shall refrain from committing, encouraging or condoning acts of subversion, hostility or aggression against territorial integrity or political independence of member states'.[42]

One factor which, surprisingly, was not raised in relation to ECOMOG, is the legality of peace enforcement action by a regional organization. The fact that this was not raised as a serious legal problem for ECOMOG, lends support to the argument that criticisms against the ECOMOG operations were not the result of genuine legal concerns. Although Article 52 of the UN Charter empowers regional organizations to deal with regional security issues in accordance with principles of the charter, there are restrictions on enforcement action by such organizations. Whilst the Charter is vague on the relationship which should exist between the UN and regional organizations in dealing with regional security issues,[43] it implies the supremacy of the UN Security Council in initiating enforcement action.[44] The collective security system envisaged by the charter outlined in Chapter VII, provides that the Security Council, in the event of failure of non-violent means of attaining peace, may take 'such action by air, sea and land forces, as may be necessary

---

[40] Tom Woewiyu, an NPFL spokesperson expressed the rebel faction's doubt on the legitimacy of the peace force, arguing that the SMC did not get the mandate from a full summit of all member states to send a military force and expressed the view that they should report back. *West Africa*, 3-9 Sept. 1990, p.2390; Furthermore, Blaise Compaore, President of Bukina Faso claimed that not all countries were fully briefed on the exact assignment of ECOMOG, also claiming that the Mediation Committee was not competent to intervene in a member state's internal conflict. *Newswatch*, 27 August 1990, p.16; and *The Guardian* (Nigeria), 8 September 1990.

[41] Captain Blaise Compaore, the Bukinabe leader opposed the ECOMOG operation on this basis. See *Guardian* (Nigeria), 8 Sept. 1990, pp.1-2; Prominent Nigerian jurists also held this view. See for example, Aguda's views in *The Guardian* (Nigeria), 21 Nov. 1990, pp.23-24.

[42] ECOWAS Protocol on Non Aggression .

[43] The vagueness of Article 52 is discussed by Bruno Simma, *The Charter of the UN: A Commentary*, (Oxford: Oxford University Press, 1994), p.687.

[44] See N.D. White, *Keeping the Peace: The United Nations and the Maintenance of International Peace and Security*, (Manchester and New York: Manchester University Press, 1993), p. 6

to maintain or restore international peace and security'.[45] Since the UN Security Council is the only organ empowered to authorize enforcement actions, the question arises as to whether approval should not have been sought before initiating the ECOMOG action in Liberia. However, it seems tacit approval[46] was obtained for this operation only after it had begun, and expressed approval two years later, in the form of a Secutity Council resolution.[47]

At first sight, the legal arguments advanced against ECOMOG's creation appear incontrovertible but on closer examination, their flaws become apparent. First, economic integration and regional security are linked. Lasting economic co-operation cannot be attained in the absence of regional stability. As Bundu pointed out,

> ... you cannot talk meaningfully about economic co-operation and integration by itself without also relating to the underpinning of political stability within the sub-region. The two are inseparable and therefore have to be discussed inter alia. It is clear to me that regional solidarity and commitment to integration will be considerably enhanced where political stability becomes a common identity and is also perceived as a shared responsibility.[48]

Thus, whilst political stability is clearly a prerequisite for economic integration, it would appear that once a crisis has occurred in an area, the nature of the organization which attempts to resolve such a conflict, whether social, economic or political becomes irrelevant, so long as such an organization is well equipped to perform this role. In the case of ECOWAS, the organization was established for the purpose of economic integration, but the recognition that such a goal was only attainable in an atmosphere of regional political stability, led to the adoption of the Non-Aggression pact and the Protocol on Mutual Defence.

Regarding the criticism that the SMC did not have the mandate to act unilaterally in Liberia without reporting back to the Authority of Heads of States and Governments which established it, the SMC members offered a response, giving their own interpretation of the situation. They argued that the Chairman of the Authority was also Chairman of the SMC and the latter's duty was simply to report outcomes to the former under Article 4 of Decision A/Dec/9/5/90 concerning its establishment.[49] This suggests that the SMC could only be reprimanded by the Authority for exceeding its mandate only after it had made its decisions. However, after demands by the rebels and their

---

[45] *Blue Helmets*, p.3
[46] This came through verbal support from UN Secretary General. See Section III
[47] S/RES/788, 19 November 1992
[48] Interview with the ECOWAS Executive Secretary in *West Africa*, 1-7 July, 1991, p.1085.
[49] Jinmi Adisa, 'The Politics of Regional Military Cooperation: The Case of ECOMOG', in M.A. Vogt (ed.) p.217.

supporters that the SMC should report back to the Authority, and at the insistence of Francophone members, in particular, Cote D'ivoire and Burkina Faso, an Extra-Ordinary Summit of the ECOWAS Authority was held in Bamako between 27-28 November 1990.

The summit settled once and for all, all questions and doubts surrounding the legality of ECOMOG in terms of lack of SMC mandate. The Authority endorsed the ECOWAS Peace Plan for Liberia contained in the Banjul Communiqué and Decisions of the SMC adopted on 7 August 1990, which established ECOMOG.[50] In addition, the Authority stated that it was satisfied that 'the ECOWAS Peace Plan had received the widest acceptance and support from the international community',[51] further lending legitimacy to the peace force. But the reality of the situation is that these legal questions and criticisms only came about as a result of political differences and interests among member states of ECOWAS, as will be discussed later.

The argument of the critics that article 18 of the Protocol Relating to Mutual Assistance on Defence was not applicable in Liberia implies interference in internal affairs of a member state and this is discussed below. The validity of the charge was challenged by commentators on a number of grounds. The Protocol on Mutual Assistance on Defence makes the provision that in the event of armed threat or aggression against a member state, 'the Authority shall, on receipt of a written request submitted to the current chairman, with copies to other members, decide on the expediency of military action in relation to the provision of Article 6'.[52] Supporters of ECOMOG argued that this requirement was met. The only evidence produced in support of their claim is the text of Samuel Doe's letter of 14 July 1990, to ECOWAS, asking for the region's assistance in resolving the conflict. This was after Charles Taylor had reneged on his promise to co-operate with ECOWAS.[53] Commentators argued that this request was not illegal since Samuel Doe was Liberia's legitimate leader at that point in time, even though he had lost control over much of greater Liberia. Since the rebel groups had not removed Doe from power or seize control of the Executive Mansion he (Doe) was still regarded by observers as Liberia's leader. Any claim that Doe was not the legitimate leader then would only support the alternative argument that there was no government in Liberia, thereby justifying intervention.

---

[50] Economic Community of West African States: Final Communiqué of First Extra Ordinary Session of the Authority of Heads of States and Governments, Bamako, 27-28 November, 1990, pp.4-5.

[51] Ibid.

[52] Article 16, *ECOWAS Protocol on Mutual Assistance on Defence.*

[53] *Official Journal of ECOWAS*, Vol. 21 See also, statement by Doe's Vice-president in *West Africa*, 25 Feb.-1 Mar. 1992.

The charge of illegality levelled against ECOMOG that could not be dismissed easily was that of the violation of the non-interference clause in the OAU and UN Charters. It is common for international organizations (ECOWAS is not an exemption) to enshrine in their charter, the non-interference in the internal affairs clause. However, the UN has moved away from this strict approach in the last few years. The Security Council resolution which permitted foreign powers to intervene in Iraq in support of the Kurds and the Shiites, was the first indication of this shift.[54] This event however, had not occurred at the time of the ECOMOG intervention. In the Final Communiqué of the 12th ECOWAS summit, it was stipulated that no state could interfere in a member-state's internal conflict, but when there is a conflict between one member state and another. The UN and the OAU allegedly were unable to mediate in the Liberian civil war because of the non-interference in internal affairs clause in their charters.[55] Strict application of these rules would mean that ECOMOG had no legal basis. However, new developments in the international community have now made it possible to classify some issues that were previously seen as internal problem, as those of international concern.[56]

A number of issues however transformed the Liberian problem from an internal affair to one of major international concern, thus giving justification to the ECOMOG intervention in Liberia. The first concerns humanitarian considerations. Both the ECOWAS chairman and OAU Secretary General argued that the savage killings in Liberia took the situation beyond the internal affair of Liberia. What began as an attempt to overthrow the corrupt regime of Samuel Doe degenerated into a brutal etnic war. Many decapitated bodies of Gio and Mano soldiers fighting on the government side were discovered on the streets of Liberia. The savage killings ensured that casualties were not limited to just soldiers, but a cross section of the civilian population. It was thus difficult for the rest of West Africa to ignore the war in Liberia. Indeed, before the deployment of ECOMOG, many African commentators condemned the indifference shown by African nations. In support of the ECOWAS involvement in Liberia, Salim Salim stated, 'I will rather make a mistake

---

[54] BASIC, *European Security: Discussion Document* ; see also Christopher Greenwood, 'Is There a Right of Humanitarian Intervention?', *The World Today*, February 1993.

[55] *Africa Research Bulletin*, 1-30 Sept. 1990.

[56] For a discussion of arguments surrounding 'humanitarian intervention', see Anthony Clark Arend and Robert J. Beck, *International law and the use of force: Beyond the UN Charter paradigm*, (London and New York: Routledge, 1993). See also Natalino Ronzitti, *Rescuing Nationals Abroad Through Military Coercion and Intervention on Grounds of Humanity*, (Dordrecht: Martinus Nijhoff Publishers, 1985).

trying to solve the problem than to remain completely indifferent in such a situation'.[57]

Other issues served to internationalize the Liberian crisis. The conflict was seen to have assumed an international dimension from the start because of the spill over of the war into neighbouring countries.[58] Charles Taylor's rebel faction, the NPFL, had cadets trained in Libya, a staging post in Burkina Faso, and conduit pipe for supplies and transborder facilities provided by Cote D'Ivoire. These made it difficult for the situation to be seen from a purely internal angle. Taylor was reported to have switched his base from Sierra Leone to Burkina Faso, where he was reinforced by a Sierra Leonean contingent from Libya. This group included former student leaders and intellectuals who had fled from Sierra Leone to Ghana and Libya in earlier years and formed a radical opposition group, Revolutionary United Front (RUF).[59] Sierra Leone's rejection of Charles Taylor's plan would later encourage his support of RUF's attack on Sierra Leone.

In addition to the refugee burden mentioned in the previous chapter, the kidnapping, holding hostage and killing of foreign nationals took the conflict beyond Liberia's national boundary, giving justification to the ECOWAS intervention.[60] These included the ransacking of foreign embassies, the violation of diplomatic immunity and indiscriminate killings of these civilians who are foreign nationals.[61] These atrocities against foreign nationals reached their peak with the deployment of ECOMOG in August 1990. As many as 3,000 foreign nationals were held hostage by the NPFL at one stage. Majority of these hostages were Nigerians, and many others belonged to the ECOMOG troop contributing nations.[62] It was difficult to challenge the right of these countries to rescue their nationals abroad. However, notwithstanding efforts to justify the ECOMOG operations in Liberia, it became apparent that the charges of illegality made mainly by NPFL and the countries supporting it were not due to genuine belief in these legal arguments. Rather, they resulted from political differences, and the legal arguments were employed to achieve political ends.

---

[57] *West Africa*, 1-7 July 1991, p.1085.
[58] Osisioma B.C. Nwolise also adopts the view that the internationalization of the Liberian crisis began at the initial stages with outside support for Charles Taylor. See his chapter, 'The Internationalisation of the Liberian Crisis and Its Effects on West Africa', in M.A. Vogt, p.57.
[59] *Africa Confidential*, Vol.32, No.10, 17 May 1991, p.3.
[60] See Natalino Ronzitti, p.xiv.
[61] *Newswatch* (Nigeria), 11 June 1990.
[62] *Daily Champion* (Nigeria), 30 August 1990, p.1.

II

THE COURSE OF THE OPERATION: EFFECTIVENESS AND SUCCESS

The effectiveness or success of ECOMOG here refers to the degree to which the force succeeded or failed to accomplish the purpose for which it was established. Thus, the section will examine the extent to which ECOMOG fulfilled the mandate it was given by its creators – the SMC/ ECOWAS. The factors, which determined the success or effectiveness of this force were a combination of political and military ones.[63] ECOMOG's efforts to implement its mandate during the period between 1990 and 1994 spanned four distinct phases. Thereafter, UN involvement became more apparent and ECOMOG conducted military operations jointly with the United Nations Observer Mission in Liberia (UNOMIL). The adoption of a peace creation strategy was more apparent in the period between 1990 and 1994. By 1997, when its mission in Liberia was nearing completion, ECOMOG's attention became focused on Sierra Leone, which had suffered a reversal after the democratically elected government of Ahmed Tejan Kabbah was toppled by the military and chaos ensued in the capital, Freetown.

The first phase concerns the initial stages of the force's deployment where a combination of factors served to undermine its effectiveness. The second phase witnessed a degree of success in the force's implementation of its mandate, brought about largely by changes in strategy and political approach. The third phase is marked by stagnation, as the force was unable to proceed to fulfil the rest of its mandate. It was fraught with incidents and developments which prevented the force from achieving much progress. The fourth phase witnessed greater UN involvement in the peace process, improving ECOMOG's chances of achieving positive results.

PHASE ONE – UNSUCCESSFUL PEACEKEEPING

Opposition within Nigeria

Although ECOMOG at the beginning of its mission in Liberia experienced tough resistance from rebel groups, a number of political problems were also responsible for the force's apparent ineffectiveness at this stage. One of the factors, which undermined the effectiveness of ECOMOG during this initial

---

[63] While the military factors have had a direct effect on the performance or success of the force, the political factors have had an effect on the force largely in terms of perceptions of its performance.

phase, was domestic opposition to its deployment in the troop contributing nations, most especially Nigeria. Nigeria's involvement in ECOMOG generated enormous controversy within the country. A number of Nigerian organizations issued a joint statement demanding that the Nigerian government should pull out of ECOMOG.[64] Prominent Nigerian jurists questioned the legality of Nigeria's involvement, further strengthening the NPFL's position.[65] Such opposition could not be ignored, given the importance of Nigeria to the entire operation. Public outcry over Nigeria's involvement in ECOMOG threatened to increase the NPFL's intransigence as Taylor expected that public pressure could bring about the withdrawal of the force.

Domestic opposition to ECOMOG in Nigeria was the result of a number of factors. One was the belief that the objective of Babangida's regime in Liberia was not benevolent.[66] Some opinion leaders in Nigeria argued that the deployment of ECOMOG was the result of the administration's self interest – the desire to protect Doe. Relations between the administrations of Samuel Doe and President Babangida were very cordial as opposed to the cool relations between Doe and the civilian administration of Shehu Shagari in Nigeria. Babangida's administration contributed generously to the Graduate School of International Relations in Liberia named after the Nigerian President.[67]

The delay of Babangida's administration in evacuating Nigerians trapped in Liberia served to fuel suspicion that the government's action in Liberia was inspired by the leader's self interest. Despite mounting public pressure and calls for the evacuation of Nigerians trapped in Liberia, especially after the British and American governments evacuated their citizens, the Nigerian government argued that the 'evacuation of Nigerian citizens at the outset of the war would have embarrassed Samuel Doe and would have heightened the fear that the situation was indeed precarious'.[68] Babangida expressed the view that it was 'not right for the government to create distinctions between fellow Africans over evacuation exercise'.[69] But many viewed the government's response as an attempt to sacrifice Nigerians to guarantee Doe's prestige and

---

[64] These organizations included the Civil Liberties Organization, Committee for Defence of Human Rights, Nigerian Union of Journalists, Gani Fawehinmi Solidarity Association, the National Association of Nigerian Students, and Women in Nigeria; *African Concord*, 21 July 1991.

[65] One of the strongest opponents of the mission was Akinola Aguda. *The Guardian* (Nigeria), 21 November 1990, p.23.

[66] See *The Guardian*, (Nigeria) 5 June 1990; and 'Nigeria's Vietnam', in *African Guardian*, 29 October, 1990.

[67] Nigeria is said to have spent $20 million towards the establishment of the Babangida Graduate School of International Relations in Nigeria. *African Concord,* 27 August 1990.

[68] *African Concord*, 27 August 1990.

[69] Ibid.

cover up the fact that the control of government was slipping from his hands. Thus Nigeria's role in ECOMOG and humanitarian explanations were considered to be hypocritical.

Another important consideration behind the domestic opposition to ECOMOG in Nigeria was the poor state of the economy.[70] The structural adjustment programme (SAP) resulted in frequent devaluation of the Naira. A direct result of this was rampant inflation, which greatly diminished the buying power of the consumer and wages and salaries became almost worthless. Thus, Nigeria's involvement in Liberia was not looked upon favourably by many Nigerians as the financial implications were well understood. Such internal disapproval coincided with strong opposition from not only the NPFL, but also countries, which initially rendered their support to the rebels. Such vocal criticisms from both external and internal sources greatly strengthened Taylor's position politically, and this in turn influenced his position on the battlefield. He utilized both propaganda and continuous assaults on the newly deployed force, to thwart the peace process. It is possible that this had some influence on Taylor's attitude and continuous opposition to the force.

Political Divisions within ECOWAS

A very important factor that affected the ECOMOG operation concerned the differences in the political positions of member states and their roles in the conflict. There can be no doubt that a cohesive alliance (ECOWAS) was one of the prerequisites for a successful peace process in Liberia. However, at the outset, the different roles played by member states undermined any seeming cohesion which may have previously existed within the organization. This in turn affected ECOMOG's chances of success. Indeed, the contradictory roles played by some ECOWAS members in the Liberian war account for much of the failure to achieve an early resolution to the conflict.

The main external sub-regional players in the war were Burkina Faso, Cote D'Ivoire, and Nigeria. Nigeria, the prime mover of ECOMOG, was initially a supporter of Samuel Doe, while both Burkina Faso and Cote D'Ivoire rendered their support to Charles Taylor and his men. The Ivorian President, Felix Houphouet-Boigny was then able to exert his influence on other Francophone states to support his position, or at the very least, adopt a stance of indifference. There was great concern that this would stir old Anglophone-Francophone rivalry. However, the differences in the political positions of these countries was largely the result of different interests in Liberia.

---

[70] See *Nigerian Tribune*, 15 August 1990, p.9.

Nigeria's position appeared to change from that of overt support for Samuel Doe, to a more neutral one as the war in Liberia assumed greater levels of violence. Its initial support for Samuel Doe's regime was apparent especially given the rapport between both leaders. President Doe's quick visit to Nigeria at the peak of the conflict was interpreted by many Nigerians as a plea for military assistance. Thus it seems Nigeria's initial suggestion to establish ECOMOG, was borne out of the desire to help a friend and neighbour in trouble. One report states that as early as March 1990, Nigeria's President Babangida was prepared to send troops unilaterally to help his friend Samuel Doe when it became clear that he could not crush the rebellion. According to other reports, however, Sierra Leone's President Momoh, his former Kaduna Army Staff College classmate, persuaded Babangida to render such assistance via ECOWAS, which could provide mandate for an intervention force.[71] Another version of events exists. This suggests that it was US President Bush who convinced Museveni (OAU Secretary-General) to persuade Nigeria to intercede in the Liberian crisis using the ECOWAS platform.[72]

However, it appeared Nigeria's real and long term interests (of regional dominance) in the sub-region far outweighed its support for Samuel Doe. The Nigerian government soon abandoned its overt support for Samuel Doe and swapped it for a supposedly neutral stance. First, it had become obvious that the situation in Liberia was not just that of removing a handful of rebels. A full scale war had emerged, which needed a more cautious approach. It had also become obvious that Doe's continued rulership of Liberia was the major factor that prevented the resolution of the conflict.[73] Lastly, under these circumstances, overt support for Doe was not in Nigeria's best interest. The desire to render assistance to Samuel Doe was only a short term goal, which if caution was not applied, could ruin a more beneficial, long term objective – that of regional dominance, and perhaps eventually, permanent membership of the UN Security Council. The success of ECOMOG would enhance Nigeria's prestige and standing in the international community as a regional power.

The situation was quite different for the other sub-regional players who supported Taylor's warring faction. The Ivorian leader supported anti-Doe forces out of a deep seated resentment for Samuel Doe. After his rise to power, Doe had murdered A.B. Tolbert, son of former President of Liberia,

---

[71] *Africa Confidential*, 17 May 1991, Vol.32, No.10, p.3.

[72] An NPFL spokesperson claimed during interview that Museveni provided him with this information.

[73] Charles Taylor's initial claim was that he was interested only in unseating Doe from power. Indeed, this was one of the major reasons which persuaded the ECOWAS mediators that peace could be restored quickly to Liberia. Obtaining Doe' resignation seemed an easy way to bring peace about.

and son-in-law of Houphouet-Boigny (the Ivorian Head of State). Doe had promised Boigny that A.B. Tolbert who was pulled out from the safe haven provided by the French embassy in Monrovia, would be unharmed. It is believed that Boigny never forgave this act.[74] Thus, it was largely on the Ivorian leader's personal interest that the fate of Liberians and ECOMOG were to hang. Boigny used another of his sons-in-law, Blaise Compaore, Head of State of Burkina Faso, to allow Charles Taylor and the remnants of the abortive 1985 coup led by Thomas Quiwonkpa, use Burkina as a base for the 1989 invasion, while allowing supplies to reinforce Taylor's men to flow through Cote D'Ivoire.[75]

This difference in political positions prevented cohesion within ECOWAS, which in turn undermined the effectiveness of ECOMOG. The level of support given by some member-states to the NPFL, largely account for Taylor's refusal to accept a negotiated settlement. His intransigence was in line with Boigny's goals. It was easy for Cote D'Ivoire to persuade her francophone allies (except for Guinea, with a track record of dissenting or differing from the other francophone states' alliance with France), to withdraw their support for, or participation in ECOMOG.

Togo and Mali, which were members of the Standing Mediation Committee (SMC) and had initially promised to send a contingent each to Liberia as part of ECOMOG, withdrew their promises. Indeed, their level of participation in SMC meetings indicated that the interests of the Francophone members of the committee were not as strong as that of their anglophone counterparts. For example, while presidents of Nigeria, Ghana and the Gambia attended all the crucial meetings relating to the peace plan, Mali and Togo sent their foreign ministers.[76] Although the real issues that led to the differences in the political positions amongst member-states of ECOWAS were not Anglo or francophone ones, the bond between francophone states appeared so strong, that regardless of the rapport between a francophone and an anglophone state such as Togo and Nigeria, the loyalty or allegiance to the francophone fraternity appeared stronger. This situation seemed to change with the death of President Boigny who for so long acted as the leader of the Francophone bloc.

It appears that every country which contributed troops to ECOMOG or played a distinct role in the Liberian crisis did so either on the basis of direct self interest, or was compelled to act in support of one of the West African power brokers – Nigeria and Cote d'Ivoire. Sierra Leone and Guinea, who both share borders with Liberia were very much interested in preventing the war from spilling over into their respective countries. Togo and Mali pulled

---

[74] *Africa Confidential*, Vol.32 No.10, 17 May 1991.
[75] Ibid.
[76] Mode of attendance was indicated in each Communiqué of SMC meetings.

out of ECOMOG amid pressures from Cote D'Ivoire's President Boigny, and Ghana, influenced by Nigeria, remained in ECOMOG.[77] The Gambia appeared to have been the only country which contributed troops to ECOMOG mainly out of a desire to produce a successful ECOMOG which would be a major achievement for ECOWAS. This desire was in turn borne out of the fact that the Gambian president, Sir Dauda Jawara, was then the Chairman of ECOWAS. The establishment of a successful and effective peacekeeping force would be a great achievement for himself and his country.

There was however, the recognition amongst member states of ECOWAS of the long term advantages such as the prestige that a successful peace force would confer on the region.[78] Cote d'Ivoire and Burkina Faso and others therefore maintained the appearance of solidarity with ECOMOG, whilst covertly assisting Taylor. No leader wanted to be seen to be openly disrupting peace and progress in the region. Burkina Faso and others offered to contribute troops to ECOMOG, while Cote d'Ivoire denied that arms were being supplied to the NPFL.

The Death of Samuel Doe

The kidnap from ECOMOG quarters and eventual killing of Samuel Doe by the breakaway rebel group (INPFL) led by Prince Yomie Johnson, weakened the ECOMOG mission during this initial phase.[79] The inability of the force to guarantee the safety of a leader of one of the conflicting parties exposed its weakness. Indeed, this factor led Charles Taylor to later express his doubts over ECOMOG's ability to protect him. The embarrassment faced by ECOWAS over this event led to the removal of the Force Commander, Arnold Quainoo.[80] This removal itself created a political problem for ECOMOG, since Quainoo's replacement was a Nigerian, giving the operation an outlook of a solely Nigerian undertaking. The friction which Quanoo's removal created between Nigeria and Ghana was eased by the Nigerian Foreign Minister's declaration that General Quanoo 'remained the overall Force

---

[77] *Africa Confidential*, 17 May 1991.

[78] OAU Secretary-General, Salim Ahmed Salim explained during an interview with *West Africa* that after extensive consultations with some leaders and foreign ministers of ECOWAS member states, all of them agreed that it was in 'the larger interest of the region and the continent for a solution to be found to the conflict'. See *West Africa,* 22-28 October 1990, p.2690-1.

[79] For accounts of events leading to Samuel Doe's death, see *The Punch* (Nigeria), 18 October 1990.

[80] For details of events surrounding Doe's death, see *The Guardian* (Nigeria), 13 Sept. 1990 and *West Africa*, 17-23 Sept. 1990.

Commander' whilst his replacement General Dogonyaro, was the Field Commander'.[81] In another respect, the death of Doe weakened the argument of critics who saw ECOMOG as a force deployed in support of Doe.

Lack of Precedent

Another factor that accounted for the apparent ineffectiveness of ECOMOG at the initial stages was the lack of peacekeeping precedent in the sub-region. The fact that the sub-regional organization did not have any prior peacekeeping experience led many (especially the NPFL and its backer states) to doubt the credibility of both the force and ECOWAS, thereby advocating that the UN or at least the OAU should carry out peacekeeping instead.[82] Despite Nigeria's clout in the sub-region, Taylor and his men doubted the ability of ECOWAS to secure Doe's resignation. It is to be expected that such a force which is unprecedented in the region, would be greeted with scepticism. The performance of this pioneering force would largely determine the response to a future force. In addition to this, the suspicion over Nigeria's role whose initial support of Samuel Doe was apparent, also led to the call for bigger organizations to take over from ECOMOG. Thus the NPFL's lack of belief in ECOMOG's capability was sufficient to create a negative response to the ECOWAS peace plan.

PHASE TWO – THE CHANGE TO ENFORCEMENT STRATEGY

This phase marked a turning point for ECOMOG. It was able to achieve some of the ECOWAS objectives in Liberia. The force successfully put an end to the violence and brutal killings that had dominated the conflict until then. Rebel forces were driven off the centre of Monrovia, with ECOMOG forces freely patrolling the city. Foreign civilians and displaced citizens were evacuated, and other humanitarian aid was delivered. Finally, a cease-fire was signed by all the parties to the conflict then – NPFL, INPFL and AFL.

A number of factors account for this measure of success in fulfilling some of its mandate in Liberia. The first was a change in ECOMOG's peacemaking approach, from peacekeeping to peace enforcement, once it became obvious[83]

---

[81] See *The Guardian* (Nigeria), 26 September 1990, p.1 and 5 October 1990, p.12.

[82] In a communiqué issued by the NPFL after the SMC meeting which established ECOMOG, a suggestion was made that ECOMOG's composition be widened to include other African states of the OAU in order to give it 'a more continent coloration'. See *West Africa*, 13-19 August, 1990, p.2289 .

[83] Following rebel attacks on the force.

that a peacekeeping strategy would not secure the objectives of the peacemakers.[84] Thus, ECOMOG was not only perceived as effective, it succeeded in fulfilling a substantial part of its mandate in Liberia. As explained earlier in section one, this adoption of a strategy of limited offensive reaped a number of benefits. First, it expedited the evacuation of thousands of refugees. These refugees included Liberians, many of whom were granted asylum in various West African countries, as well as nationals of many other West African countries. Although figures on the actual number of refugees have varied, most reports have estimated the number of Liberian refugees at 500,000, nearly one quarter of Liberia's population.[85]

Second, ECOMOG rendered security protection to, and facilitated the work of the humanitarian organizations whose previous attempts to provide relief were hindered by the atrocities of the warring factions. In addition, the limited offensive strategy enabled the force's ability to curtail the excesses of the warring factions. The INPFL was restricted to a sector of Monrovia, while the AFL was confined to the barracks, and the NPFL driven out of the firing range of Monrovia.[86] The enforcement action also made it possible, for the Interim Government of National Unity (IGNU), to shift its base to Monrovia from Freetown where it governed Liberia by proxy. Hospital facilities were restored, as well as schools, hotels, and return of normal economic activities. Many foreign embassies were also able to resume some level of diplomatic activity. Thus, it would seem that the effects of the use of force by ECOMOG, were largely humanitarian. What was perhaps the most vital achievement of the limited offensive strategy was that it persuaded the various factions to accept a cease-fire agreement under ECOWAS/ECOMOG supervision after denying them a military solution.[87] The use of force created an atmosphere in which peace talks could be conducted.

---

[84] This change in strategy was made possible by the readjustment of ECOMOG's mandate by the Mediation Committee. See *Africa Research Bulletin*, Vol.27, No.9 Sep.1-30 1990, p.9837; See also *The Peacemaker*, Vol.1 No.1, p.11.

[85] One of such reports was from the office of the UN Co-ordinator of Emergency Relief Operations.

[86] This had an immediate advantage although Taylor remained in control of over 80% of the Liberian land mass.

[87] *Africa Research Bulletin*, 1-30 November 1990.

Diminishing Credibility of the NPFL

Some political factors added to ECOMOG's increasing credibility and effectiveness during this phase. One was the NPFL's loss of credibility. Charles Taylor, who was initially seen as the man to rescue Liberia from Samuel Doe's reign of terror himself committed many atrocities against not only Doe's Krahn tribe, but also against the Gio and Mano people who were part of his rebel faction. For example, there were reports that Taylor, largely out of insecurity or fear of being overthrown by his own army, ordered the execution of some NPFL leaders, including Gio politician, Jackson Doe.[88] Fear of torment by Taylor, drove many Gio members of the NPFL across the border.

Taylor's failure to lay down his arms after Samuel Doe's death (since Doe was his sole rationale for fighting), or at least seek to co-operate with ECOMOG to achieve a peaceful settlement, made it increasingly obvious that his own intentions were not as ingenuous as he initially led many to believe. His continued intransigence or at best inconsistencies suggested a determination to protect his own personal interest which was the ultimate prize – the leadership of Liberia. However, Charles Taylor's inconsistencies gave ECOMOG a political victory and improved the way in which the force was perceived (not by the NPFL), lending it more legitimacy.

UN and OAU Endorsement

Another political factor was the backing which ECOMOG received from the OAU and the UN despite NPFL calls for OAU and UN intervention. This, coupled with the political and financial support from the US further instilled confidence in the peace force. The UN did not heed calls for intervention but rather, the UN Secretary-General (then Perez de Cuellar), wrote to the ECOWAS chairman, wishing the organization's initiative every success.[89] A reaction from the UN Security Council came in January 1991, when the Council's President (on behalf of the Council), commended '... the efforts made by the heads of state and government of the community to promote peace and normalcy in Liberia'.[90]

---

[88] *Africa Research Bulletin*, 1-30 November 1990, p.9911; This is not incompatible with claims made by Prince Johnson during my interview with him.

[89] Dawda Jawara revealed this at a briefing to diplomats based in the Gambia, when the question of ECOMOG's legitimacy was again raised. See *West Africa*, 13-19 August 1990, pp.2289-2290.

[90] UN Doc. S/22133.

The full backing of the OAU for the ECOWAS initiative in Liberia was also evident from the start. The Secretary-General of the OAU did not at any stage consider the possibility of OAU intervention in the Liberian crisis. Rather, his comments on the crisis only served to stamp legitimacy on the activities of ECOMOG in Liberia. For example, in reaction to the argument that the ECOMOG force in Liberia had no legal basis, Salim A. Salim took the opposing viewpoint, seeing the ECOWAS initiative as a timely and bold decision, as the West African countries could not justifiably leave Liberians to fight each other.[91] His controversial statement on the principle of non-interference in the internal affairs of states further served as a strong support for the ECOWAS initiative. He argued that 'non-interference should not be taken to mean indifference' and thus called for this principle of non-interference to be examined in a broader context.[92] Similarly, the OAU Chairman, Yoweri Museveni of Uganda, was also supportive of the ECOWAS action. [93]

Support from the Local Community

The humanitarian intervention argument was difficult to challenge, given the enormous human suffering, with many civilians starving and trapped in Liberia. The wider civilian populace in Liberia welcomed the presence of ECOMOG in the country. ECOMOG was able to restore calm to Liberia and an extent of normalcy to life in the war torn country. The continued presence of the force restored enough confidence to many Liberians in exile, that they began returning home in large numbers. Thus, the ECOMOG force was regarded by many Liberians as the 'deliverer', who rescued them from the horrors of the war. This view was however predominant in the city, where ECOMOG was stationed. The impression of people in greater Liberia, is not clear. ECOMOG's arrival in Liberia and its success in restoring calm to the country, resulted in the slogan 'Thank God for ECOMOG'. Many Liberian citizens who were interviewed commended the efforts of ECOMOG and expressed gratitude to the force, whilst the main Liberian opposition to its presence has come from NPFL quarters. However, some of the civilian

---

[91] Salim A. Salim's interview with *West Africa*, 22-28 October, 1990, p.2690.
[92] Ibid. During his address at an inaugural lecture at the Africa Centre in London, he further argued that 'Africans are one people. It is hence unacceptable that a part of that people should stand in silence and in seeming helplessness when another part is suffering'.
[93] *The Guardian* (Nigeria), 8th August 1990, p.10 and 23 September 1990, p.1.

populace were sceptical of ECOMOG's ability to make any progress beyond that which it achieved by putting an end to the violence.[94]

Positive Changes in the Political Positions of NPFL Backers

Another important factor that helped the effectiveness of ECOMOG was the seeming change in political position by the main backers of Charles Taylor – Burkina Faso, Cote d'Ivoire and Libya. The first two agreed to participate in the peace plan which they had earlier opposed, and to withdraw their support for the NPFL, playing active roles in the peace negotiations. Libya also promised to withdraw its backing of NPFL.[95] Following diplomatic pressure on Libya, to withdraw its support, Colonel Qaddafi promised to 'contribute, with his moral and ethical effort, towards the success of the West African effort, for the sake of peace and stability in Liberia, and respect for the will of the people'.[96] It is believed that Libya persuaded Taylor to sign the cease-fire document.[97] In addition to this, troops were deployed from Mali and Senegal (francophone states), giving more balance to the force. Taylor had initially attributed his lack of co-operation to the one-sided appearance of the ECOMOG force.

THE TEST FOR PEACE CREATION

The decision to either maintain the enforcement strategy or discontinue it, proved to be very crucial to ECOMOG's continued effectiveness. Having obtained a cease-fire and secured the agreement of all parties to the conflict, the question arose as to whether ECOMOG should have continued to employ enforcement until the NPFL was denied any means of constituting a credible military threat, or whether the strategy should have been stopped. This is the dilemma which confronts the peacemaker in resolving such complex violent conflicts; the dialectical relationship between the military and political wings of a peacemaking process; and the limitations of the enforcement strategy.

Both options had dire implications for the peace process. Whilst ECOMOG's military superiority (in relation to all the warring factions), would

---

[94] These are documented in a recorded interview with both members of the warring factions in Liberia, and other citizens, by Gabumo Publishing Press. My interviews with a cross-section of Liberian people confirm their appreciation of ECOMOG. See also, Bill Frank Enoanyi, *Behold Uncle Sam's Step-Child.*

[95] *The Vanguard,* (Nigeria), 22 November 1990, p.1.

[96] *Africa Research Bulletin,* November 1-30, 1990, p.9912.

[97] Ibid.

have enabled it to maintain the cease-fire by force, and completely neutralize Taylor's forces, herein lay its weakness, which was political. This strategy would only have denied all parties the capability to pursue the conflict via violent means. Lasting peace was not guaranteed by this option, leaving a real possibility of future outbreak of violence. This demonstrates that attainment of real peace is dependent upon a political factor: the ability of the peacemaker to secure an agreement from conflicting parties to settle their conflict peacefully.

The decision to discontinue or proceed with the strategy of 'limited offensive' in Liberia was determined largely by ECOMOG's mandate, which was in turn dependent upon the objectives of the Standing Mediation Committee (SMC). Thus, once the cease-fire agreement was obtained, the enforcement action was stopped and ECOMOG reverted to a traditional peacekeeping role. This decision gave an indication of the real purpose of the enforcement action. It was not to render one party excessively weak in relation to the others. Rather, this strategy was meant to protect the force and other humanitarian establishments in Liberia, to secure safe passage of humanitarian aid, and to create an atmosphere conducive to negotiations. Any objective contrary to this would have robbed the organization of its peacemaking credential, which was still being challenged by the NPFL and its supporters. However, after enforcement was swapped for peacekeeping, it soon became clear that the progress made by ECOMOG could not be converted into a real settlement. This decision was to give way to another phase, where the force was unable to proceed with efforts to attain the rest of its mandate in Liberia.

PHASE THREE – STAGNATION

This phase, which spanned December 1990 to October 1992, was one of stagnation for the ECOMOG operation. The progress that was expected to follow the cease-fire agreement, failed to materialize. There was disagreement over the provisions of the cease-fire agreement, but efforts to reach a compromise with Charles Taylor proved futile. Whilst mediators were actively pursuing a peace plan acceptable to the NPFL, the rebels launched attacks on Sierra Leone and Guinea. The entry of another faction further compounded the situation. The stalemate that emerged was attributed by many, to Charles Taylor's inconsistencies, whilst others blamed flaws in the agreement. A major problem however, was the apparent failure of, and the inherent contradictory effects of the peace enforcement strategy earlier adopted (though later discontinued) by ECOWAS. This same strategy which produced a cease-fire, was also in many ways, responsible for the impasse which ensued.

Problems with Peace Agreements

Within weeks of signing the cease-fire agreement, it became clear that the cease-fire was only a fragile one, as relations between ECOMOG and NPFL remained tense. This prevented ECOMOG from progressing as expected, to disarm the factions and allow the election process to begin. A number of issues gave rise to this situation. First was Taylor's dissatisfaction with the offer of six seats out of thirty in the interim government. Taylor expected that he would have a greater say in the new administration than any other faction.[98] This was not altogether unfounded, given the fact that about ninety percent of the Liberian land mass was under his control. Opponents however argued that even though this was the case, Monrovia contained close to 1.5 million people, and these constituted about three quarters of the country's population. In addition to this, the question of disarmament and confinement of troops could not be resolved. Discussions aimed at settling this issue ended in an impasse. However, the main problem rested with the NPFL, as the AFL accepted the cease-fire document as presented, while the INPFL agreed to the confinement of its troops, but not to their disarmament.

A third area of disagreement was the inspection of all ships, aircraft, and vehicles entering Liberia. The NPFL wanted the inspection to be carried out by two ECOMOG representatives as well as two delegates from each of the warring factions. Whilst ECOMOG agreed to having two representatives from each faction, it rejected the idea of having only two ECOMOG inspectors, as this 'would impede its right to implement its responsibility'.[99] Moreover, ECOMOG argued that it would not accept such restrictions, since it was not a party to the conflict.[100]

In view of these unresolved issues, efforts were intensified to break the deadlock. Such efforts resulted in a series of broken peace agreements. An extra ordinary summit on the Liberian conflict took place in Lome, Togo on 12 February 1991. Agreement was reached to confine and disarm troops from the three factions. The INPFL was to be at Caldwell base, the AFL at the Barclay Training Centre and Camp Schieflin, while the NPFL were to be in various assembly points outside the capital. Troops and surrendered weapons were to be registered at ECOMOG reception centres.[101] However, a deadlock quickly set in. An agreement was reached to convene an all-Liberian conference from 15 March 1991 which would decide on an interim government acceptable to all parties. But Charles Taylor indicated his desire to lead the

---

[98] *Africa Research Bulletin*, 1-31 January 1991, p.9732.
[99] *Africa Research Bulletin*, 1-31 Jan. 1991, p.9732.
[100] Ibid.
[101] *Africa Research Bulletin*, 1-31 Mar. 1991, p.10022.

interim government and thereafter run for presidential elections.[102] This contradicts the provision in the original peace plan which stated that the leader of the interim government could not run for elected office.

The all-Liberian conference which was held from 15 March to 20 April 1991 was inconclusive despite the efforts of all other groups to move closer to the NPFL's demands. Among the concessions made was that a three-member executive council be established which would consist of a chairman and two co-chairmen, one of whom would be Charles Taylor. Whilst the chairman would not be eligible to contest elections, the co-chairmen may run for elected office.[103] This option would make it possible for Charles Taylor to be part of the interim government, and still be able to contest in the elections. However, the NPFL later walked out of this conference.[104] The conference went ahead to form an Interim Government of National Unity (IGNU), with Amos Sawyer, still as President, and Dr. Peter Naigow of the INPFL as its Vice-President.

NPFL Invasion of Sierra Leone, Entry of New Faction

Whilst attempts were being made to reach some compromise with Charles Taylor, the NPFL took the conflict beyond Liberia's border, into Sierra Leone, further complicating ECOMOG's task. On 23 March, NPFL rebels invaded two Sierra Leone border towns, prompting a series of battles with Sierra Leone forces.[105] Captured guerrillas stated that they were Liberian members of the NPFL trained in Burkina Faso and Libya.[106] It soon became apparent that the effects of this incident would be far greater than previous rebel attempts to disrupt life in neighbouring countries.[107]

The announcement by a former Corporal in the Sierra Leonean army of his intentions to establish a rebel army to overthrow President Momoh's government, further compounded the situation.[108] In spite of condemnation by the US[109] and neighbouring states, the NPFL took control of some strategic areas in Sierra Leone, including Zimi which is located in the country's rich mining

---

[102] Ibid.

[103] *Africa Research Bulletin*, 1-31 April 1991, p.10095.

[104] Nwolise, p.282

[105] *Africa Research Bulletin*, 1-31 April 1991, p.10072.

[106] Ibid.

[107] In January of the same year for example, NPFL rebels looted and attacked Guinean villages on the border with Liberia, provoking intervention by the Guinea army. Reports by *Agence France Presse* (AFP), 9 Jan. 1991.

[108] *AFP*, 10 April 1991.

[109] *Africa Research Bulletin*, 1-30 April 1991, p.10073; and *West Africa*, 15-22 April 1991.

and agricultural region.[110] It is believed that a combination of political motives and a severe food shortage experienced by NPFL rebels located in north-west Liberia, led to the incursions into Sierra Leone.[111] It later became clear that Sierra Leone had been plunged into a civil war, and that the rebels were a mixture of genuine Sierra Leonean dissidents and Liberians connected to Charles Taylor's NPFL. Sierra Leone was plunged into a civil war, which would shape developments in the country. This is discussed later in this chapter. This incursion into Sierra Leone and Taylor's unflinching intransigence led many to become suspicious of his primary motivation. The entry of another faction into the Liberian war made the attainment of a political solution even more difficult. The new group, known as United Liberation Movement of Liberia for Democracy (ULIMO) was supposedly 'born out of the desire of displaced Liberians to return home and continue their search for democratic freedom'.[112] This group stated that its main objective was to force the NPFL to the negotiating table.

The Yamoussoukro Accords

The meetings held in Yamoussoukro constitute a significant step in the efforts of the sub-regional leaders to find lasting peace to the crisis. The role played by the Ivorian leader confirmed that consensus was returning to ECOWAS. A meeting was held in Yamoussoukro (Cote d'ivoire) from 29-30 June 1991, chaired by President Houphouet-Boigny. The Ivorian leader persuaded Charles Taylor and Amos Sawyer to accept a cease-fire as the first part of efforts to find peaceful solution to the conflict. Both leaders promised to pursue reconciliation.[113] At the 14th session of the Authority of Heads of State and Government in Abuja, Nigeria from 4-6 July 1991, the establishment of a Committee of Five as an adjunct to the SMC was approved by the Authority. These included Heads of State of Cote d'ivoire (as Chairman), Guinea-Bissau, Senegal, The Gambia, and Togo.[114]

The first meeting of the Committee of Five was held in Yamoussoukro, Cote D'ivoire, on 29 July, 1991. Efforts were made to build the parties' (especially the NPFL's) confidence in order to move toward the goal of organizing free and fair elections in Liberia. This meeting did not achieve much as Taylor's position had not shifted although the fragile cease-fire was

---

[110] *Daily Telegraph* (UK) 30 April 1991.
[111] *The Guardian (UK)*, 3 April 1991.
[112] *Africa Research Bulletin*, 1-30 June 1991, p.10176.
[113] See M.A. Vogt, p.283, and *Official Journal of ECOWAS* Vol. 21, p.22.
[114] *Official Journal of ECOWAS*, Vol.21, p.47.

still holding. The third meeting in Yamoussoukro held on 16 September 1991, which was the second meeting of the committee of five, made considerable progress. It was unanimously agreed that ECOMOG should be remodelled and reinforced. The parties agreed to continue to observe the cease-fire. In addition to this, the parties agreed to encamp and disarm their troops, under ECOMOG supervision. ECOMOG was to liaise with the conflicting parties to arrange the procedures for implementing the agreement. In addition to this, agreement was reached to establish an electoral commission, and monitoring of the elections by the International Negotiations Network, founded by former US President, Jimmy Carter.[115]

The acceptance of ECOMOG was a significant shift in the NPFL's position despite the absence of UN or OAU troops as Taylor had previously requested. A number of factors have been attributed to this change. First was the decision of Senegal to send troops to ECOMOG. Charles Taylor had always opposed Nigeria's dominance in ECOMOG.[116] Secondly, it is believed that the attacks against NPFL territory by ULIMO led Charles Taylor to become amenable to ECOWAS peace moves.[117] Armed conflict had broken out on 4th September between the two warring factions, after ULIMO rebels attacked those of the NPFL from the north-west area of the country. This situation had threatened to create new problems for ECOMOG.[118] However, ULIMO, which was not a party to this agreement, rejected it, stating that it was 'prejudicial to the interests of Sierra Leone and Guinea'.[119]

However, the Yamoussoukro IV agreement (which was the third meeting of the Committee of Five) was the most significant. It went a long way to clarify many of the ambiguities in previous agreements. Furthermore, it provided a comprehensive programme of implementation and a timetable for encampment and disarmament.[120] Nonetheless, this accord could not be implemented.

The Geneva Agreement

A meeting held in Geneva on 6th and 7th April 1992, attended by the Committee of Five and the conflicting parties, resulted in the Geneva agreement which created a buffer zone along the Liberia – Sierra Leone

---

[115] Ibid.
[116] *Africa Research Bulletin*, 1-30 Sept. 1991, p.10274.
[117] Ibid.
[118] Reports by *AFP* on 6 & 11 September 1991.
[119] *AFP*, 19 Sept. 1991; and *Africa Research Bulletin*, 1-30 Sept. 1991, p.10274.
[120] *Official Journal of ECOWAS*, Vol.21, pp.26-27.

border, and reaffirmed the role of ECOMOG.[121] It was agreed that the Yamoussoukro IV accords presented the best framework for lasting peace in Liberia, and that ECOMOG should implement this accord without further delay.[122] By 30th April 1992, ECOMOG troops had begun deploying in areas under NPFL control. It was reported that over 7,000 ECOMOG soldiers were to be sent out from Monrovia into the countryside. This coincided with reports that Charles Taylor had reneged on the agreement, arguing that he was forced to sign it.

Events leading to the NPFL Attack – Operation Octopus

The incidents which followed this ECOMOG deployment quickly revealed that the previous negotiations and agreements had done little to change the position of the NPFL. The rebel group captured the ECOMOG contingents that had been deployed in their territory, killing six Senegalese soldiers. In spite of the NPFL's initial denial of the death of Senegalese soldiers in their custody, the deaths were eventually confirmed.[123] The ECOWAS Committee of Five called for the establishment of a commission of inquiry into the deaths.[124]

From here on, events in Liberia deteriorated and ECOMOG found it impossible to fulfil its mandate. The kidnap of the ECOMOG troops coupled with intense fighting between the NPFL and ULIMO led ECOMOG to withdraw its troops from Kongo and Bombo, around the Liberian border with Sierra Leone.[125] Disarming the NPFL was fast becoming an impossible task. Thus for the first time since the beginning of the conflict, ECOWAS leaders gave serious consideration to imposing economic sanctions if the NPFL did not honour the peace agreement within one month.[126] Charles Taylor stated that he would take the imposition of sanctions as 'a declaration of war'.[127] Peace talks in Cotonou on 17th August 1992 which were to include the ULIMO for the first time, were unsuccessful.[128]

ECOMOG's efforts to progress with its mandate in Liberia were dealt major blows by the NPFL during this phase by two crucial developments. First, the NPFL captured five hundred ECOMOG soldiers, disarming and

[121] *Africa Research Bulletin*, 1-30 April 1992, p.10524.
[122] *Official journal of ECOWAS* Vol. 21, p.49.
[123] *Africa Research Bulletin*, 1-30 June 1992, p.10600.
[124] Ibid.
[125] *Africa Research Bulletin*, 1st-31st July 1992, p.10658.
[126] *Africa Research Bulletin*, 1-31 August 1992.
[127] Ibid.
[128] Ibid.

depriving them of food in what was seen as a 'dehumanising campaign'.[129] The NPFL having lost a substantial measure of its territory to ULIMO rebels, accused the ECOMOG soldiers of collaborating with this rival group.[130] Rescuing these soldiers was a difficult task as they were dispersed among various rebel held areas. This incident led the Force Commander to order the withdrawal of ECOMOG troops from NPFL territory.[131] The second development was the massive attack, code named 'Octopus', launched by the NPFL on Monrovia from 15 October 1992, in a bid to finish the job it had started in 1990, controlling the whole of Liberia. This created a major set back for ECOMOG which was surprised by the NPFL attack, and had to revert to its earlier enforcement strategy, halting the shelling, and rocket attacks from the NPFL.[132]

The fact that the NPFL was regrouping and rebuilding its forces whilst taking part in peace agreements strengthens the argument of those (mainly rival groups and the peacemakers), who argued that Taylor's goal had always been to control the reigns of power. Others, including some legal experts and NPFL supporters, blamed Taylor's uncompromising attitude on fundamental flaws in the agreements. They argued for example, that agreements were not accompanied by documents defining keywords, terms and clauses used.[133] Some argued that the emergence of ULIMO, coupled with NPFL suspicions of ECOMOG accounted for the NPFL's intransigence.[134] Taylor also argued that he could not disarm and encamp his troops in the face of ULIMO threat. Whilst this position is understandable, it is also the case that Taylor did not agree to disarm even when ULIMO was not in existence.

THE FLAWS OF PEACE CREATION

The peace enforcement strategy adopted during the second phase largely accounted for the NPFL's unyielding stance. ECOMOG's heavy military presence in Liberia did not reassure Charles Taylor that his forces would not be decimated if they disarmed.[135] This was compounded even more by the fact that ECOMOG defeated the NPFL forces in battle, driving them out of

---

[129] *Africa Research Bulletin*, 1st-30th September 1992, p.10719.

[130] Ibid.

[131] *West Africa,* 12-19 Sept. 1992, and *Daily Telegraph (UK)*, 12 Sept. 1992.

[132] *Associated Press*, Liberia; *BBC Focus on Africa*, 31 Oct. 1992; *AFP*, 2 Nov. 1992; and *Reuters*, 3rd November 1992.

[133] The NPFL spokesperson interview.

[134] Former US President Jimmy Carter expressed this in a letter to ECOWAS leaders. *Liberian Studies Journal*, Vol. XVIII 1992, p.262.

[135] Ibid.

Monrovia which would have been their ultimate prize. The psychological effects of this on the NPFL were great. The loss of face that the physical act of having to surrender their arms to ECOMOG would bring, appeared difficult for Charles Taylor to bear. Thus, a military solution seemed a more attractive option.

The animosity of the NPFL troops toward the Nigerian contingent in particular was an indication of their deep sense of loss from the ECOMOG intervention. Their attitude toward Nigeria partly derived from the fact that had it not been for the sheer strength (numerical, military and financial) of the Nigerian troops that intervened, Taylor would perhaps have defeated the AFL and assumed leadership of Liberia. NPFL leaders and soldiers alike had gone on record to say that they would never surrender to the Nigerian troops.[136] Thus although ECOMOG initially managed to halt the violence and carnage in Liberia through the use of force, the lasting peace which was expected to follow did not occur. This very act which created the atmosphere in which peace negotiations could occur, was also partly responsible for the collapse of the peace process.

This situation revealed the inherent weaknesses and contradictions of terminating violence through the use of force, and then seeking to arrange and keep peace. It sometimes becomes necessary to stop violence regardless of the parties' willingness to seek peaceful solution to the conflict, as was the situation in Liberia. Termination of such violence is the sole essence of enforcement action. This strategy can only create a peaceful atmosphere, but it cannot bring about lasting peace. Thus enforcement is only a military means employed to satisfy a political end. Peacekeeping on the other hand, is politically attractive, but incapable of enforcing any agreements, or at least terminating the violence which may erupt. Thus, the very strategy which created progress for ECOMOG, was also responsible for its setback.

OPTIONS IGNORED BY ECOWAS

ECOWAS could perhaps have prevented the conflict from persisting this far (making its mandate easier to fulfil) had it exercised one or more of a number of other options. First, instead of swapping enforcement for peacekeeping, ECOMOG could have continued with the former until it had neutralized Taylor's forces. Adopting a peacekeeping strategy allowed the NPFL to rebuild its forces. However, one could only argue this clearly with the benefit of hindsight. There had been strong political factors which prevented the force

---

[136] For example, interview with a high ranking soldier in the NPFL on *Sky News Special Report* on 9 February 1994 revealed that the force was determined never to disarm to Nigerian troops.

from continuing with the enforcement strategy. A second option was to use different troops for the enforcement operation whilst fresh troops from other West African troops would come in to perform peacekeeping functions. Thus the Nigerian troops whose presence the rebels objected to would have been withdrawn while troops from other countries would be brought in to calm the situation and perform a traditional peacekeeping role. A more attractive option which ECOWAS surprisingly did not take, was to impose an embargo on the movement of arms into this area. This would not only have prevented the NPFL from rearming, it may have been difficult for ULIMO to join the conflict.

The absence of an arms embargo after the use of military force stopped only confirms the arguments of critics that ECOWAS did not conduct thorough research into the Liberian conflict, and thus did not understand the intricacies of the conflict before jumping into it.[137] It is also argued that West African leaders were excited over the challenge that the Liberian conflict presented. Nigeria in particular, welcomed the opportunity to show that it deserved a permanent seat on the UN Security Council.[138] Thus, ECOWAS leaders, imprisoned by their own perceived ideas of what was happening in Liberia, did not make adequate preparation before going in. However, a combination of all these factors led ECOMOG to be largely unsuccessful in this phase. Indeed, the force appeared to revert to the initial lack of progress experienced during the first phase.

PHASE FOUR – RETURN TO ENFORCEMENT STRATEGY

During this phase, ECOMOG employed the enforcement strategy for the second time but it was not without its costs. Accusations of partiality and violations of human rights were levelled on ECOMOG. But it was in this same phase that the UN became more actively involved in the crisis. Its support of ECOWAS to a large extent served to legitimize ECOMOG's actions, but it also exposed the UN to some criticisms. Most of all however, the phase witnessed the first concrete agreement between the parties, involving the UN and including concessions made to the NPFL.

---

[137] See Lord Avebury's comments in *Africa World Review*, Nov. 1993 – April 1994. Also, General Emmanuel Erskines, UNIFIL Commander, warned against failure to impose an arms embargo on all the factions. See *The Guardian* (Nigeria), 14 September 1990.
[138] Interview with Senior NPFL spokesperson..

Allegations of Human Rights Violation

In its bid to protect itself and wrench control of some parts of Monrovia from the invading NPFL, ECOMOG increased its forces in Liberia. However, ECOMOG not only re-established control over Monrovia, it launched a campaign to strike at NPFL supply and communication lines. This is a departure from ECOMOG's initial position when it used just enough force to secure control of Monrovia and allow the passage of humanitarian aid. This time, the goal of the force was apparently to neutralize Taylor's forces, denying them the means to regroup and re-attack Monrovia. The ECOMOG force commander at the time, Major-General Adetunji Olurin, stated that 'you can be sure that anywhere Taylor is using to launch any attack on us will be a target'[139]

ECOMOG bombed the American-managed Firestone rubber plantation, where according to military sources, Charles Taylor was storing munitions.[140] Charles Taylor himself was to later acknowledge the loss of three strategic strongholds to ECOMOG. These included Robertsfield International Airport, Harbel and Kakata, which made it virtually impossible for the rebels to launch any attack on Monrovia, and they were also deprived of some of the lifeline for their campaign.[141] Whilst Kakata was a military base, Harbel and Roberts-field Airport were used by the rebels to evade the sanctions imposed on Liberia by ECOWAS.[142] Taylor also lost the ports of Greenville[143] and Buchanan. ECOMOG warships had blockaded shipping in order to enforce the ECOWAS embargo.

The use of force by ECOMOG in this way was however not without political costs. There were reports of civilian casualties which were incurred as a result of ECOMOG actions. The bombing raids at the Firestone plantation left one hundred and twenty-five civilians dead, according to the NPFL, while others estimated the number dead at thirty-eight.[144] There were also reports that ECOMOG launched air attacks (by Nigerian planes) against Liberia's border with Cote d'ivoire, where a clearly identified relief convoy was stationed, killing and injuring a number of local people.[145] However, some ECOMOG supporters argued that the incident '... was a clear navigation

---

[139] *Associated Press*, Monrovia, 04 November 1992.
[140] Ibid.
[141] *BBC Focus on Africa*, 27 Feb. 1993.
[142] Ibid.
[143] *Reuters*, 03 May 1993.
[144] *Associated Press*, Monrovia
[145] Press Release by *Medecins Sans Frontieres* (a humanitarian agency), on 4 Mar. 1993; and *Reuters*, 5 Mar. 1993, which also reported that a high-level Nigerian delegation was dispatched to Ivory Coast to discuss the incident.

error'.[146] There were also claims that other towns in the north of Liberia were targeted by ECOMOG for similar raids, damaging hospitals and relief compounds.[147] The UN special envoy to Liberia, Mr. Gordon-Somers after a visit to Taylor's territory, Gbarnga, later confirmed that he saw some evidence that there had been hits on civilians and civilian targets, but he could not say if they resulted from misguided missiles, bombs, cluster bombs, etc.[148]

Thus, the employment of the peace enforcement strategy in this phase attracted sharp criticisms in ways which were not expressed during the earlier phase when ECOMOG adopted the same strategy. This situation appears to be the result of a combination of factors. First, the weapons brought to bear in this second enforcement action were different from those used in the earlier phase and their effects were more damaging. For example, it has been argued that in 1990, ECOMOG was able to drive Taylor's 'ragtag' force as well as other forces out of Monrovia very easily.[149] Brigadier Malu, ECOMOG Chief of Staff at the time, argued that reports that Taylor used untrained children to fight his battles were not totally correct. Rather, the rebel leader spent the two years after the first cease-fire agreement, training and arming a cadre of fighters.[150] ECOMOG, which was not prepared for war, had to immediately build up its forces in Liberia, following new orders from ECOWAS to enforce a cease-fire in the country.[151]

The troops that had previously numbered about 7,000 were doubled. Nigeria landed battle tanks and armoured personnel carriers, and long range artillery guns, and a squadron of Alpha jets to back up the force.[152] In addition to these were Guinean MiG warplanes and an artillery crew with B-21 multiple rocket launchers, and Ghanaian warplanes.[153] The outcome of this combination of forces was that while NPFL shelling was silenced, civilian casualties were incurred, especially from the air raids. The extent to which the weapons used were effective is another issue which, is discussed in the next chapter.

Second, unlike the previous phase when ECOMOG had halted the use of force immediately after they were able to force the NPFL and other parties back, the attacks on the NPFL continued this time even after the force had left the vicinity of the state capital. The goal this time seemed to be to deprive the NPFL any means to conduct further military operations, and force the rebels

---

[146] *Reuters*, 5 Mar. 1993.
[147] Ibid.
[148] *BBC Focus on Africa*, 25 April 1993.
[149] *Associated Press*, Monrovia, 26 Nov. 1992.
[150] Ibid.
[151] *Reuters*, 15 Nov. 1992.
[152] Ibid.
[153] Ibid.

to the negotiating table. Thus, after defending itself and the capital from NPFL attacks, ECOMOG itself went on the attack. This totally changed its image from a peace force, to one which had made itself a party to the conflict. The effects of the economic sanctions by ECOWAS and the UN in addition to those of the air raids, made life more difficult for the local population in the territory controlled by Taylor.[154]

Claims of Partiality

The charges of partiality directed against ECOMOG came not only from the fact that the NPFL was the only party left which was challenging ECOMOG presence in Liberia, but also because ECOMOG utilized the support of the other factions in their battle with the NPFL. The INPFL had been defeated by ECOMOG and its leader Prince Johnson had been taken to Nigeria, in ECOMOG's bid to neutralise his forces. The AFL had long been rendered incapable of fighting any major battle. ULIMO, though at war with the NPFL, was not opposed to ECOMOG's presence. However, ECOMOG's inferior knowledge of the territory, led it to employ the services of both Prince Johnson and the AFL. The peace force also enjoyed the co-operation of ULIMO. These groups offered to show ECOMOG the escape routes used by the NPFL.[155]

The decision to employ the assistance of these rebel groups in countering the NPFL offensive, proved costly for ECOMOG. The image of the force was badly compromised and accusations of partiality came from many quarters. It is alleged that ECOMOG armed the AFL and ULIMO.[156] There were reports of instances where AFL or ULIMO soldiers formed the front-line of the attack, while ECOMOG troops came behind with heavy artillery.[157] However, ECOMOG made a major error of leaving the rebels alone to hold surrounding territory, as preparation was made for a major assault. These forces, already well known for gross indiscipline went on rampage in Monrovia, looting and harassing innocent civilians.[158] This poor conduct of the rebel groups worsened ECOMOG's position and created fresh problems for the force.

---

[154] The reaction of Liberians in territory under Taylor's control is analysed in *Africa political Intelligence Review* (APIR) fact sheet, 16 April 1993.

[155] *West Africa*, 23-29 Nov. 1992; and *Africa Watch*, June 1993.

[156] *Africa Watch*, 'Waging War to Keep the Peace: The ECOMOG Intervention and Human Rights', June 1993 p.14.

[157] Hillary Anderson, *BBC Focus on Africa* (News Magazine), Jan-March 1993.

[158] *West Africa*, 23-29 Nov. 1992.

ECOMOG had to withdraw these troops from the streets of Monrovia, ordering them back into the barracks.[159]

This experience however indicates that there is a major contradiction between human rights protection and military operations designed to enforce peace. Many supporters of ECOMOG argue that guaranteeing human rights was not an explicit part of ECOMOG's task.[160] Rather, its job was the enforcement of a cease-fire and implementation of the Yamoussoukro IV accord. Amos Sawyer, for example, argued that human rights was part and parcel of the peace process. Thus if a cease-fire was obtained and the peace process was completed, human rights would automatically be guaranteed.[161] Abbass Bundu, the ECOWAS Executive Secretary also pointed out that

:d in peace enforcement, a situation which was a far cry mission. Thus he expected the co-operation of all :f agencies.[162] The controversy over what the role of e in such multifaceted operations is likely to continue ks of relief agencies and ECOMOG in Liberia were so hey were all working toward one ultimate goal – the id security in Liberia. After these experiences, efforts nate the activities of ECOMOG and relief agencies.)ticed after the signing of the first Abuja Agreement of

The Role of the United Nations

e notable contributions to the Liberian war in terms of :e from the earlier stages of the conflict, its first real ' came in November 1992, nearly three years after the :solution 788 was adopted by the UN Security Council . The resolution called on conflicting parties to observe a cease-fire, and it endorsed an arms embargo on deliveries of weapons and military equipment into Liberia, with the exception of those meant for the use of ECOMOG.[163] This resolution also requested the UN Secretary-General to

---

[159] Ibid., and *Reuters*, 3 Nov. 1992.

[160] *Africa Watch*, June 1993.

[161] Ibid.

[162] Statement from Abbass Bundu. Document obtained from *BBC Focus on Africa*, 10 May 1993.

[163] *Associated Press* Monrovia, 19 Nov. 1992; *Reuters*, 20 Nov. 1992; *Africa Watch*, June 1993; S/RES/788.

dispatch a Special Representative to Liberia urgently, to evaluate the situation and report back to the Council with any recommendations.[164]

The UN Special Representative, Trevor Gordon-Somers, submitted a report in March 1993, following visits to Liberia from November to December 1992, and January to February 1993. He recommended the dispatch of two hundred UN observers to monitor a new cease-fire agreement.[165] This resulted in the formation of the UN Observer Force in Liberia (UNOMIL). The UN Secretary-General described this situation in Liberia as representing 'a good example of systematic co-operation between the United Nations and regional organizations, as envisaged in Chapter VIII of the Charter'.[166] Charles Taylor's unwillingness to disarm to ECOMOG especially in its current form, led to suggestions that ECOMOG should be broadened to include other ECOWAS members, although the current command structure would be retained.[167] Over 2,500 soldiers were to be deployed from Tanzania, Uganda and Zimbabwe. They began to arrive in Liberia in December 1993.[168]

The Cotonou Agreement of 25 July 1993 was signed between the Interim Government of Liberia, the NPFL and ULIMO, in the presence of representatives of ECOWAS, OAU and the UN. This agreement was a major political victory for the NPFL, largely because Taylor's refusal to disarm to ECOMOG, led to the expansion of the force to include troops from other African nations as well as UN observers. However, firm UN support for ECOMOG was evident in the agreement. ECOMOG was given the power to enforce peace if the agreement was violated by any of the parties, although the agreement stipulated conditions for enforcement.[169] Although the Cotonou Accord still constituted the basic framework for co-operation between ECOMOG and UNOMIL, there were other peace agreements, following Cotonou's collapse.[170]

ACHIEVING A SETTLEMENT OF THE LIBERIAN CONFLICT

A settlement of the Liberian conflict was not achieved until 1997, when elections were successfully staged in Liberia. After Cotonou, a number of attempts were made before disarmament and elections were finally accom-

---

[164] S/RES/788.

[165] *Africa Watch*, June 1993, p.29.

[166] Report of the Secretary-General on the question of Liberia, *UN Doc. S/25402*, 12 March 1993.

[167] Ibid.

[168] *New Democrat Weekly* (Monrovia), 23-29 Dec. 1993, p.24.

[169] *Cotonou Accord*, Article 8(1-3).

[170] These included Akosombo, Accra and Abuja Agreements.

plished. The first was in Akosombo, Ghana, where an agreement to supplement agreement was signed, which gave greater participation to the Liberian National Transitional Government (LNTG) and the warring factions in the management of the transition efforts in the country. Within three months, another agreement was needed to supplement the Akosombo accord. Its main purpose was to clarify the Akosombo accord, and also to include new factions as signatories to the accord. However, the parties could not reach an agreement over the membership of the proposed new Council of State and this constituted a main set back in the peace process. The Abuja agreements of August 1995 and August 1996 respectively were the most successful of the accords as they resulted in the highest level of disarmament witnessed in the seven year process, and paved the way for the July 1997 elections. In the period after the 1995 Abuja Accord there was a comprehensive disarmament, demobilisation and reintegration plan, which was stalled as a result of the outbreak of another crisis in April 1996 in Monrovia.[171] The agreement was however brought on track in 1996 following another meeting in Abuja, Nigeria. This led to the disarmament and demobilization of more than 70% of the combatants. In the elections that followed, Charles Taylor won with a convincing 75% majority, making a second ballot unnecessary.

BEYOND LIBERIA TO SIERRA LEONE

The civil war in Sierra Leone, which began in 1991 was overshadowed by the war in Liberia and there was no significant attempt from outside the subregion to intervene in Sierra Leone. ECOWAS member states were stretched thin by the peace operation in Liberia and could only manage a small presence in Sierra Leone. The force that was present in Sierra Leone consisted largely of Nigerian troops and their initial task was mainly to render assistance to Sierra Leone in the protection of the border areas that were vulnerable to invading troops from Liberia. However, by 1995, international efforts, largely by the UN, to achieve a negotiated settlement in Sierra Leone intensified. Unlike Liberia, where efforts to address the crisis focused on achieving a negotiated settlement prior to the staging of elections, the peacemakers in Sierra Leone saw the staging of elections as one of the ways of achieving a lasting settlement to the conflict. Thus, elections were held, in which Ahmed Tejan Kabbah emerged president of Sierra Leone in 1996.

---

[171] For detailed analysis of the developments in the peace process from Cotonou to elections see Abiodun Alao, John Mackinlay, and 'Funmi Olonisakin, *Peacekeepers, Politicians and Warlords: The Liberian Peace Process,* (United Nations University Press), 1999.

There was initial optimism that Kabbah would be able to achieve national reconciliation, and address many of the grievances of the rebels, thereby making the continuation of the civil war unnecessary. Kabbah's predecessor had employed mercenaries (Executive Outcomes), in the bid to crush the rebellion. Although the rebels were contained, they continued to operate in the hinterland. Kabbah ended the use of mercenaries and sought to rebuild a new national army. A bilateral defence pact was signed with Nigeria as part of the long term restructuring plans but these plans were disrupted in May 1997, when a band of soldiers led by Major Johnny Paul Koromah ousted President Kabbah. In the ensuing chaos, a Nigerian force based in Sierra Leone attempted to reverse the coup without success. The military option was later substituted for another approach: the imposition of sanctions on the military junta in Sierra Leone. This had some success. A peace accord was eventually signed in Guinea in October 1997 between ECOWAS and Koroma's Armed Forces Revolutionary Council (AFRC), which outlined a plan that would culminate in the re-instatement of President Kabbah in April 1998. There were indications that the rebels would renege on this within two months of this agreement. Although this process was due to end in April 1998, hostilities flared again in Sierra Leone in February 1998, at which time the Nigeria-led ECOMOG troops overwhelmed the troops of the AFRC, opening the way for the restoration of Kabbah.

The intermittent switch between peacekeeping and enforcement seen in Liberia, was not prominent in Sierra Leone, but Nigeria's readiness to use force was immediately apparent. Although the crisis here did not escalate to the scale seen in Liberia, it was difficult to challenge a decision to intervene, if only to restore order. The *coup d'etat*, which removed the elected government of Ahmed Tejan Kabbah, after just over a year in power, was a bloody one which was not confined to military quarters alone. The *coup* makers, led by Major Johnny Paul Koroma, and their Revolutionary United Front (RUF) allies, wrought havoc on Freetown, Sierra Leone's capital, and its residents. In their bid to release political prisoners from jails, they let criminals loose, who joined in the raping, looting, arson and killings that ensued. The evacuation of foreign nationals and civilians became necessary as the crisis rapidly escalated. President Kabbah fled to Guinea, where he requested assistance from Nigeria, with whom Sierra Leone had a bilateral defence pact. Two battalions of Nigerian troops, stationed in Sierra Leone under this bilateral pact failed to foil the *coup*. Nigeria's immediate response was to dispatch troops to Sierra Leone, to reverse the *coup* and to restore order. Although this was a predominantly Nigerian operation, carried out under the ECOWAS umbrella, the condemnation of the *coup* by many Sierra Leoneans, and international organisations such as the UN, OAU, and the Commonwealth, gave legitimacy to the Nigerian-led effort to reverse the *coup*.[172]

Nigeria and Guinea appeared to be the only states in support of the use of force whilst other ECOWAS member states advocated the imposition of sanctions against Koroma's regime, and simultaneously sought a diplomatic resolution of the conflict. The military option was abandoned for sanctions and diplomacy, which led in October 1997, to the signing of a peace deal in Guinea under which President Kabbah would be reinstated by April 1998. There were early signs that the peace agreement would not succeed, given additional demands by the junta in Sierra Leone. In February 1998, ECOMOG capitalised on an incident in Sierra Leone, using all necessary force to overwhelm the troops of the Armed Forces Revolutionary Council (AFRC) and ejected them from Freetown. This was in marked contrast to Liberia, where solely diplomatic options were relied upon after the first enforcement operation in 1990. The idea of sanctions were not initially considered in Liberia until 1992, by which time, the NPFL had seized the opportunity to re-arm for a show down with ECOMOG. However, the Sierra Leone situation deviated from *Peace Creation* in many respects. Initially, it was more of an attempt by Nigeria to restore President Kabbah to power under a bilateral arrangement rather than an attempt to bring about peaceful resolution of conflict between warring parties.

The willingness of the sub-regional power, Nigeria, to take forceful measures to restore order in West Africa is striking. Such willingness and decisiveness are hard to come by in the wider international community. It is not often in the immediate national interest of states, to expend human and material resources in conflicts that do not have a direct impact on their security. It is usually only in the immediate interest of neighbouring states that are faced with a mass influx of refugees and other security threats, to find a solution to these crises and they may not have the capacity to respond. It is however arguable that Nigeria was able to intervene in Liberia and Sierra Leone on such a huge scale because of a military regime, which was not accountable to an electorate. As such, the regime was able to spend over 30 billion Naira (more than 3 billion US Dollars) in Liberia, without any political repercussions. Whilst a civilian regime in Nigeria may find it difficult in future to conduct such an expensive operation or, indeed, to get away with the casualty level incurred in Liberia, the desire to remain a sub-regional super-power might tempt such a regime to conduct peace operations.

---

[172] The role of Nigeria in Sierra Leone and the implications of its actions in the West African sub-region are discussed in greater detail by this author in "Mercenaries Fill the Vacuum", *The World Today*, June 1998.

CONCLUSION

The establishment of this ECOMOG operation in the face of serious legal problems, indicates that implementation of such activities are determined more by political will, than international law. Indeed, the failure of the UN to subject the ECOMOG operation to serious scrutiny, in terms of legality of its conduct and of the operation, reinforces the view that post-Cold War Africa holds little interest for the international community. Thus, the ECOMOG operation appeared to be convenient for the UN, and the US in particular, given its reluctance to intervene militarily in Liberia, and the UN's reluctance to take decisive action in Sierra Leone.

The political circumstances, which dictated the level of ECOMOG's effectiveness in Liberia, have reinforced the argument that peace can only be achieved with the co-operation of the conflicting parties. The lack of co-operation from just one party adversely affected ECOMOG's capacity to fulfil its mandate in Liberia. Furthermore, the Liberian experience has shown the need for the peacemaking body to be cohesive. Division within ECOWAS itself over the Liberian conflict created problems for ECOMOG. This is perhaps the greatest disadvantage of multilateral conflict management or peacemaking.

The ECOMOG experience has illustrated the capabilities and limitations of the use of force to create peace. It is useful only to the extent that it is able to terminate violence and hence reduce human suffering and guarantee the flow of humanitarian aid. It may go beyond this to neutralize the forces of conflicting parties, thereby denying them the means to pursue conflict through violence. However, real peace can only be achieved with the agreement and desire of the parties to seek it.

Lastly, ECOMOG employed peacekeeping and peace enforcement intermittently within the operation. This was not the original intention of the organization. The strategy was developed as the conflict proceeded, in response to the situation the ground. This task calls for a combination of skills, most of which are military. However, separating such skills from political issues proved to be a more difficult task. These are examined in the following chapter.

CHAPTER FIVE

The Operational Dimensions of the ECOMOG Mission

INTRODUCTION

The previous chapter analyzed the politics surrounding the ECOMOG operation in Liberia and, to some extent, in Sierra Leone. However, there were issues at the core of the planning and execution of the operation, which undermined the mission and accounted for some of the outcomes discussed in the earlier chapter. This chapter discusses these factors and the extent to which they affected the success of the operation. In particular, this chapter seeks to examine the military issues, which confronted ECOMOG in its attempt at peace creation. These issues are discussed under two major sections. The first section focuses on the planning and the nature of the operation during the different phases. It analyses some of the operational difficulties confronting the force. The second focuses on ECOMOG's organization and the difficulties posed by problems of command and control, differences in training and doctrine and logistics and how all these affected the operation. The chapter concludes with an overall assessment of the effects of these factors on the entire operation.

Much of the data used in this chapter were obtained from field research conducted in the mission area in Liberia and some other West African countries. The data were obtained through interviews, observation and questionnaires. The discussion of the ECOMOG operation during the second enforcement phase and the ensuing peacekeeping period benefits the most from the data obtained from the field research. This is largely because the troops on the ground during the field research were those who had participated in the second enforcement action and the peacekeeping operation, which followed. A tiny proportion of the force had been in Liberia throughout the entire operation. A small number of troops was serving in the operation for the second time, after being rotated. Discussion of the operation during the first two phases thus relies on both secondary sources and interviews with the few who had been around during these periods. Special attention has been devoted to the Nigerian military in some sections largely because Nigerian troops formed about seventy percent of ECOMOG. Thus factors which are peculiar to the Nigerian military invariably had a noticeable impact on ECOMOG. These factors are discussed here only to the extent that they influenced the course of the operation.

I

PLANNING OF THE OPERATION

Operation Liberty (the codename given to the ECOMOG operation in 1990), was plagued with flaws right from the planning stages. Both the political and military leadership failed to prescribe a response that corresponded to the situation in Liberia. Although the operation was authorized by political leaders in order to attain certain objectives (discussed in Chapter Four), adequate attention was not given to the military means through which these objectives would be secured.

It appears that the need to win international and domestic support led the political planners to authorize a 'peacekeeping' mission when events unfolding in Liberia indeed indicated that peace enforcement was unavoidable, if the overall objectives were to be achieved. Indeed, one of the West African politicians who was present during the decision to deploy ECOMOG to Liberia confirmed that the intention of the SMC was to impose peace in Liberia.[1] However, by camouflaging such intentions (to impose peace) under a peacekeeping umbrella, the force, which was mandated to keep peace, was paralysed and thus prevented from using a more effective means to attain its objectives.

Apart from the unusual and perhaps unsuitable mandate, clear directives were not issued to the force, to guide it in certain areas of its operation. For example, what the response of the force should be to warring factions especially those who supported ECOMOG's deployment (the INPFL and Doe's forces) was not clear. This led to some fundamental errors in dealing with Prince Johnson and his men and further hampered the peacekeeping image of the force. On arrival in Monrovia, the force was welcomed at the Freeport by the INPFL leader, while the NPFL attacked it. In addition to this precarious situation, Prince Johnson's relationship with ECOMOG was allowed to transcend the limits of peacekeeping. This tarnished the peacekeeping credibility of the force, as it was unable to maintain an impartial outlook. Indeed, it is believed that such relationships with this warring faction contributed to the death of Samuel Doe, further jeopardizing the mission.

The planners did not envisage a multifaceted operation which would entail humanitarian activities such as the handling of refugees. Thus there were inadequate directives on how to deal with the refugees when the entire mission was in fact justified on this humanitarian ground. This initially created some problems for the force. According to Iweze:

---

[1] Interview with the Ghanaian Foreign Minister Obed Asamoah in *Africa Report*, Nov./Dec. 1990, pp. 17-20.

The refugee situation was reviewed at the planning stages. But surprisingly, in spite of this, the ECOWAS HQ did not treat this issue with the same degree of importance it deserves. When we arrived at the Freeport of Liberia and the advancing troops moved forward, the refugees started pouring into our position. ... Their presence was to pose a problem to us.[2]

In addition, the military leadership failed to make adequate preparations for the mission. The troops were hurriedly dispatched to Liberia without careful analysis of the tasks they were expected to perform, their chances of success and the best way to achieve that success. The situation in Liberia indicated that the troops would use force albeit in self defence, but they were not adequately prepared for such an eventuality. A Nigerian General for example remarked that 'the planners did not heed warnings at the planning stage, to prepare the troops for possible combat in Liberia'.[3] The troops were not mentally prepared for what to expect in Liberia.[4] Nigerian troops for example were told that they were going on a peacekeeping assignment in Liberia, not war, and that they were going to earn some US Dollars.[5] This affected the disposition of the troops to the operation. Indeed, morale was seriously weakened when the troops arrived in Liberia only to face heavy artillery fire from the NPFL.

This lack of preparedness for the use of force is demonstrated by a number of other factors. First, many of the troops turned up without personal weapons such as side arms.[6] Furthermore, a proper analysis of the category of soldiers suitable for the operation was not conducted. For example, some of the contingents initially deployed consisted largely of para-military forces who performed customs and immigration duties in their country.[7] This suggests that it was not impressed upon contributing nations that fighting troops were needed for the operation. A command and control centre was not earmarked during the planning and at start of the operation.[8] The troop strength was not

---

[2] C.Y. Iweze, 'Nigeria in Liberia: The Military Operations of ECOMOG', in M.A. Vogt and A.E. Ekoko (eds.), *Nigeria in International Peacekeeping 1960-1992*, p.236. General Iweze was ECOMOG's first Chief of Staff and he was present at the planning stages of the operation..

[3] Personal interview with General Williams who was involved with the initial planning of the operation in July 1994. *(Hereafter, the Williams interview).* He confirmed that despite the conviction of some of them at that time, that the troops would have to enforce peace in Liberia, plans continued for a peace keeping operation.

[4] Ibid.

[5] Ibid., also, some of the Nigerian soldiers interviewed in Liberia indicated that they were not given a proper picture of events in Liberia. Thus they left Nigeria under the guise that they were coming on a normal peacekeeping operation. The adverse economic situation in Nigeria and the low pay received by other ranks made the prospect of going to Liberia a particularly attractive one.

[6] Iweze, 'Nigeria in Liberia: The Military Operations of ECOMOG', p.220.

[7] Ibid.

[8] The Williams interview.

based on any clearly defined area of operation – whether it would monitor the cease-fire only in Monrovia or move into the hinterland.[9]

Furthermore, there were inadequate intelligence reports on the situation in Liberia. According to General Iweze:

> If the saying that "a general who goes into battle without intelligence report is like a blind-folded boxer in the ring" is true, the inception of ECOMOG proves the point.[10]

He claims that although some effort was made to appraise the situation in Monrovia, an accurate assessment of the situation was not made and thus a clear picture of events was not provided.[11] The force had no access to military maps of Liberia. A tourist map had to be relied on for the initial planning.[12] A military map was later obtained from the US embassy.[13]

Logistic officers were not present at the initial planning and staffing of the logistic areas of the operation. In the bid to achieve a balanced representation by participating nations, officers who had no logistic training or experience were selected to handle the logistical aspect of the operation.[14] This is another indication of how politics prevailed over military issues.

This state of preparedness was discussed in many different quarters and attributed, to a number of factors. The most common argument was that time was not given to evaluate the political and military problems of the mission before the force was deployed to Liberia. Different commentators remarked that:

> Maybe the mandate was quite clear, but things were happening fast. So the political and military leadership may not have had enough time to launch an operation of this magnitude – lives of troops, their sustenance and the mission.[15]

> The force was not adequately prepared. The haste with which the force had to be assembled is responsible for this. There is a lesson to be learnt with respect to preparation : there cannot be a quick fix.[16]

> ECOMOG was set up on August 7. It entered Monrovia on August 24, just a little over two weeks of preparation. I should like to think this was a record in peacekeeping but this inadequate preparation was to be felt at the early part of the operation.[17]

---

[9] Iweze.

[10] Ibid. p. 240.

[11] Ibid. p.221.

[12] Ibid.

[13] Ibid., and this was also confirmed in the Williams interview..

[14] Iweze, p.236.

[15] Personal interview with General Opande, the Commander of the UN Observer Mission in Liberia (UNOMIL) in June 1994 *(Hereafter the Opande interview).* This is his personal opinion of the ECOMOG operation.

[16] Personal interview with Professor Amos Sawyer, the former Interim President of Liberia in June 1994 *(hereafter the Sawyer interview).* Professor Sawyer was an ardent supporter of the concept of ECOMOG. This gives extra weight to his criticism of the operation.

Secondly, it appears that ECOWAS and ECOMOG leaders under-estimated Charles Taylor's rebel forces. Many dismissed the NPFL as an insignificant force, which would capitulate at the sight of a supposedly mighty ECOMOG force. Major General Iweze sums up the views amongst ECOWAS members through the comments of one of the officials that:

> With the calibre of soldiers all the warring factions had, the sight of tanks, armoured cars and aircraft would scare the living daylight out of them and we would just walk over the area.[18]

This notion amongst ECOWAS leaders perhaps accounts for the lacklustre way in which the operation was planned.

However, one argument, which was not generally expressed but nonetheless compelling is that which ties the flaws in the ECOMOG operation to Nigeria's domestic situation. General Williams argued that the involvement of the military in politics has affected the selection process into key offices. Thus military personnel are appointed into important positions on the basis of their support of the leadership instead of competence.[19] This adversely affected the ECOMOG operations in the ways which are discussed below.

The ECOMOG force that was expected to browbeat the NPFL force into submission consisted of the following[20]:

Ground forces consisting of:
One Rifle Company from the Gambian Armed Forces
One Battalion[21] from the Peoples Republic of Guinea Armed Forces
One Battalion from Nigerian Armed Forces with a Platoon of Reconnaissance, A battery of Artillery 105mm Howitzer, a troop of Engineers and a squadron of Signals
One Battalion from Ghana Armed Forces with its support weapons including A Reconnaissance platoon, a platoon of 120mm Mortars

---

[17] Abass Bundu, 'The Role, Experience and Lessons of Security Co-operation Within ECOWAS: The Lessons in Liberia' (Paper presented at a High-Level Workshop on Conflict Resolution, Crisis Prevention and Management & Confidence-Building, Organized by UN Department for Disarmament Affairs, Cameroon, 17-21 June 1991), p.20. Abass Bundu was the Executive Secretary of ECOWAS at the time of ECOMOG's formation and for two years after that.

[18] Iweze, p.220.

[19] The Williams interview.

[20] These details of the composition of the initial ECOMOG force deployed for Operation Liberty are derived from Iweze, p.219-20; and from Olatunde A. Oladimeji, 'Nigerian Navy's Contributions to International Peacekeeping' in Vogt and Ekoko (eds.), p.273. Commodore Oladimeji previously held the position of Director of Plans at the Naval Headquarters, Lagos.

[21] The number of troops in a battalion varies from one country to another. The ECOMOG troop strength analysed later in this book indicates the level of disparity between these figures.

A Battalion from the Republic of Sierra Leone Army with four ar-
moured vehicles (AFV)
Ghana Navy, consisting of:
   Two Fast Attack Crafts (FAC)
   Two merchant ships
Nigeria Navy, consisting of:
   Two FACs
   Two mine countermeasure vessels
   One landing ship tank (LST)
   One oil tanker
   One Tug boat
   Three Merchant ships
Ghana Air Force, consisting of:
   Four NB 339 FGA – this was up until 20 October 1990
Nigerian Air Force was to later join those listed above. It consisted of:
   Four Alpha Jets FGA
   Two Super Puma Helicopters
   Nine c-130s on call.

At first sight, the composition of ECOMOG at this initial stage seems a
contradiction between ECOMOG's stated purpose and its actual intentions at
that time in Liberia. For a force whose mandate and stated objective was to
keep peace in Liberia, its make up suggested an intention beyond that of
traditional peacekeeping. The arms were beyond those of light arms required
for conventional peacekeeping. However on closer examination, the force was
indeed a reflection of the desire of the political and military leadership that a
show of strength would be sufficient to deter continued violence from the
rebels. ECOMOG leaders had since confirmed that the force was not originally intended to be engaged in combat. According to General Olurin :

> ... from the very limited mandate of ECOMOG and from its size, composition and opera-
> tion strategy, the force was not initially expected to become directly involved in combat.
> It was merely expected to monitor a cease-fire which, it was then expected would be
> successfully brokered by the Mediation Committee.[22]

Apart from such declarations, the fact that emphasis was not placed on the
deployment of only fighting troops, and that the air task force was not geared
for combat further lends weight to the argument that this composition was
only intended as a show of strength. The belief that the presence of heavy
weapons in the area of operation is necessary in order to deter rebels intending

---

[22] General A.I. Olurin, 'Peacekeeping in Africa : The Liberian Experience', in *The Peacemaker*, Vol.2. No.1, Sept. 1992 – Sept. 1993, pp. 20. General Olurin was ECOMOG's Field
Commander during the second enforcement period.

to attack is widespread among ECOMOG officers. For example, General Inienger remarked that:

> The rebel is a determined person. He wants to test your will even if you have superior forces. Heavy weapons are necessary to prove superiority, not annihilation. You may not even need to use them.[23]

THE OPERATION

The concept of the operation was largely based on its terms of reference[24] but some strategies evolved in response to the circumstances on the ground. The operation changed in nature and scope during the different phases. The difficulty in operating strictly according to its terms of reference was relieved largely through the alteration of its mandate to suit the changing situations. The rest of this section is devoted to a discussion of the conduct of the operation during the different phases.

The Early Phases:
Unsuccessful Peacekeeping and the Change to Enforcement

The effects of defective planning were apparent from the early stages. The force was unable to embark on peacekeeping as instructed due to the hostile environment in which it landed. In addition, insufficient troop strength led the force to establish its Headquarters at the Freeport where it landed, exposing it to greater risks. However, the choice of this location enabled the same men to defend the FHQ and the Freeport simultaneously.[25] Above all, the force was confronted with the multifaceted nature of its tasks. Apart from its military assignment, a fundamental part of its task was the delivery of humanitarian assistance.

Although ECOMOG's mandate was not changed to one of enforcement until September 1990, the force appeared to have adopted this stance from the very beginning. The fierce attacks from the NPFL meant that the force had to

---

[23] Personal interview with General Inienger, ECOMOG Field Commander, July 1994. **Hereafter the Inienger interview.**

[24] Particularly its mandate and regulations, contained in *Decision A/DEC1/8/90* of the SMC on the Establishment of ECOWAS; & Regulations for the ECOWAS Cease-fire Monitoring Group (ECOMOG) in Liberia – *ECW/HSG/SMC/1/6/Rev.1* of 13th August 1990; Also in *Official Journal of ECOWAS* Vol. 21 1992, pp. 35-40.

[25] Iweze, p. 224

defend itself and at the same time hold some ground. According to General Olurin:

> Having established a firm base at the Freeport by pushing back Taylor's fighters from this area, a three-pronged strategy was adopted, aimed at establishing a foot-hold in more areas of Monrovia municipality. ...The initial objective was to push back the rebels up to the bridge on Montserrado river.[26]

This strategy made peacekeeping more difficult to achieve as ECOMOG's neutrality had been compromised.

The change in ECOMOG's mandate to one of enforcement led to an increase in troop strength[27] but its activities were not significantly different from the initial ones. It continued to repel NPFL attacks with the use of force although emphasis was placed on the minimum force required to achieve this. It was therefore easier to justify ECOMOG as a peacekeeping force. Moreover, the enforcement action allowed the force to create an atmosphere where peacekeeping and other humanitarian activities could be embarked upon.

The peacekeeping activity which followed the enforcement phase (December 1990 to October 1992) in some ways resembled conventional peacekeeping operations. ECOMOG troops were interposed between the warring factions at different points. General Olurin describes the pattern of this operation:

> ... ECOMOG created buffer zones between the NPFL and the other warring factions that existed then, that is the AFL and INPFL. In Mount Barclay and Schieffelin, buffer-zones were created between the NPFL and the AFL while between the NPFL and the INPFL similar buffer was created with the deployment of ECOMOG troops in White Plains.[28]

The functions of the air and naval task forces during this period mainly entailed air supply and transport, and supplying relief through sea routes.[29] These extra tasks however appears to have taken the mission beyond a traditional peacekeeping, to one resembling 'wider' or 'second generation peacekeeping'.[30]

---

[26] Major-General Adetunji Olurin, Text of a Lecture on Military Operations in Liberia, delivered to student-officers at the National War College (NWC), Lagos. 2-5 October 1993, p. 10

[27] One battalion each from Ghana and Nigeria. Iweze, p.234

[28] Olurin, NWC Lecture, p. 11

[29] The Inienger and CNO interviews.

[30] See Chapter One.

The Latter Phases:
Stagnation and Return to Peace Enforcement

The operation assumed interesting dimensions with the NPFL attack on ECOMOG and Monrovia in October 1992. ECOMOG was again forced to embark on enforcement. The magnitude of the NPFL onslaught attracted a heavy-handed approach from ECOMOG as peace enforcement was employed to its limits. Thus ECOMOG's activities from this stage strongly demonstrated the practical problems of employing both peace enforcement and peacekeeping in one operation. It also illustrates the very thin line between peace enforcement and war.

After almost two years of peacekeeping,[31] the surprise attack by a rejuvenated NPFL almost paralysed the force. Its peacekeeping posture meant that ECOMOG possessed neither adequate manpower nor the right type of weapons and equipment, to deal with this attack. The inadequacy in manpower led for example, to the deployment of administrative staff in the Headquarters, and the Engineers as riflemen.[32] But the force struggled to contain the NPFL onslaught. General Olurin remarked that:

> ... Due to our unpreparedness for war in both equipment and strength after one week, our troops were forced to withdraw to the immediate surroundings of Monrovia.[33]

The immediate task facing ECOMOG was to defend itself, after which it would force the rebels back to the negotiating table. Operating in a mission area far from the home base, the force needed immediately to adapt to new conditions in order to achieve these tasks.

ECOMOG'S INITIAL STRATEGY

The initial strategy adopted by ECOMOG in meeting this threat resulted largely from both its perception of the aims of the NPFL and the available resources on the ground. The fierce attacks launched by the NPFL on ECOMOG headquarters, the air and sea ports left ECOMOG officers in no doubt that Taylor's intention was to defeat the force in Liberia and prevent it from reinforcing through the ports. This would thus allow the NPFL to capture the Executive Mansion unchallenged.[34] General Olurin for example asserts that:

---

[31] The events following the first cease-fire agreement of November 1990 have already been discussed in the previous chapter.
[32] Major B. Musah, 'An Operational Overview of Ghanbatt 7', in *EXODUS II*, Vol.7, p.8.
[33] *The Peacemaker* Vol.2, No.1 p.16.
[34] This was the prevalent view within ECOMOG and many other quarters in Monrovia.

> Charles Taylor's main plan was to first seize the ECOMOG Headquarters and simultane-
> ously seize the Freeport and the Airport to prevent any re-supply and reinforcement of
> ECOMOG troops. ... He knew the capability of ECOMOG in its peacekeeping posture
> and has calculated that he could overwhelm the troops in 2-3 days.[35]

The ECOMOG Chief Naval Officer was equally convinced that the sea port
came under fierce attack by the NPFL because 'Taylor wanted to prevent
troops reinforcement via the sea.'[36] Charles Taylor's radio broadcast in which
he vowed to be in Monrovia by seventeen hours on the day of the attack and
make a presidential broadcast by nineteen hours makes it difficult to challenge
the claim of the ECOMOG chiefs.

ECOMOG chose initially to maintain a defensive posture in containing the
NPFL attack, abandoning a plan to go on the offensive. General Olurin
confirmed that:

> ECOMOG's plan to go on the offensive at the initial stages of the war was shelved.
> ECOMOG as at then maintained a static posture. This was in conformity with our man-
> date to defend ourselves decisively if attacked.[37]

It however seems that the force had little option as inadequate manpower
would have prevented it from going on the offensive.

This defensive stance did not continue for long. The force was increased
from seven thousand during peacekeeping times, to about fourteen thousand.[38]
Nigeria was the only country which provided additional troops. These
included the crack 72 Airborne battalion, The 33 Artillery Brigade, two
Infantry Brigades, and one reconnaissance battalion.[39]

Having successfully prevented the capture of its Headquarters and the
immediate environs by the NPFL, ECOMOG altered its strategy and went on
the counter-offensive. Still tying the decision to ECOMOG's mandate, the
Field Commander, General Olurin argued that:

> To be in a better position to implement the mandate of ECOWAS, ECOMOG moved out
> to check the excesses of NPFL. Also ECOMOG could not have defended itself by sitting
> in one position containing attacks from NPFL. That was proving too costly in men and
> material. ECOMOG fanned out by 22 December 1992 to check and discourage NPFL the
> only faction attacking ECOMOG...[40]

---

[35] *The Peacemaker*, Vol.2, No.1, p.16.

[36] Personal Interview with the Chief Naval Officer (CNO) in July 1994. **Hereafter the CNO
interview.**

[37] Olurin, in *The Peacemaker*, p.17; and Lecture at National War College.

[38] *BBC Focus on Africa*, 04 November 1992. The FC in this phase, General Olurin, indicated
that ECOMOG's strength 'had risen to over 11,000 all ranks', Lecture at National War College,
p.6 For details of ECOMOG troop strength as at June 1994, see Table 6.1 in Chapter Six.

[39] Ibid.

[40] *The Peacemaker*, p.19.

This decision to go on the counter-offensive was a necessity if the force was to minimise casualties amongst its men as well as innocent civilians. The NPFL was able to shell Monrovia at will.[41] The NPFL is believed to have inflicted heavy casualties on ECOMOG at the beginning of Operation Octopus. The actual figures of the casualties sustained by ECOMOG has been a closely guarded secret within the force. General Olurin however (in his statements above and below) admits that ECOMOG suffered some casualties:

> The constant rebel attacks led to some casualties on our part. The design of the enemy was to make sure ECOMOG force continued to lose men by attrition... ...To avert losing men by attrition and to weaken the rebels' will to fight we planned a major move forward to make our positions in the field less precarious.[42]

The Role of the Naval Task Force

Apart from ground forces, the Navy and the Air force were also actively involved in the efforts to control the NPFL onslaught. The navy's role was a marked contrast to its previous peacekeeping role. Apart from effecting an economic blockade, the navy was tasked to carry out the bombardment of specific targets. Economic targets were selected for bombardment in order to deny Taylor the means of pursuing the conflict. ECOMOG's Chief Naval Officer confirmed that:

> Taylor wanted to prevent troops reinforcement via the sea. Therefore the navy was crucial to the operation during Octopus. There were target bombardments in Buchanan and Harper. The port of Buchanan, a major port, supported the logging business which was NPFL's life line.[43]

The Naval Gun Fire (NGF) unleashed on these strategic targets were intended to weaken the defences of the NPFL rebels as well as their will to fight. The enforcement of the economic embargo by the Navy were also expected to drastically reduce the supplies of the NPFL.

The Role of the Air Task Force

The air force during this period was to perform armed reconnaissance and provide close air support to ground troops.[44] ECOMOG's air offensive was to focus on areas identified as the NPFL's centres of gravity. These included its

---

[41] Ibid.
[42] Olurin, Lecture at the National War College, p. 18 & 19.
[43] The CNO interview.
[44] The CAO interview.

command structure, its forces on the battlefield, and its transportation systems. The offensive was to be conducted in three phases. The first which was deemed the shortest was to gain 'command of the air'. Air superiority was not difficult to achieve since the rebels did not possess any air force. They only had a few anti-aircraft artillery. This was achieved by attacking known radar locations, anti-aircraft gun positions as well as civil/military airfields.

The second phase concentrated on the attack of ground forces whilst the last was the selection of strategic targets for bombardment. This was mainly the NPFL's entire logistic infrastructure – ammunition dumps, petroleum products, tank farms, communication centres. The ECOMOG Air Task Force also had the job of conducting regular patrols of the sea lanes and air space. In addition to this, it was responsible for providing logistic support to the ground forces. Commenting on the importance of the air force to the ECOMOG operations, the ECOMOG Chief Air Officer said:

> The air force has been crucial here. The terrain is difficult. People are cut off here due to bad bridges, etceteras. Movement of troops are still done largely by roads but the air force is used to achieve flexibility and mobility.[45]

The Cotonou Accord brought the peace enforcement phase to an end and ushered in another peacekeeping phase, where ECOMOG's activities were similar to those of the earlier peacekeeping period. The Ground Task Force resumed the monitoring of the cease-fire. The air task force mainly carried out air supply and transport assignments. Helicopters were largely used for these tasks.[46] Although they still carried out continuous patrols to enforce a blockade, they provided assistance to humanitarian organizations by giving security cover, and transporting relief supplies to areas which could not be assessed by land.[47] The South east of Liberia for example is said to have been heavily forested and accessible only by sea.[48]

OPERATIONAL DIFFICULTIES

Despite ECOMOG's eventual success at repelling the NPFL attack, certain factors served to undermine the ECOMOG operation. These were a combination of rebel activity and problems relating to the force's own execution of the operation. The advance of the 7 ECOMOG Brigade to Buchanan for example met with serious obstacles. The NPFL rebels caused maximum delay in the

---

[45] Personal interview with the ECOMOG Chief of Air Staff in July 1994, ***Hereafter referred to as the CAO interview.***
[46] The Inienger and CAO interviews.
[47] The CNO interview..
[48] The Inienger interview.

advance by blowing up some bridges,[49] blocking others and felling trees across the road. The advance which began on 20 March 1993, was expected to last only three days, covering about eighty-five kilometres.[50] However, Buchanan was only captured fifteen days later due to obstructions created by the NPFL.

Land mines as well as ambushes by the NPFL created problems for the force and hampered the operation at different times. For example, two soldiers in Nibatt 13 confirmed that on 11 January 1993, the Guinean tank spear heading the advance fell into enemy minefield and was blown up, killing one Nigerian officer and two Guinean soldiers.[51] In the same month, two Nigerian soldiers in the same battalion were killed in an ambush.[52] During the previous month, the Commanding Officer of Nibatt 13 and his team fell into an ambush while adjusting defences. The casualties sustained included one soldier killed in action and the Commanding Officer and a company commander wounded in action.[53]

In addition to these problems, cases of friendly fire created set-backs for ECOMOG.[54] In November 1992, its air task force dropped two bombs on the ground troops while in combat with the NPFL but there were no fatalities. In January 1993, three soldiers were wounded in friendly mortar fire while in defences at Upper Johnsonsville. The casualties sustained in this manner and during combat with the NPFL had psychological effects on the troops.

The constraints on the Air and Naval Task Forces also created some problems for the operation. The greatest difficulty confronting the navy during this period was the poor state of the guns on the Nigerian naval ships. Obsolete ammunition was used which had little effect on the rebels.[55] The close air support and armed reconnaissance missions were crucial to the entire operation throughout this period. However, the air force did not possess all weather and night bombing capability and this created problems for the air operations. According to General Olurin,

> The ingenuity of the pilots to fly at night homing on the lights of vehicular movements lasted for a short time. Subsequently, the enemy resorted to switching off their lights at the sound of the aircraft. At the later stage of the operation, some of the aircraft had to

---

[49] The advance to Buchanan for example was halted on 27 March with the NPFL destruction of Mechlin Bridge. It took another three days for ECOMOG to successfully construct a bridge to enable it continue. Three different sources confirmed this particular event – A Lieutenant and two Lance Corporals who were part of the advance to Buchanan.

[50] Major B. Musa, in *EXODUS II* p. 8.

[51] Personal interview with the soldiers and written record of one of the soldiers.

[52] Ibid.

[53] Ibid.

[54] Brigadier-General M.A. Balogun, Lecture at National War College (NWC), Lagos.

[55] Olurin, NWC Lecture, p.24; and Balogun, NWC Lecture.

be equipped with ground positioning system to improve on their navigational systems and potency.[56]

Interception of coded messages by the rebels also undermined the air operations.[57] The Air Task Force thus resorted to deception tactics which were effective in preventing the NPFL's interception of information. This was done by transmitting their communication in local dialects, instead of English. Another aspect of these deception tactics was deliberate misinformation over the radio, to confuse the NPFL. Such deception tactics played a crucial role in the capture of St. John's Bridge.[58] The air operations were further limited by the fact that only visual air reconnaissance was performed throughout. Aircraft were not fitted with 'sensors like aerial photographic cameras', infrared line scan, etc.[59] Thus information obtained was limited to what the human eye was able to observe. In the words of the FC, '... the achievements of the NAF [Nigerian Air Force] were tremendous because we operated against an enemy without air power'.[60]

ECOMOG's tasks were made more difficult by a number of other factors. One was the haphazard deployment within the Nigerian contingent which by now constituted at least 70% of the entire ECOMOG force. Troops were taken from different units within Nigeria, many of whom had not been soldiering together, and deployed as part of the same unit in Liberia. The effect of this was that Commanding Officers found it more difficult to control the units at the crucial stage of the operation. A Nigerian Commanding Officer recalled his experience at the early stages:

> We were sent here without any time to prepare. I did not know many of the boys in my unit. There are things I would normally tell the boys in my unit and they would immediately understand. It was difficult to get such understanding from the new ones. Some of them did not even know what I meant by arrow formation.[61]

This problem was compounded by one which is closely related to the problem of logistics discussed below. The fact that many of the troops were deployed from different units meant that many of the men did not know themselves. At the same time, many of the Nigerian soldiers were not supplied with dogtags. The effects of this were disastrous. Commanding Officer of Nibatt 14 gave a vivid picture of the impact of this on the operation:

---

[56] Olurin, Lecture at NWC, p. 23.
[57] Ibid.
[58] Personal interview with Chief of General Staff, Nigerian Contingent.
[59] Olurin, NWC Lecture, p. 23.
[60] Ibid.
[61] Personal interview with the Commanding Officer of Nibatt 14 during Octopus, July 1994.

Many soldiers did not know themselves in the unit. As a result, when a soldier dropped in the heat of the battle, nobody knew who he was. Many had no dog tags. Their identities were only known later, by the number of people missing.[62]

This operation also revealed in greater depth the problems posed by many different armies fighting together as part of the same force. The differences were usually less obvious under the traditional peacekeeping situation because combat operations were not conducted. Differences in soldiering qualities of troops in the various contingents began to show and this had some effect on the operation. Soldiers in each contingent had some interesting views about troops from other countries. The most prominent views were expressed by the soldiers from the Nigerian contingent who felt that the performance of the Sierra Leoneans at times undermined the entire operation. Amongst this group, the Sierra Leoneans are dismissed as 'cowards', 'mere women'. Two occurrences where the Sierra Leoneans fled rebel attacks are often cited in support of this view by those soldiers who witnessed the NPFL's operation Octopus.

CO-OPERATION WITH OTHER ORGANIZATIONS

One area of its operation which was not envisaged by ECOMOG planners was that of co-ordinating its activities with civilian humanitarian organizations and United Nations observers. The difficulties of co-operating with humanitarian organizations became prominent during peace enforcement. Efforts to co-ordinate the delivery of relief items with ECOMOG's movement were not successful. ECOMOG had to give advance notice of its operations to prevent relief agencies from going to those areas, and it was thought that this would undermine its operations.[63] ECOMOG's destruction of some civilian structures including a relief convoy during peace enforcement prompted criticisms from some relief agencies who argued that the former's bombing raids jeopardized aid operations.[64] A real problem however was the tendency for elements within the different organizations to favour one of the warring factions.[65]

---

[62] Ibid.

[63] Personal interview with the Senior Protection Officer, UN High Commission for Refugees, Monrovia, July 1994.

[64] Press release by Medecins Sans Frontieres (MSF), 04 March 1993. Source: *BBC Focus on Africa*.

[65] The UNHCR Senior Protection Officer interview.

Effects of UNOMIL's Deployment

The deployment of the UN Military Observer Mission in Liberia (UNOMIL) had conflicting effects on ECOMOG and on the operation. In particular, it revealed the practical problems of co-operation between the UN and a regional organization in resolving regional conflicts.[66] The latter's presence in Liberia created some confusion in the minds of many ECOMOG soldiers. They were of the opinion that UNOMIL was in Liberia to monitor ECOMOG's activities as well as those of the warring factions. Others believed that UNOMIL was despatched to Liberia after ECOMOG had completed the 'dirty job' and that the former would therefore collect all the glory that was rightfully ECOMOG's. Indeed, this last view is shared by other ranks as well as officers in ECOMOG. These beliefs, coupled with the obvious comfort in which the UNOMIL observers lived, created some resentment in ECOMOG circles.

Whilst the officers were more diplomatic in expressing this opinion and exhibited fairly cordial relations with UNOMIL officials, other ranks expressed such resentment more openly. According to General Inienger,

> At the soldier level, it is difficult to understand why UNOMIL is here. At the officer level, we understand they are here and we try to educate the soldiers.[67]

On the general response to UNOMIL's presence, the Camp Commandant said:

> Those ordinary people who enjoyed ECOMOG facilities since 1990 appreciate ECOMOG. They do not feel the practical effects of UNOMIL. Many feel that UNOMIL has yet to prove their reason for being here.[68]

Remarking on the feeling within ECOMOG toward UNOMIL, he said:

> In appeasing NPFL, UNOMIL was despatched under the Cotonou Accord. In short it is (UNOMIL) like an inconvenience. Monitoring ECOMOG symbolises mistrust.[69]

ECOMOG officers were however more critical of their accommodation, particularly office accommodation at the HQ. The arrival of UNOMIL on the scene made ECOMOG's office accommodation appear substandard. Remarking on this, the CLO said:

> Accommodation is very poor. Particularly the offices. The offices are ordinary in comparison to UNOMIL.[70]

---

[66] A recent study by John Mackinlay and Abiodun Alao examined the problems of cooperation between UNOMIL and ECOMOG: ECOMOG and UNOMIL Response to a Complex Emergency, *Occasional Papers Series* No. 1 (Tokyo: UN University, 1995).

[67] The Inienger interview.

[68] The Camp Commandant/ Gamcon Commander interview.

[69] Ibid.

[70] The CLO interview.

To add to this feeling of resentment toward UNOMIL within ECOMOG, it appears that the latter's presence only served to create fierce competition for ECOMOG troops amongst the female population in Monrovia. This factor is given greater attention in the next chapter.

However, although there were constantly areas of friction between ECOMOG and UNOMIL, both organizations tried to work together. According to General Opande the UNOMIL Commander:

> There is no conflict of interest between ECOMOG and UNOMIL. We have a good working relationship. May be minor problems may occur on the way. But so far, we have succeeded in settling them.[71]

Coupled with their boosted morale by successes during peace enforcement, UNOMIL's presence made ECOMOG troops even more determined to achieve success in Liberia. The single factor which generated fierce determination among ECOMOG soldiers is the desire to see Africans succeed at resolving their own conflict. This is one of the issues discussed in the next chapter.

ALTERNATING BETWEEN PEACE ENFORCEMENT AND PEACEKEEPING

This operation demonstrated the practical problems involved in ending an enforcement action and switching to a peacekeeping one and vice versa. ECOMOG's composition on the ground at the start of operation Octopus demonstrated the problems of maintaining a peacekeeping stance in an area of operation where its presence is opposed by at least one of the parties. Although the para-military forces that were deployed during the first phase had all been replaced by regular fighting forces, the force was very much a peacekeeping one. Eyewitness accounts suggest that the force was almost overrun largely due to the calibre of men on the ground. The Nigerian troops in particular were seen to contain many middle aged soldiers who were not very mobile.[72] The peacekeeping operation which preceded this period led to the choice of such men as it was perhaps assumed that they would not have to be engaged in combat.

The events following the Cotonou agreement highlighted some of the problems of switching between both strategies. It is immensely difficult for troops who had sustained serious casualties at the hands of factions they regarded as enemies to immediately alter their posture to a friendly, neutral

---

[71] The Opande interview.

[72] Personal interview with a senior Nigerian diplomat at the Embassy of Nigeria in Monrovia. The lack of political presence on the ground from ECOWAS led Nigerian ECOMOG officers in particular to work closely with embassy officials.

one. The Gambian Contingent Commander who was a part of Operation Liberty during both enforcement periods commented on the problems of changing to a peacekeeping stance:

> The transition from peace enforcement to peacekeeping is not always smooth. We need to look into this. The apprehension was on all sides. You suspect everyone, read in-between the lines, you overreact. We need to look into these areas.[73]

Many soldiers who participated in the second enforcement operation also admitted that this was a real problem. They expressed the underlining suspicion with which the rebels were regarded.[74]

In addition, several ECOMOG officers commented on the problems of switching between peace enforcement and peacekeeping. Here are some of their remarks:

> On a peacekeeping mission, a soldier has his mind and whole self built for negotiation and peace brokering and once the warring parties see him that way, this is good. But the automatic switch over to enforcement which requires force might have some initial negative effects on the soldier. This can be overcome quite easily and quickly though once the troops are threatened.[75]

> The combatants you have been fighting against will not trust you. It is difficult to treat well, or be friendly with a person you have seen killing your fellow soldiers or officers.[76]

> The problem lies mainly in behaviour. Soldiers are tempted to continue with the same behaviour that they could get away with during peace enforcement operations.[77]

> Mental and operational posture of troops would be unbalanced. There is a need for additional heavy support weapons. Mutual trust which previously existed between peacekeeping and warring factions would be shattered.[78]

> The two operations cannot be carried out the same way because one is pacific and the other is forceful.[79]

> After having applied peace enforcement on a stubborn faction and achieved cease-fire, the faction would no longer trust your peacekeeping strategies.[80]

> There is the problem of logistics – you need more resources in peace enforcement. There is the issue of goodwill- in peace enforcement, some parts of the populace may not support you. The force will have to contend with this. [81]

---

[73] Personal interview with the Gambian Contingent Commander.
[74] Personal discussion with a group of soldiers from Nibatt 13, 14 and Ghanbatt 8.
[75] Sierra Leonean Major (Respondent 46).
[76] Tanzanian Contingent Commander (Respondent 40).
[77] Ghanaian Colonel (Respondent 2).
[78] Ghanaian Major (Respondent 3).
[79] Guinean Contingent Commander (Respondent 60).
[80] Nigerian Lt. Commander, Naval Task Force (Respondent 8).
[81] Nigerian Major (Respondent 10).

From peace enforcement to peacekeeping, enmity is created and the seed of bitterness is sowed in the hearts of the warring factions and the peacekeepers. The psychology of the rebels becomes apprehensive and ruthless.[82]

There is the problem of orientation from an aggressive posture to a friendly posture. The situation does not build trust. Where there is no trust, reconciliation is often difficult.[83]

Switching from peacekeeping to enforcement requires logistics for the execution of peace enforcement. The zeal of troops to fight may be low when they are not prepared mentally to fight and enforce peace.[84]

A human is not a machine to switch automatically from peace enforcement to peacekeeping. Element of aggression lingers on for sometime. Reflex action too continues to make soldiers overreact. Human defensive nature keeps soldiers on the path of war even in peacekeeping role.[85]

Language barriers however appeared to account for some of the problems of alternating between both strategies. Recalling some of the events in the mission area after the cease-fire, a Nibatt 14 Private remarked:

Most of the soldiers were disciplined but the Guinean problem was because they don't speak English. There was a case where some rebels approached some Guinean soldiers, indicating that they wanted to surrender. Since the Guineans did not understand them and clearly did not want to take any chances, they opened fire on the rebels. The rebels were always more afraid of the Guinean soldiers.[86]

ECOMOG's peace enforcement action as a result of NPFL's operation Octopus had profound effects on the approach of some of its commanders to the peace process in Liberia. The force's near defeat at the hands of the NPFL coupled with Taylor's inconsistencies heightened ECOMOG's mistrust of the former. It reflected in the approach of the officers to peacekeeping during the last phase. Their approach was that of caution. Their treatment of the other warring factions appeared more relaxed than that given to the NPFL. One area in which this was more pronounced was in the movement of weapons. This prompted accusations of partiality from the NPFL, claiming that ECOMOG was arming the LPC.

Although there was no glaring evidence that ECOMOG was arming any of the warring factions, there was some indication that it relaxed its approach to other factions apart from the NPFL from time to time. Some ECOMOG officials did not deny that ECOMOG occasionally looked the other way when the LPC passed its check points. As a Nigerian Headquarters official remarked:

---

[82] Nigerian Lieutenant (Respondent 19).
[83] Nigerian Major (Respondent 28).
[84] Nigerian Lieutenant (Respondent 68).
[85] Nigerian Lt. Colonel, Commanding Officer, 221 Light Tank Battalion (Respondent 67).
[86] Personal interview with Nibatt 14 Private.

We feel that as long as there is a buffer between us and the NPFL, it will be difficult for them to attack us. Since the LPC started attacking NPFL positions, they have been kept busy and prevented from attacking ECOMOG.[87]

This approach was not the official standpoint of ECOMOG but rather, the attitude of some Nigerian ECOMOG officers. This also highlights the depth of the Nigerians influence in the force. The Nigerians appear to have been the most hurt by the NPFL's challenge not just because of Taylor's constant opposition of the Nigerian participation but also due to the national pride at stake. Many Nigerians believe in the saying that the country is 'the giant of Africa' notwithstanding its acute political and economic problems. If Charles Taylor had successfully removed ECOMOG from Liberia, Nigeria would have been humiliated. General Olurin confirmed this by his statement that:

... Whilst Nigeria increased her troops contribution after the launching of Charles Taylor's "Operation Octopus" no other troops contributing country increased her strength. The reason being the inability of these nations to mobilize additional troops, and Nigeria in the majority had a lot to lose in case of defeat by the NPFL.[88]

Thus the Nigerians were tougher in their approach toward the NPFL. This approach led some Nigerians to interpret the Ghanaian soft approach in meetings as support for NPFL.[89]

A number of ideas aimed at addressing the problems emanating from changing to peacekeeping from an enforcement posture have been proposed. The most plausible appears to be one which suggests an immediate rotation of troops by each contributing country after an enforcement action. A fresh set of troops would perhaps maintain a peacekeeping image more readily. There are however problems surrounding swift rotation of troops in ECOMOG. These are discussed below. A second idea which appears workable at first sight is that the troop contributing nations in an enforcement action should be changed altogether during a peacekeeping period. This opinion was influenced by the NPFL's stiff opposition to the Nigerian contingent in ECOMOG. Thus it is thought that if Nigerians participated in enforcement and were withdrawn while countries like Togo, Guinea Bissau etc. came to keep the peace, the problems may be greatly reduced. Apart from the fact that financial constraints would prevent this system from working, this view has been strongly opposed especially in Nigerian quarters. They argue that 'those who did not participate in winning the peace are likely to be reckless with it.'[90]

This section has argued that faulty planning created problems for the operation. It has analyzed some of the difficulties faced by ECOMOG in

---

[87] Personal interview with a Nigerian Colonel at Nigcon Headquarters.
[88] Olurin, NWC Lecture, p. 6.
[89] Ibid.
[90] The Nigerian Diplomat interview.

adapting to the different changes in the area of operation. In particular, it discussed the problems involved in co-operating with other military and civilian organizations, and the problems of alternating between peacekeeping and peace enforcement. It now remains to be seen, the extent to which issues of command, control, logistics, training and doctrine affected the operation at different stages.

II

COMMAND, CONTROL AND COMMUNICATION

ECOMOG was forced to confront different issues relating to command and control during the different stages of the operation. Many of the command problems faced were characteristic of similar multinational forces while others resulted from the fact that these national forces were working together for the first time. These problems were dealt with as they went along.

A number of factors undermined command and control during the initial phase. Amongst these were political considerations. The need to have an international command in order to portray the mission as a truly multinational effort meant that every participating country had to be represented in the chain of command regardless of their ability to meet the requirements of that position. Amongst Nigerians especially, there was the need to allay the fears of some of the factions in Liberia, as well as other West African countries that Nigeria was out to dominate the sub-region and satisfy its self interest in Liberia.[91] Thus political considerations prevailed over competence. This view however changed over time in Nigerian circles, especially after the death of Samuel Doe and the controversy surrounding the conduct of the Force Commander. Nigeria thus assumed command of ECOMOG.

The original arrangement was that the force would be commanded by a Ghanaian of the rank of Lt. General, while the Deputy Force Commander would be a Brigadier from Guinea. The Chief of Staff would be a Nigerian Brigadier and Chief Logistics Officer, a Nigerian Colonel. The Chief of Personnel was to be a Gambian, the Chief of Operations a Sierra Leonean, the Chief of Communications, a Nigerian and a Gambian Camp Commandant. However, some of these countries did not have officers of the ranks or experience required to fill these positions. For example, the only Brigadier in the armed forces of the People's Republic of Guinea was the Head of State and the next in rank was a Lt. Colonel. Asking Nigeria to provide a Chief of Staff of the rank of Brigadier would create command problems. Guinea eventually provided a Lt. Colonel who was promoted to the rank of a Maj.-

---

[91] This factor was discussed in the previous chapter.

General after having arrived on the ECOMOG scene. This was seen to have undermined discipline and control. The Gambia's situation was somewhat similar. The most senior Gambian officer in ECOMOG, was a Captain.

The lack of qualified staff led to rearrangements in this structure. An arrangement was reached between some contributing states to swap appointments; for example, the position of Chief of Operations given to Sierra Leone was swapped with Ghana. At the time of conducting the field research, the post of Deputy Military Information Officer which was originally allocated to Ghana, was occupied by a Sierra Leonean. The Chief of Personnel who was supposed to be a Gambian was replaced by a Nigerian Lt. Colonel. A Nigerian Major-General replaced the Ghanaian Field Commander after the death of Samuel Doe while a second Deputy Field Commander (DFC) position was created – DFC 1 was a Ghanaian while DFC 2 was a Guinean. This is however not reflected in the organizational chart held by ECOMOG (see Figure 5.1).

Active political involvement and direction from ECOWAS was lacking especially in the latter half of the operation. The organizational structure designed by ECOMOG (Figure 5.1) reflects this point. Theoretically, the Executive Secretary of ECOWAS under the Authority of the Heads of State and Government should control ECOMOG's activities. In practice however, such control from ECOWAS was absent on many occasions.[92] It should also be noted that the positions of Political and Legal Advisers (PA and LA) had been unoccupied since the start of the mission as a result of shortage of funds.[93] Thus ECOMOG had no civilian officials.[94] The Special Representative was apparently withdrawn from the early phase and reintroduced in 1995.

A number of incidents demonstrated the difficulty in controlling multinational forces of this nature. There was the tendency for contingents to put their national interests above those of the force. For example, instructions given for a loading procedure which would enable swift advance on landing was ignored by the troops who gave preference to the loading of rations for their different contingents. As Iweze remarked,

> we were lucky that the opposing forces did not meet us with higher degree of opposition, if not we would have been sitting ducks.[95]

The unwillingness of some ECOMOG officers initially to receive orders from senior officers from countries other than their own made command of

---

[92] See Chapter Six.

[93] This was confirmed by ECOMOG's Chief Operations Officer (COO), a Ghanaian Colonel, during my interview with him in June 1994. This interview is *hereafter referred to as the COO. interview.*

[94] Ibid.

[95] Iweze, p.222.

Figure 5.1 ECOMOG Organization**

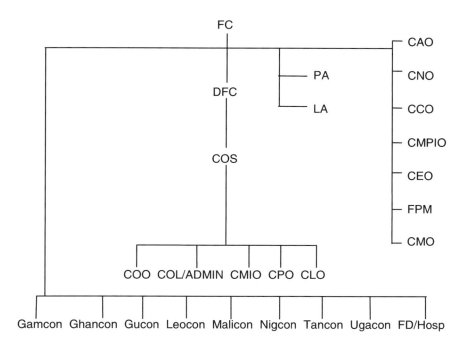

FC	– Field Commander
DFC	– Deputy Field Commander
COS	– Chief of staff
COO	– Chief Operations Officer
COL/ADMIN	– Chief of Logistics/Admin.
CMIO	– Chief Military Information Officer
CPO	– Chief Personnel Officer
CAO	– Chief Air Officer
CNO	– Chief Naval Officer
CCO	– Chief Communication Officer
CMPIO	– Chief Military Press Information Officer
CEO	– Chief Engineer Officer
FPM	– Force Provost Marshall
CMO	– Chief Medical Officer
LA	– Legal Adviser
PA	– Political Assistant
CLO	– Chief Liaison Officer

** This organizational chart was provided by the ECOMOG Headquarters in Monrovia during the field research.

this multinational force more problematic. Iweze cites an instance where a Ghanaian Battalion Commander expressed reservations about handing over the parade to the ECOMOG Chief of Staff, arguing that 'it was impossible for him a Ghanaian to hand over to a Nigerian'.[96] He states that 'this type of reaction to orders was a common feature at the initial stage of the operation'.[97] However, this type of command problem is common to multinational forces as has been demonstrated by experiences in Somalia. As discussed in Chapter Two, some countries are totally opposed to their officers being placed under the command of another country's officer(s).

The importance of the Force Commander to the success or outcome of a mission was made all too clear by this operation right from the start. The commander's leadership style, and the lack of unity within the ECOMOG high command, appeared to have created problems which at times, brought the operation to the brink of collapse. Prince Johnson and his men were allowed frequent visits to ECOMOG headquarters without being disarmed. The decision by the Chief of Staff of ECOMOG to disarm the NPFL before entering the FHQ was reversed by the FC who was careful not to provoke the rebel leader.[98] This decision to allow the INPFL leader to continue frequent visits to FHQ without being disarmed, was to create complications for the force. Following an unannounced visit by Samuel Doe to the FHQ, Prince Johnson and his armed men also arriving unannounced, captured Samuel Doe whom they (INPFL) later executed. This event damaged ECOMOG's credibility.

The INPFL leader was able to utilize the absence of cohesion in the ECOMOG high command to his advantage. For example his demand for a 105mm Howitzer to blow up the executive mansion following Doe's death was agreed to by the FC but refused by the Chief of Staff. This resulted in the INPFL seizure of a platoon of Nigerian soldiers who were released only after negotiations were made to release some weapons to him.

Different interpretations have been given of the FC's approach and the absence of unity in command during this phase. The less objective view simply dismisses him as a soft man, hardly a soldier. Others argue that this was due to the fact that the FC selected was in the 'evening of his career' and thus should not have been made to command an operation where fighting was imminent.[99] However, apart from these issues of personal style and lack of active military service, a more plausible reason for these problems in command was the differences in background, both in training and doctrine, of the various national forces. This made it difficult to achieve cohesion and

---

[96] Ibid. p.223.
[97] Ibid. pp.223-4.
[98] Ibid. p.227.
[99] Ibid. p.240.

uniformity in command. Such differences also account for the distinct views within the Nigerian camp.

Some degree of flexibility had been introduced in the command by the time NPFL launched Octopus. Some officers operated under the command of officers from other countries. General Olurin confirmed that:

> Operation instructions issued were executed by unit commanders, some of whom were placed under the command of other contingents without recourse to the home governments for clarification.[100]

This demonstrates the need to be able to adapt to changing circumstances in an operation of this nature.

The command problems faced by ECOMOG during Octopus mainly concerned the forces in the field. Fresh from home territory without adequate preparation for what they were to expect in Liberia, many of the troops were reluctant to obey orders to advance and capture some areas. The Commanding Officer Nibatt 14 during Octopus observed that:

> ... Not battle tested, some of the soldiers refused to move forward, crying. Some went on AWOL due to fear.[101]

Also recalling the troops' reaction to casualties suffered and the events following the orders to advance into the Iron Factory, a Nigerian Corporal stated:

> It took serious threats and persuasions to get the unit to dig in for the night because of the experiences of previous units that returned into the area and were disastrously beaten back.[102]

The conduct of some ECOMOG troops during the peacekeeping period created immense difficulties for the operation. This issue was not apparent during the enforcement period. Elements within the original ECOMOG had resorted to looting. It is generally believed that cases of looting occurred within every contingent but it was rampant amongst Nigerians and to a lesser extent, the Guineans. Many within ECOMOG agree that looting was not so common with the Ghanaians who were regarded as the most disciplined (after Senegal). However, they seemed to be well known for buying looted goods. The size of the Nigerian contingent made the looting problem within its camp even more prominent. It appeared to be common knowledge to Liberians both inside and outside the country that ECOMOG troops participated in the looting of their properties. Whilst the Liberians inside seemed to condone this

---

[100] Olurin, in *The Peacemaker*, p.2.

[101] Personal interview with CO Nibatt 14.

[102] Personal interview with a Nigerian Corporal who gave his account of his unit advance into the hinterland which eventually led to the capture of Buchanan.

behaviour because of the protection rendered to them by ECOMOG,[103] the Liberian refugees outside the country appeared particularly bitter.[104]

This looting problem though carried out by only a small fraction of the force, tarnished the image of ECOMOG in the eyes of observers in Liberia, especially the Americans. In addition, it provided justification for Taylor's claims of incompetence on the part of ECOMOG. For the Nigerian contingent, the cases of looting especially amongst other ranks has been linked to the long delay in paying the soldiers. It has been suggested that more frequent payment of allowances would reduce the number of soldiers who loot little items:

> The small allowance paid to the troops is irregular and this adds to the problem. For example, some people from bad homes would be tempted to steal or loot from shops.[105]

The greater problem however lies with the few officers who have looted not out of desperation for small cash, but for personal enrichment.

The failure of the ECOMOG high command to curb this problem has served to compound it. For example, it was thought that the FC was reluctant to discipline officers who had given decades of service to their country.[106] The other difficulty of control stemmed from the fact that the powers of the high command to discipline troops from other countries was greatly limited. General Olurin discussed this problem:

> By the provisions of the ECOMOG Standard Operating Procedures, disciplinary powers of command are vested in contingent commanders....One had to resort to quasi-diplomatic means in effectively exercising command. It should be noted that obedience of command in military parlance stems from fear of sanctions. The only effective sanction that can be employed is repatriation of an erring subordinate or junior commander.[107]

The force encountered immense communication problems particularly at the initial stages, which affected command and control, hence operational effectiveness. The lack of standardization also created problems in this area. Each contingent brought its own different communication equipment which was incompatible with the rest, thereby making communication with the troop contributing countries difficult.[108] Attempts by Nigeria to remedy this problem were not effective. According to Major-General Iweze:

---

[103] Liberians in the capital, Monrovia are generally grateful for the protection rendered by ECOMOG that any wrong doings on the part of the troops are often swept aside.

[104] Statements made during personal interview with members of the Women's Unit at the Liberian Refugee Camp in Oru- Ijebu, Nigeria in June 1994. This interview was conducted for The Panos Institute for their Women and Conflict Program. The data from these interviews are used in this work with the permission of Panos.

[105] The CPO interview.

[106] The Nigerian Diplomat interview.

[107] Olurin, NWC Lecture, p.30.

[108] C. Iweze, The International and Multinational dimension of ECOMOG Joint Operation, Lecture delivered at the National War College (NWC), Lagos, 15 February, 1994, p. 9.

Nigeria eventually issued RF 301 radio sets to all participating countries but there was the problem of interpreters since there was no common language all the troops could speak. This problem contributed in no small way to the killing of Doe.[109]

The Ghanaian airforce which originally provided support for the mission relied on radio messages relayed via Ghana to the base in Sierra Leone.[110] Thus responses were not received in good time.

Communications were not as effective as was expected during peace enforcement. There was no centralized communication equipment. The three companies in a battalion had only one radio.[111] The equipment taken to the mission area did not last long. Although the manpower was available to repair them, there were no spare parts and no funds. Thus maintenance was diffi-cult.[112] The effects of this on the operation were described by the CPO and the CLO:

... Communication equipment were only given at battalion level. Some soldiers have been lost in the bush in some cases.[113] If a soldier was stranded in the bush, it was difficult to contact him as he had no communication equipment.[114]

The Deputy CCO summed up the communication problems during the second enforcement period:

During peace enforcement, the problems were greater. Equipment broke down easily or enemy would capture equipment. Enemy could jam your radio. But the enemy had no capability to conduct electronic warfare ... . Also, it was not possible for battalions to come here to collect their mail.[115]

At the beginning of the last peacekeeping phase, the force was hardly left with any communications equipment to conduct effective peacekeeping. The Field Commander stated that the force could not perform any peacekeeping duties unless it had the tools to do so.[116] It required 'petroleum products, vehicles, and communications gadgets in order to put the troops in the right frame of mind for disarmament'. [117]

The US offered 'limited assistance'[118] to ECOMOG in these areas, providing a short term solution. It enabled the now expanded ECOMOG to

---

[109] Ibid., p. 10.
[110] Ibid.
[111] Personal interview with ECOMOG Chief Communication Officer (CCO) and Deputy CCO.
[112] Ibid.
[113] The CPO interview.
[114] The CLO interview.
[115] Deputy CCO interview.
[116] *BBC Focus On Africa*, 8 February 1994; Personal interview with the Field Commander and with the CLO.
[117] *BBC Focus on Africa*, 8 February 1994.
[118] *BBC Focus on Africa*, 21 February 1994; Also confirmed in the Inienger, and the CLO interviews. The implications of this limited assistance are discussed further in this chapter.

begin its peacekeeping duties along with the newly deployed United Nations Observer Mission in Liberia (UNOMIL). The US assistance via the UN enabled communication equipment to be provided at platoon level.[119] Despite this however, effective communication links could not be maintained with all areas due to inadequate equipment. ECOMOG's Deputy Chief Communications Officer highlighted the problems with check points and vehicles: 'check points should have radios, but they have none. Vehicles also have no radios.'[120] The vehicles fitted with radios are those belonging to commanding officers and higher ranks.[121]

Effects of Language Barriers

Language barriers affected command right from the outset. ECOMOG troops who were present during the enforcement period in 1990 admit that language barrier created a few problems during this phase. The Camp Commandant who was a platoon commander during the operation in 1990, argued that though not a major obstacle, the language differences between the Francophone and Anglophone states was a hindrance.[122] His account of his personal experience during this phase provides an indication of some of the problems created by language barrier in the field :

> ... During that operation, Guinea was on our right flank while Ghana was on the left. Things were happening very quickly and there was no interpreter. Communication was difficult. My little knowledge of French and Mandingo[123] were combined with sign language to communicate with the Guinean platoon commander and I in turn interpreted this to the Ghanaians. It was like a linguistic cocktail yet they got it quick.[124]

A Nigerian battalion commander argued that language barriers seriously affected command initially. He recalled desperately attempting to use sign language to a Guinean soldier amidst the chaos which followed a rebel attack, and the soldier walked away, not quite understanding what he wanted.[125] Some in the anglophone camp argued that soldiers from the francophone states

---

[119] The CCO and Deputy CCO interviews.
[120] Ibid.
[121] Ibid.
[122] The Camp Commandant interview.
[123] The Mandingo ethnic group can be found in a few West African countries. They are in Liberia, Guinea, Sierra Leone and some parts of the Gambia. They all speak a common language. While this has eased the problem of communication amongst the Mandingo speaking members of ECOMOG, it also threatened to create a problem of partiality due to tribal allegiance.
[124] The Camp Commandant interview.
[125] Personal interview with Lt. Col. Moses in July 1994.

sometimes refused to follow orders, under the pretence that they could not understand the instructions.

The overall effect of language barriers on the operation was summed up by a Commanding Officer:

> Ordinary conversation particularly with Francophone countries (Mali, Guinea and Senegal) is as difficult as passing a camel through the eye of a needle. Translation of ideas does not exactly carry the meanings. Communication in terms orders (sic) are misunderstood. The military way of appreciation varies.[126]

The Gambian Contingent Commander also commented on the effects of language barrier at this stage:

> ... It slows down the speedy flow of orders. You have to wait for the interpreter to interpret the order. Therefore time is wasted.[127]

Attempts were however made to solve the problems created by language barrier. Interpreters were provided to enhance communication at a number of levels. Remarking on the problem and efforts to reduce it, General Olurin stated:

> ... This (language barriers) to a large extent slows down command. A typical example of this is passing operations orders or instructions through the Deputy Field Commander of 15 Nig Bde. In an ideal situation the CO of the Guinean battalion should receive orders from the Bde under which it comes.[128]

The Air Force and Navy had fewer command and control problems. The Task Forces were directly responsible to the Field Commander. Task Forces consisted mainly of Ghanaians and Nigerians (anglophone) and command and control was unified. The absence of language barrier made command and control easier. The smaller size of the task forces compared to the ground forces makes for easier command and control. According to the Chief Naval Officer (CNO) :

> Command and Control is unified. Any of the navy ships could be tasked on any assignment. There is even tasking. Command and control is more effective because we are smaller. Command ability is also important.[129]

The CNO however added that numbers are irrelevant when talking about the effectiveness of the navy :

> The Navy is about four hundred. But you don't talk about numbers. Sophistication and technology are the important things. You need highly skilled personnel for good performance.[130]

---

[126] Personal interview with the Commanding Officer, ECOMOG Ground Task Force/221 Light Tank Battalion, July 1994. He also expressed this in a self completed questionnaire – Respondent 67.
[127] The Gambian Contingent Commander interview.
[128] Olurin, NWC Lecture, p. 31.
[129] CNO interview.

The Chief Air officer also commented on the ease with which the NAF and
the GAF worked together:

> We share a lot of training institutions and staff courses. Therefore, working together was
> quite easy.[131]

Other issues which affected command and control were those relating to
training and doctrine, and logistics distribution. These are discussed below.

TRAINING AND DOCTRINE

Opinion is divided as to whether ECOMOG generally had a doctrine.
However, at different phases of the operation, the force not only blended the
differences in training and doctrine of the different contingents, it also
developed its own doctrine in response to the changing situation on the
ground. At first glance, the ECOMOG force was characterized by two broad
divisions with respect to training and doctrine – those of anglophone and
francophone states. The Gambia, Ghana, Nigeria and Sierra Leone belonged
to the former, while Guinea, Mali and Senegal[132] were in the latter grouping.
The post-independence armies of these countries were modelled after those of
their erstwhile colonial masters. Thus while the anglophone countries adopted
the style of training handed down by the British, the francophone states
adopted the style of the French. Although many agree that the principles of
war are generally the same, there were noticeable differences between both
camps. The Guineans for example were found to possess a more offensive
concept of operations.[133]

However, among the Anglophone contingents, there is not exactly uniformity of style. For example, although Ghana and Nigeria originally adopted the
British pattern of training, these have been modified to suit national policy in
each country. According to the ECOMOG Camp Commandant who is a
Gambian, 'the differences in anglophone countries is on emphasis and
experience'.[134] Ghana is the most experienced West African country in
peacekeeping, although Nigeria has participated in a number of peacekeeping
missions. Peacekeeping is considered the major specialization of the Ghanaian
army. This is seen as an attempt by President Rawlings to keep the army busy

---

[130] Ibid.

[131] The CAO interview.

[132] Senegal withdrew from the operation during the second enforcement period.

[133] The Gambian Contingent Commander.

[134] Personal interview with ECOMOG Camp Commandant, a Captain who is also the Gambian
Contingent Commander, in July 1994. ***Hereafter the Camp Commandant or Gambian
Contingent Commander interview.***

and divert its attention from political issues.[135] Sierra Leone has a lot less experience than others, while for the Gambia, it was the army's first outside operation. Since its establishment in the 1980s, the Gambian military has been trained by the Nigerians. An ECOMOG Battalion Commander described the force in a nutshell:

> ... the Ghanaian contingent are good in peacekeeping. On the other hand, the Nigerian contingent is a crack force for peace enforcement or out right combat. The Sierra Leonean and Guinean contingents blend the two extremes.[136]

This peacekeeping specialization of the Ghanaian army determined the response of that contingent in ECOMOG to the situation in Liberia. As a force which is trained only in traditional peacekeeping principles, the use of force in ECOMOG has been totally strange to the Ghanaians in ECOMOG and has affected the operation as discussed below. This adherence to traditional peacekeeping principles largely affected the attitude of the Ghanaian FC in the first phase. Some commentators have argued that his 'relaxed style is more suited to peacekeeping than offensive action ...'[137] It is also not unlikely that Arnold Quanoo adopted the style of Ghana's first General to head a peacekeeping operation. General Emmanuel Erskine who commanded UNIFIL between 1974 and 1981, went to great length to appease armed factions, in his bid to keep the peace.[138] Thus there were sharp distinctions between the Ghanaians and the Nigerians who were more prone to enforcement.

The disparity in the backgrounds and skills of the different forces affected the operation right from the outset. The first Guinean contingent in Liberia for example consisted largely of troops with a paramilitary background. That this happened at all is a reflection of the lack of proper planning and co-ordination prior to the operation. This created problems for the operation. Although the Guinean contingent was able to capture objectives given to them, they were often unable to hold ground. At the initial phase, it was common for the Guinean troops to capture a particular territory and then vacate the area. This act of abandoning their position resulted in the loss of the ground which was gained, adversely affecting morale and ultimately, the operation.

The diverse background also brought some friction in the chain of command. The Guinean Contingent Commander for example objected to the system which obtained whereby objectives were given to each country's battalion separately, under their commanders. He preferred a system whereby

---

[135] This view was expressed for example by Margaret Vogt, during the Vogt interview.

[136] Remarks made by a Nigerian Lt. colonel – Commanding officer of 221 Light Tank Battalion during my interview with him . He also made similar comments in a questionnaire.

[137] See *West Africa*, 1-7 October 1990, p.2557.

[138] Emmanuel A. Erskine, *Mission with UNIFIL: An African Soldier's Reflections*, (1989), p.31.

all the contingents would be mixed and then split into platoons and tasks would be allocated on this basis. However, others disagreed on the grounds that this method would create even more command problems. The Nigerians in particular were not in favour of mixing troops up below platoon level. General Inienger for example remarked:

> Contingents do not operate in isolation. We mix them up. There are two major formations – 15 & 7 Brigades. It enhances command. But at the low level, you cannot afford to mix people up...[139]

The differences in training and doctrine were highlighted in the enforcement phases (i.e. phases II and IV) by two different issues. First was the training background of the soldiers. The peacekeeping background of the Ghanaians served to slow down the operation in two major ways. First the preference for peacekeeping among the Ghanaians led them to delay the use of force until diplomacy had been exhausted.[140] Secondly, the Ghanaian troops were particularly cautious in executing directives that on occasion it took eight days to perform a task that was expected to take only one day. This is also partly the effect of peacekeeping specialization, which would have taken the focus away from training for combat.

Second was the effect of the differences in the fighting capability of the force. The deployment of troops with diverse background and experience also occurred at contingent level. This for example resulted in variation in the capability of Nigerian troops. While the second and third Nigerian battalions were very efficient in carrying out their tasks, Nibatt 1 (the original battalion deployed to Liberia) was particularly slow. They were not as mobile as other units.[141] Many of the casualties sustained by the force during Octopus resulted from poor tackling of rebel ambush.[142] The composition of this battalion is further confirmation that the planners were not really expecting serious combat in Liberia. It was expected that the force would succeed in intimidating the rebels into an agreement to go to the negotiating table.

ECOMOG's doctrine and tactics during the enforcement periods were largely determined by the tactics employed by the guerrilla force. With practically no training and experience in guerrilla warfare[143], many ECOMOG troops were initially thrown off guard by the fact that after having advanced and taken control of a territory, they were attacked by the rebels from the

---

[139] The Inienger interview..
[140] Personal interview with a Nigerian Major in 221 Light Tank Battalion. This was also implied by the Gambian Contingent Commander.
[141] Iweze.
[142] M.A. Balogun, NWC Lecture.
[143] The Tanzanian and Ugandan troops who were well trained in guerrilla tactics were not a part of the force at this time. They only arrived after the cease-fire and the decision to expand ECOMOG.

rear.[144] The NPFL's probing attacks coupled with its tactics of delaying the ECOMOG advance in order to have enough time to regroup posed a few problems for the ECOMOG force. A Ghanaian Lt. – a Mortar Platoon Commander – aptly describes the troops' experience of the guerrilla tactics:

> During the advance to Buchanan, it was envisaged that rebels would concentrate at a point and try to halt the advance. It was realized, however, that they would allow the forward elements to move well ahead, adopt a bypass taking advantage of their knowledge of the terrain, and attack from the rear. This explains the numerous times that the gunners had to battle it out seriously at the rear to overpower them.[145]

Commenting on the rebels' probing attacks, he remarks:

> They would try to test your pulse irrespective of your strength by sending out few men to fire at your general direction. When you return fire your position is given away and the bulk of them now pour maximum fire on you.[146]

These tactics posed great difficulty for the ECOMOG ground forces. The commanders were faced with the task of devising effective ways to counter them. Unusual tactics were adopted in order to successfully overcome the rebels. The remarks of the Operations Officer of the Ghanaian seventh Battalion provides an interesting description of the doctrine and tactics employed by ECOMOG in dealing with the rebels:

> My impression about the ECOMOG operations is that it is unique and of a peculiar nature. Its doctrine does not correspond with what we read from our military books. The tactics is neither Conventional Warfare nor Counter-insurgency. During the advance to Buchanan, rebel contact was dealt with in ECOMOG's own way. The known military approaches of frontal and flanking attacks, envelopment and encirclement could not be adhered to strictly.[147]

The general approach adopted by the ECOMOG Ground Task Force in its effort to capture strategic targets (especially in the hinterland) from the NPFL however, was to advance in large numbers and capture a target. The advance was usually led by armoured tanks while the infantry followed and were closely supported by the Air Task Force. On capturing a target, a unit would remain behind to hold the ground. The comments of a Lance Corporal on the advance and capture of Buchanan provides an interesting description of the pattern of advance:

---

[144] Almost every ECOMOG officer and soldier who experienced Octopus that I had cause to interview talked about this particular problem. Battalion commanders argue that this served to weaken the morale of their men..

[145] Lt. Ansoma Yeboah, 'The Rebel's Tactics', in *EXODUS II* Vol. 7, Feb.- Sept. 1993, p.13. EXODUS II is a news magazine of the Ghanaian contingent serving with ECOMOG in Liberia.

[146] Ibid.

[147] Major B. Musah, 'An Operational Overview of Ghanbatt 7', pp. 8-9.

Nibatt 10 took over the lead of the advance for the second leg while Nibatt 8 deployed covering the whole length of the distance covered in the first leg of the advance.[148]

Defences, in form of trenches were developed and continuously improved whilst the activities of the rebels were contained. Even in such positions, rebels managed to trickle in and attempted to seize these positions from ECOMOG troops. But through aggressive patrols, fortification of defences, ECOMOG managed to maintain its hold over the grounds it gained.

LOGISTICS AND ADMINISTRATION

ECOWAS failed to meet the logistic requirements of the force, making a centralized distribution impossible. The agreement reached by ECOWAS (SMC) was that each contributing nation would provide logistic support for its contingent which would be self sufficient for the first thirty days of the operation. After this, ECOWAS was to take over the administration.[149] However, this take over did not occur as the ECOWAS Secretariat did not have the means to provide the needed logistics. The contributing states thus continued to supply their troops despite the strain on their weak economies. The comments of the CAO best describe the impact of this logistic situation on the operation:

> The force is a combination of inter-related units working together. Operationally, it is under the FC's command. Logistically, it is controlled by different governments.[150]

This absence of centralized logistic distribution meant lack of uniformity in almost all aspects of logistics and the effects were profound. There were huge gaps between the logistics capability of the different contingents. ECOMOG officers were particularly concerned about the effects of this on command, control and morale. General Olurin for example remarked that:

> The lack of centralized logistics has inherent command and control problems for the commander. Besides, it is bad for morale of troops who share the same accommodation or office or check points to have different standards of feeding and welfare amenities...[151]

General Bakut also expressed a similar concern:

> ... financial constraints have made it impossible for uniformity to be maintained in feeding standards. This tends to reveal inequalities and affects the morale of the troops...[152]

---

[148] Records of a Nigerian Lance Corporal.

[149] This arrangement was confirmed by General Williams in my interview with him; also in personal interview with ECOMOG Chief of Logistics (COL), in Liberia in July 1994, *(hereafter the COL. interview);* as well as remarks by ECOMOG's former Chief of Logistics, Col. A. Etukudo, in *The Peacemaker*, Vol.1, No.1 Sept.91-Sept.92.

[150] The CAO interview.

[151] Olurin, in *The Peacemaker* p.13.

Nigeria's problem with logistic distribution had an immediate impact on the force. The economic and political problems within Nigeria quickly began to tell on its large contingent in ECOMOG. Many Nigerian troops arrived without uniforms and boots.[153] This particular problem led Prince Johnson of the INPFL to provide these items as gifts to the troops.[154] This very act affected the peacekeeping image of the force as it meant that many now saw Prince Johnson as a friend. Thus the peacekeeping principle of impartiality had been undermined. The size of the Nigerian contingent in relation to the others meant that its logistic problems affected the force as a whole. Apart from Ghana, the other contingents were relatively small and it was therefore easier for them to make adequate provision for their troops. The Ghanaian contingent was generally considered to be the most organized and to a large extent, well provided for in terms of logistics.

The administration of rations suffered immense problems. Rations were brought in for the troops by ship from Nigeria, including cattle and bread. On arrival in Monrovia, the cattle were sometimes dead and the bread mouldy and soaked in water. General Olurin remarked that:

> ... As a result of the extended line of communication between the troops contributing countries and Liberia, most essential raw rations get spoiled enroute. In the case of NIGCON, bread and onions grow mould before they get to Monrovia. The need for preservation should be taken into consideration in future.[155]

Bread and other perishable items which could be found within Liberia were later purchased locally[156].

Whilst all the logistic issues discussed here had adverse effects on the troops and served to weaken their morale, the issue of operational allowance proved to have the worst effect on morale within ECOMOG. A small operational allowance of five US Dollars per day was negotiated at the start of the mission. This came to a monthly average of one hundred and fifty Dollars. It was agreed that each contributing country would be responsible for the payment and upkeep of their own troops. There were however noticeable differences both in the amount and the pattern in which some contingents were paid. The Sierra Leonean government paid its troops only one hundred Dollars a month on average. This was a source of discontent within that contingent.

---

[152] Personal interview with Maj. Gen. Ishaya Bakut, former ECOMOG Field Commander, in Nigeria, April 1993.

[153] Personal interview with Margaret Vogt at the Nigerian Institute for International Affairs (NIIA), Lagos in June 1994. Margaret Vogt worked extensively with the Nigerian military on its role in the ECOMOG operations in Liberia. General Iweze also mentions this particular logistic problem within the Nigerian contingent in his chapter in Vogt and Ekoko, (eds.).

[154] Iweze, 'Nigeria in Liberia ...'

[155] Olurin, NWC Lecture .

[156] Personal interview with ECOMOG Chief Personnel Officer, Monrovia – July 1994.

This feeling was shared by Sierra Leonean officers and soldiers alike. A Sierra Leonean Lieutenant summed up the general opinion within the contingent:

> We would like the increase of our operational allowance to the standard of the other contributing nations.[157]

The problem in the Nigerian camp was of a different kind. Although operational allowance was paid at the agreed rate of five Dollars per day, the allowance was not regular. Troops were sometimes not paid for three months. This had an adverse effect on morale of troops within the contingent but its effects on the operation became more apparent during the peacekeeping period which followed.

The supply of uniforms was one of the most glaring aspects. Every country had its own different type of uniform right from the start of the operation. Some events during Octopus revealed the shortcoming of this practice. There were cases where rebels captured and killed some ECOMOG soldiers and wore their uniforms. At other times, rebels made replica uniforms of some contingents. Five Guinean soldiers died as a result of this problem.[158] Another problem with uniforms was the inability of some countries to adequately supply their troops. Nigeria's case was the most glaring. According to the ECOMOG Chief Logistics Officer and the Chief Personnel Officer :

> Some of the countries are unable to re-supply their people. Nigeria for example, you need to see some of our soldiers in the bush. Their condition, uniforms and so on, is appalling.[159]

> The troops, especially Nigcon, were deployed without adequate supply of uniforms including boots. Some have resorted to buying from other contingents. There is now a sale point on the premises. However, recently, attempts were made to transfer the uniforms intended for Babangida's[160] Presidential Guard to the troops.[161]

ECOMOG's Field Commander during this period commented on the appalling condition of Nigerian troops:

> ... It is however disheartening to note that of all the contingents in Ops. [sic] Liberty the Nigerian contingent is the mostly badly turned out. Most of the soldiers had only one pair of boots and uniform. Our troops can easily be seen in tattered camouflage uniforms. Of late they have resorted to purchasing uniforms and boots from Ghanbatt and Leobatt Contingents[162]

---

[157] Expressed in questionnaire (respondent no.52) and also during discussion held with some Sierra Leone officers based near Monrovia Freeport.
[158] Ibid.
[159] The CLO interview.
[160] Nigeria's former military President.
[161] The CPO interview.
[162] Olurin, NWC Lecture, p.30.

The concern over the supply problem with uniforms in the Nigerian contingent was shared by officers and other ranks alike. Many soldiers are however very bitter that they had to resort at times to buying their uniforms with their own money. A Nigerian private for example narrated his experience when he was newly deployed to Liberia:

> When I arrived here, a Guinean soldier was kind enough to give me one of his uniforms. Although it was a bigger size, it was much better than what I had. Other countries do not have this problem of uniform.[163]

Commenting on the uniform problem, a Nigerian Lance Corporal said:

> I had to buy my uniform from the allowance that they gave us. I don't think this is good enough.[164]

The lack of centralized distribution also created problems with medical facilities, especially at the initial stages. The Ghanaian contingent was the best equipped in terms of medical supplies. Although there was a policy that all ECOMOG medical resources (both equipment and manpower) should be combined for effective medical administration, a situation was created in which Ghanaian soldiers were given preference over others in surgery.[165] The Field Hospital at the ECOMOG Headquarters was used for the entire force. There were however general problems surrounding the delivery of medical care to the troops. Medical facilities were generally considered sub standard. Commenting on this problem, the CLO said:

> Apart from consumables, facilities are poor. There are no laboratories to carry out basic tests. Therefore the town hospital is used for this. This has a lot of problems. Blood samples are sometimes exchanged and people receive treatment they are not supposed to.[166]

Troop Rotation

The adverse effects of switching from peace enforcement to peacekeeping as well as the problems of discipline discussed above are partly attributable to lack of frequent rotation of the troops. Although it was initially agreed that the contingents would be rotated every six months, this pattern has not been followed. The Ghanaian contingent rotated most frequently while the Sierra Leoneans, Guineans and Nigerians rotations were the least frequent.[167] This only served to lower morale and diminish productivity.

---

[163] Personal interview with a Private in Nibatt 12.
[164] Personal interview with a Nigerian Lance Corporal in Nibatt 13.
[165] Iweze, 'Nigeria in Liberia', p.237.
[166] The CLO interview.
[167] Responses in questionnaires and personal interviews.

The psychological effects of lack of frequent rotation on the force were profound and they were most noticeable in the Nigerian camp, given its size. In theory, officers and other ranks could obtain passes to travel home to see their families. However, they were expected to pay their way from the allowance that they were paid.[168] The cost of transportation to Nigeria prevented majority of soldiers from going home whilst officers often managed to travel home to see their families. Invariably, a soldier remained in the mission area until he was rotated. This did not enhance morale within the force. This was compounded by the fact that many of the troops remained in the mission area after the enforcement period without any rehabilitation. Commenting on the problems of infrequent rotation, General Inienger said:

> ... Having been away from home for too long, they (soldiers) sometimes behave differently at check points. For example they have mood swings. The same soldier who acts erratically today, may act calmly tomorrow.[169]

The effects of long stay on the social life of soldiers is discussed in greater detail in the next chapter.

Whilst the ECOMOG high command undoubtedly realized the need for regular rotation of troops, it was unable to achieve this or some standardization in rotation pattern amongst the contingents. The most commonly cited reason for this is the cost of rotation. According to General Inienger:

> Rotation is advisable ideally every six months. Lack of this could lead to familiarity, fatigue, boredom and efficiency diminishes. It is however costly to rotate on the meagre resources of different countries.[170]

Since each contingent is responsible for the cost of rotating its troops, rotation was not uniformly done within the force. Each country rotated as frequently as it could. The costs included those of transporting the troops to the mission area and providing weapons, equipment, uniforms amongst other things to every soldier.[171] Nigerian troops deployed during Octopus for example were transported to the mission area in commercial aircraft and not by sea or military transport planes,[172] further raising transportation costs.

However, it is believed that other reasons account for Nigeria's troops remaining in Liberia for unduly long periods. Promises and plans to return some troops home were made on several occasions and then reneged upon. A view held by some Nigerian other ranks is that their home government was concerned that returning them to Nigeria under an unstable political climate could lead to insurrection in the army. The attitudes of some of the soldiers

---

[168] Ibid.
[169] The Inienger interview.
[170] Ibid.
[171] The CLO and CPO interviews.
[172] Olurin, NWC Lecture, p.27.

makes it easy to believe this claim. Having gained confidence from the successes of peace enforcement, some proclaimed that they were battle tested while their colleagues at home were not.[173] Indeed it was not uncommon to find soldiers who had participated in enforcement dismissing some officers as cowards while exhibiting greater respect for those whom they considered to have fought gallantly at the battle front.[174] The extremists expressed their readiness to join a rebel army if there was one in Nigeria.

Transportation and Combat Supplies

The method by which troops were lifted from Nigeria to the area of operation created logistic problems. During Octopus, there was a sharp departure from the initial practice of bringing the troops in by sea from Freetown. Troops had to be airlifted from Nigeria on commercial aircraft. On the problems of airlifting rotating troops, General Olurin remarked:

> ... Most battalions and units came in piece-meal leaving behind their organic support weapons and troops' carrying vehicles. Most of the problems in this regard could have been avoided if rotating troops are brought on by ship to the Mission Area or had military transport planes been used.[175]

Inadequate supply of vehicles and shortage of spare parts was a major problem and it served to slow down the operation. From the start of the operation vehicles at ECOMOG's disposal were mainly those originally imported from Asia for the AFL as well as those from NIGCON.[176] However, apart from being inadequate, lack of spare parts rendered many of the vehicles useless as maintenance could not be carried out.[177] The troop carrying vehicles as well as the Armoured Personnel Carriers from Nigeria did not have the appropriate spare parts. Many vehicles were sent to Liberia without spare tyres.[178] Remarking on the problem with vehicles in Nigcon, the CLO said:

> The force was assembled in 1990. Since then there has been no re-supply of spare parts. Most vehicles are now grounded.[179]

ECOMOG also had problems with the storage and supply of Petroleum Oil and Lubricant (POL) such as Automated Gas Oil (AGO). Inadequate storage

---

[173] This feeling is common amongst Nigerian soldiers I held discussions with.
[174] This issue is discussed further in the next chapter.
[175] Olurin, NWC Lecture, p. 27.
[176] Ibid. p. 29.
[177] Ibid.
[178] Ibid.
[179] The CLO interview.

facility led the force to use the facilities of the Liberian National Petroleum Company (LNPC).[180] According to General Olurin:

> ... Delays are experienced due to the bureaucratic procedure of making demands. Most times vital operations are kept on hold due to lack of AGOs mainly used by heavy vehicles like Armoured Fighting Vehicles and gun-towing vehicles.[181]

The supply of ammunition presented its own problems, but some contingents coped better than others. Each contingent depended on its home government for the supply of ammunition. Some contingents managed to cope with problems of inadequate supply. For example, the Gambian Contingent Commander remarked:

> Every country supports its contingent but it all works. If I run out of ammo, I go to Guinea, because they have the same thing.[182]

All three services of the Nigerian contingent however had to cope with problems of a different nature regarding the supply of ammunition. The contingent at times received weapons and ammunitions in very poor condition from home. General Olurin remarked on this on this problem:

> In some cases, unserviceable and expired rounds of 7.62mm along with malfunctioning hand grenades were shipped to ECOMOG. ... Ammo was equally not available at times for the airforce thereby limiting the number of sorties that were flown.[183]

The supply of fuel was about the only aspect of the logistic distribution that had been continuously centralized. This was largely because Nigeria provided all the petroleum for the force although the Nigerian ECOMOG officers were concerned about the amount of responsibility that was shouldered by the country. The fuel supply was however made with the expectation that Nigeria would be reimbursed by the ECOWAS Secretariat at some stage. The Chief Logistics Officer for example expressed this view:

> Nigeria has been supplying the fuel, passing it through ECOWAS, in the hope that it can be paid for in future. However, this is almost impossible.[184]

The Air and Naval Task Forces

The logistic problems in the Nigerian camp affected Nigerian elements of The Air Task Force from the time it was deployed. They were heavily reliant on the Ghanaians for logistic supplies at the initial stages. Provisions for feeding

---

[180] Olurin, NWC Lecture, p.28.
[181] Ibid.
[182] Personal interview with the Gambian Contingent Commander.
[183] Olurin, NWC Lecture, p.29.
[184] The CLO interview.

and accommodation were not made when the force arrived in Sierra Leone where the ATF was based. Other items essential to the operation such as POL and storage facilities and area maps were not available for the NAF unit. The Ghanaian unit which was already operating in the area came to the rescue of the Nigerians by providing all of the required logistic items in the first few weeks. Tents had to be brought in from Ghana due to the unavailability of this item in Nigeria.

Budget restrictions created a huge maintenance backlog for the NAF and this affected the state of the aircraft that were despatched for the ECOMOG operation. The Nigerian detachment of the ATF had to contend with long delays in NAF HQ responding to request of logistic items. This led at times to the 'cannibalisation of aircraft for spares', in order to avoid total grounding of the operation. Nigeria's C-130s were grounded and this led to the lifting of troops with commercial aircraft during Octopus.[185]

The Air and Naval Task Forces were also affected by the lack of spare parts. They were dependent on the supply of spare parts from home governments. Ghana appeared to be more effective at doing this than Nigeria. The same was the situation with the navy. The Nigerian element at times had to rely on the local market in Liberia which traded in maritime equipment but they were not readily available. According to the Chief Naval Officer (CNO):

> Virtually everything on the ship is precision equipment. Spare parts are not available here. Time is critical. The time lapse can affect you. The local market trades in maritime equipment but the critical area is weapons and standard equipment. You therefore have to adapt. Luckily, the other side has no strong navy that will pose a threat. Therefore equipment needed to be used only during Octopus.[186]

The FC also commented on the state of disrepair of the guns on Nigeria naval ships:

> ... the naval ships and their equipment are not maintained at regular intervals. The situation would have been different at sea if the rebels had naval capability.[187]

The immense logistic problems faced by ECOMOG at different stages of the operation appear to have resulted from two major factors. First was the poor financial circumstances of the West African nations. This made it virtually impossible for them to provide adequate support for their troops. The second factor is related to Nigeria's domestic situation. This factor is difficult to ignore given that the country contributed over 70% of the ECOMOG force. Although other contingents had their own shortcomings, those of the Nigerian contingent appeared to overshadow the rest and dictate the image projected by the force in most circumstances.

---

[185] Balogun, NWC Lecture.
[186] The CNO interview.
[187] Olurin, NWC Lecture, pp.24-25.

The active involvement of the Nigerian military in politics seriously weakened its ability to maintain a high level of professionalism or conduct military operations effectively. As a result, many commentators argued that the poor planning and execution of the ECOMOG operations in Liberia was a reflection of the disorganized state of the Nigerian military.[188] The participation of the Nigerian military in politics had weakened its professional posture in two significant ways. First was the tendency of the military personnel in power to appoint on the basis of the support they got from certain individuals rather than on competence. This had an indirect effect on the operation in the sense that personnel selected to plan and execute the mission were not necessarily the best people for those positions.

The second factor had a more direct effect on the ECOMOG operations. This was the fact that for the entire period of the ECOMOG operations, the Nigerian military sought to maintain itself in power. As a result, the ECOMOG operation in Liberia was not given the necessary attention. Nigerian ECOMOG officers were frustrated by the length of time it took the government to respond to requests for spare parts or indeed the payment of allowance. The home government was preoccupied with domestic political issues.

A third factor was the fact that the ECOMOG operation appeared to have been more of a personal mission of the former president and so the pattern of its maintenance was handled in that personal manner instead of devising a standard procedure for maintaining it. It was common practice for example, for the Nigcon Commander to go straight to the President to seek approval for its funding, allowance, etc. But after the departure of that leader, it became more difficult to do this.

Notwithstanding these difficulties, ECOMOG was successful in enforcing a cease-fire but a few factors made this task easier to achieve. First was the absence of a credible air or naval threat from the NPFL. Second was the fact that the NPFL had to turn to conventional tactics in order to defeat ECOMOG in the capital, Monrovia. This was a particularly difficult task. It was thus easier for ECOMOG to defeat the rebels in the capital through conventional means, no matter how unprepared it was.

CONCLUSION

This chapter has analyzed how different problems undermined ECOMOG's effectiveness, deeply complicating its task of achieving the political objectives for which it was established. The first of these was the flawed planning which

---

[188] The Williams interview.

set the scene for a catalogue of errors in the execution of the operation. These included amongst others, failure to anticipate a combat role for the force and the multifaceted nature of the operation. The planners obviously saw peacekeeping in the traditional sense, entailing creation of buffer zones and interposition between combatants. Events in Liberia however dictated otherwise.

ECOMOG's experience demonstrated how quickly an operational environment can change when dealing with conflicts like the Liberian one, and the challenges which face a force that has to adapt to these changing circumstances. It revealed the character of a peace creation force, where the air force and navy could perform crucial combat roles along with tactical support such as transportation. The character of parties to this internal conflict who could not be relied upon to abide by agreements highlighted the need to prepare for the use of force in such operations. The ECOMOG operation also illustrated the importance of giving troops adequate training to meet the challenges posed by irregular forces with unconventional doctrine and tactics. Above all, it highlighted the need for flexibility in order to effectively employ peacekeeping or enforcement strategies as situations may require when seeking to create peace.

Apart from challenges posed by the nature of the conflict and the changing operational environment, there were those which resulted from the fact that different national forces were working together for the first time. These included the problems of command and control and differences in training and doctrine. Others were the result of financial constraints and the domestic circumstances in contributing states. The logistic problems were a reflection of this. These problems made a high level of integration extremely difficult to achieve within ECOMOG, further affecting the force's ability to attain its objectives.

Many of these problems are however not peculiar to ECOMOG. Many UN peacekeeping operations have been found to lack efficient command and control system and adequate training of some units, amongst other things.[189] However, for a force which, constantly had to shift between peacekeeping and enforcement, these shortcomings were more pronounced in ECOMOG. In UN operations where enforcement was embarked upon (e.g. Somalia), a task force largely under the command of a single nation would usually perform such duties, whilst the more regular type of peacekeeping would be conducted under a multinational command. This would reduce the command and control problems during enforcement. In the case of ECOMOG, the peace enforcement activities were conducted under a multinational command.

---

[189] This was discussed in Chapter Two.

Indeed, ECOMOG's measure of success in creating peace in Liberia was largely due to the type of opposition it faced. The rebels were ill equipped and poorly trained in comparison to ECOMOG. The force may perhaps have suffered a terrible defeat at the hands of a better equipped rebel army. This should not, however, remove the fact that ECOMOG succeeded in bringing a semblance of peace to Liberia through its enforcement operations. There were other factors which worked in favour of ECOMOG, increasing the level of cohesion in the force, and enhancing its ability to sustain the operation. These constitute the focus of the next chapter.

CHAPTER SIX

The Sociological Dimensions of the ECOMOG Operation

INTRODUCTION

The two preceding chapters analysed ECOMOG's mandate and stated objectives, and the extent to which the force succeeded or failed to achieve these, given the political and military situations under which it had to operate. This analysis addressed two major questions about the role of a force seeking to create peace. The first relates to factors outside the control of a military organization (e.g. political influences), which, impact on its ability to create peace. The second concerns the characteristics of a force, which enhance its capacity for peace creation. It has long been recognized that organizations (particularly large multinational forces), often experience difficulty in operating effectively, no matter how well meaning the intentions of their founders. According to Van Doorn,

> In the past, the truly successful, reasonably adequately functioning organizations consti-
> tuted exceptions to the rule that organized co-operation can slip as easily into conflict and
> anarchy as it can degenerate into a reign of terror by the few over the many. Only in re-
> cent times has the awareness grown that such danger can be avoided by recognizing the
> three-fold character of each organization: i.e. its character as a rational construction, as
> a unit of co-operation and as a social institution.[1]

Thus, the effectiveness of an organization can be understood in terms of its purpose; the characteristics of its constituent units and how its members perceive their role in the organization; and its social composition. The last two are likely to determine the level of cohesion within an organization. This cohesion, which Janowitz describes as 'the feeling of group solidarity and the capacity for collective action', is an important feature which contributes to the capacity of any military organization to function effectively.[2] A force such as ECOMOG, seeking to conduct peace creation is no exception. The previous chapter already analyzed how organization, differences in training and doctrine, and operational experience affected ECOMOG's internal cohesion and its ability to carry out its mandate in Liberia.

---

[1] J.A. A. Van Doorn, *The Soldier and Social Change: Comparative Studies in the History and Sociology of the Military,* (Beverly Hills, California: Sage Publications, 1975), p. 5
[2] See Morris Janowitz, *The Military in the Political Development of New Nations: An Essay in Comparative Analysis.* (Chicago and London: The University of Chicago Press, 1964), p.67

It is the purpose of this chapter, however, to examine ECOMOG's potentials and limitations for conducting peace creation, from the point of view of its internal social organization. This includes the dimensions of social origin, ideology, cohesion and cleavage, and the influences of these features on the development of attitudes and patterns of behaviour favourable to peace creation. These factors are discussed in three main parts. The first discusses the social organization of ECOMOG and how this impacted on the operation. It examines how commonalties and differences throughout the force influenced the operation. The second section examines how organizational politics in ECOMOG weakened or strengthened cohesion in the force. The conflict approach is adopted in this analysis, identifying the different sources of cleavage within ECOMOG and their impact on the operation. The third and last section assesses how the findings in the two preceding sections influenced the development of peace creation attitudes. The analysis conducted in this chapter relies on documentary material and responses to questionnaires and interviews conducted during field trip.

I

ECOMOG'S SOCIAL ORGANIZATION

Common Features

ECOMOG troops had a combination of similarities and differences, which inevitably had some degree of influence on the operation. First, all the national contingents which participated in the ECOMOG operations were of sub-Saharan African origin with similar political and economic experiences, and all broadly shared a common African culture. Although variations exist in different African countries when their culture is subjected to deeper scrutiny, there are many common grounds in African tradition. All these countries (unlike Liberia), experienced European style colonialism and attained independence at about the same period, mostly following the development of nationalist movements.[3] They have passed through similar stages of political development, experiencing military rule or civilian authoritarianism. Guinea, Mali and Nigeria, and Sierra Leone were under military rule at the time, while Ghana was under the civilian rule of the former military leader, Gerry Rawlings. The only country which at that time could perhaps boast of stability and civilian rule untainted by military coups (not for lack of coup attempts),

---

[3]   The last section focuses more on similar issues of nationalism in the contingents and the effects of this on the mission.

was that of the Gambia, under Sir Dauda Jawara. However, this government was overthrown in a military coup in 1994. Tanzania, like Gambia, had a long history of one party authoritarian regimes, while Uganda (like Nigeria), had had its experience of military dictatorship and war. In addition, these countries shared similar economic experiences – poor economies characterized by low Gross Domestic Product (GDP), many resulting from gross mismanagement. They have some of the lowest GDP per head in the world.[4] Their GDP per head (in US$) in 1988 for example, were: 369, 416, 217, 287, 233, 123 & 204, for Ghana, Guinea, Mali, Nigeria, Sierra Leone, Tanzania and Uganda respectively.[5]

The broad similarities in culture appeared to be a strong unifying feature. The troops were all initially from West Africa until ECOMOG was expanded to include contingents from Tanzania and Uganda, both from East Africa. The sharp variation in the Liberian culture, especially in the capital, Monrovia, accentuated the cultural similarities among all the contingents. Officers and other ranks from almost all the contingents reflected on the sharp differences between the Liberian culture and those of its West African neighbours. In Monrovia, as in other cities, the culture seemed to be at wide variance from what obtained in Liberia's rural areas and in other West African countries. Influenced by what they perceived as the American way of life, many Liberians adopted 'liberated' life styles. For example, the concept of 'single motherhood' which is frowned upon in many other parts of West Africa has for long been an accepted practice in Liberian cities. It was also common practice for women to co-habit freely with men without being married. Similarly, a woman could marry as many times as she wished without the fear of being stigmatized.[6] This lifestyle shocked many ECOMOG men who were not accustomed to African women being that 'Liberated' nor to the general lacklustre attitude of the Liberians whom they came across.[7]

The similarities in culture among officers and men from contributing nations had some positive effects on ECOMOG. One noticeable area of such influence was that of command within the force. Reflecting on this point, the Gambian Contingent Commander commented:

---

[4] See The Economist, *The Book of Vital World Statistics*, (The Economist, October 1992), p. 35.

[5] Ibid.

[6] Discussion with a group of Liberian women in Monrovia, interviewed for the Panos oral testimony programme.

[7] This view was expressed freely by a cross section of ECOMOG officers and other ranks.

> ... you cannot complain about discipline from another contingent. A soldier from another contingent gives you respect. The African culture and heritage of giving respect to the elder enhances this.[8]

This natural expression of respect applied even in cases where officers performed similar duties, irrespective of rank.

> One thing makes you stand out. That is your rank. My peers are Colonels and Generals. I am considered a son in their midst. There is a bit of pressure to live up to expectation.[9]

Whilst these shared experiences had some positive influence on the operation, the sharp differences between Liberian attitudes and those of the vast majority of the ECOMOG participating nations created a major set back for the operation.[10] The lack of detailed knowledge of the Liberian people and culture by both the force and their negotiators soon became apparent. This illustrates Avruch's point (discussed in Chapter One), that mediators will encounter problems when attempting 'to convey messages across linguistic and cultural barriers'. The assumption that there were no major cultural differences between Liberians and other sub-Saharan Africans turned out to be an erroneous one which significantly impacted on the peace efforts. ECOMOG officers and other ranks were almost unanimous in their opinions of Liberians. They described the Liberians they dealt with as generally unreliable and inconsistent people, who could not be trusted to abide by an agreement. Officers complained that at negotiations, representatives of conflicting parties changed their stories and positions unbelievably frequently, grounding negotiations to a halt on many occasions. ECOMOG's Chief Logistics Officer remarked on this attitude:

> Liberia should be taken as an isolated case. ... other Africans do not behave in this way. They would sit on the same table with you tonight, agree on a decision and by the morning, they would have changed their minds.[11]

At the informal level, many officers and other ranks held similar views of many of the Liberian women with whom they associated, believing them to be unreliable and unstable. This attitudinal pattern was not envisaged by the creators of ECOMOG, who believed that a resolution to the Liberian conflict would be swift once an agreement was reached.

---

[8]   The Gambian Contingent Commander interview.

[9]   Ibid. The Gambian Contingent Commander was a Captain, one of the most senior ranks in the relatively young Gambian army.

[10] Although attitudes and practices in the Liberian cities varied sharply from those of the rural areas, a large proportion of Liberian leaders were based in the capital and were accustomed to the 'liberated' practices here.

[11] The CLO interview.

Differences

Despite the broad similarities in culture and political and economic experiences however, there appeared to be basic differences between the attitudes of troops in the ECOMOG contingents, to the mission. There was, for example, a sharp variation between the attitudes of the expanded ECOMOG, Uganda and Tanzania, and the rest of the force. Whilst the original ECOMOG troops reacted positively to the need to create peace and majority were willing to use force if it became necessary to switch from a peacekeeping stance, the expanded ECOMOG were not so willing to do this. This attitude by the expanded ECOMOG, although apparently similar to that of the Ghanaian ECOMOG which often refused to use force until diplomacy had been exhausted, is at variance with it on closer examination. The Ghanaians eventually followed the use of force option whilst the expanded ECOMOG would not even consider it. The East Africans were strictly in support of a peacekeeping operation rather than one of peace creation, which entailed the use of force. Indeed, one of their conditions (particularly Tanzania), for agreeing to deploy troops to Liberia was that they would not participate in any fighting. According to the Tanzanian Contingent Commander,

> The force[12] came here on the understanding that it will keep peace and disarm the factions. If the situation goes beyond this, then they will have to be withdrawn.[13]

However, many officers in this group considered the operation (which was then in a peacekeeping phase), to be extremely monotonous.[14] Their anti-enforcement attitude appeared to have resulted from political pressures rather than a general abhorrence of the use of force. This is discussed further in the third section below, which deals with peace creation attitudes. These contingents withdrew in 1995, following complaints of inadequate funding. The original ECOMOG force, consisting of only West Africans, subsequently remained in Liberia attempting to cope with the continuing conflict.

The late deployment of the expanded ECOMOG partly accounted for the differences in attitude between the original and expanded ECOMOG. Had the former shared the same initial experiences as their original ECOMOG counterparts, there might perhaps have been greater pressure to employ more severe methods of conflict resolution, as the rest of the force, if and when it

---

[12] Referring to the Tanzanian Contingent.

[13] Personal Interview with the Tanzanian Contingent Commander, July 1994. (**Hereafter the Tanzanian Contingent Commander Interview.**)

[14] Discussion with a group of Ugandan ECOMOG officers. These officers ranked from Second Lieutenant to Captain. Their boredom could also been seen from the viewpoint of an army which is accustomed to being in combat situations, following Uganda's relatively recent experience of a civil war.

became necessary. This was perhaps compounded by the proximity of the participating countries to the area of conflict. The East Africans were sufficiently far from the Liberian conflict geographically, that they could afford to be removed from it. There was no urgent need to achieve stability in the region, at all costs. Certainly not at the cost of Tanzanian and Ugandan lives. The fact that these countries were not a part of the sub-regional organization may have also contributed to this problem. Nigeria could not exert influence on them in the same manner it did its West African neighbours. However, some degree of pressure may have been brought to bear if it became necessary to switch to enforcement.

This expansion of ECOMOG to include East African troops undoubtedly affected integration within the force. Whilst the decision to expand ECOMOG increased Charles Taylor's confidence or at least removed justification for NPFL's intransigence, integration with the original force was more difficult to achieve. For one, it was impossible immediately, to assign officers from these countries, to staff positions in the ECOMOG headquarters. However, as will be discussed below, there was regular contact between senior officers from Uganda and Tanzania and other contingents based at the ECOMOG headquarters. The issue of integration was compounded by the effects of UN/US funding of the expanded force. Although the US rendered assistance to the expanded ECOMOG via the UN, this appeared to create a 'two-tiered' ECOMOG. The US stipulated that the funds could only be used for areas relating to peacekeeping and not those which would enhance enforcement. Thus assistance was provided in areas of communications, drugs and petroleum products. The original ECOMOG considered this assistance inadequate in comparison to that which was rendered to the Tanzanian and Ugandan troops who comprised the expanded ECOMOG.

The allowance paid to the expanded ECOMOG was a major source of discontent among the original ECOMOG troops. Whilst they were generally paid an average of one hundred and fifty US Dollars a month,[15] their East African counterparts were promised three times this amount. The latter did not have the same logistics problems encountered by the others. This further lowered the morale within the original force. General Inienger emphasized the effects of such policies:

> The US donated specifically for the expanded ECOMOG. This has raised objections that it would create two ECOMOGs not one... The difference is quite obvious. The expanded ECOMOG is better funded. Their food is better and this creates command problems.[16]

---

[15] One hundred US Dollars in the case of Sierra Leone.
[16] The Inienger interview.

In terms of their recruitment and formation, there were not substantial differences between all the contingents in ECOMOG. The officers and other ranks from all the contingents were composed entirely of regular career soldiers. This was the case throughout the operation except for the earlier stages when Guinea deployed men who performed police and immigration duties at home (see Chapter Five). There were however differences in the recruitment patterns of some of the countries. The Guinean and Sierra Leonean armies for example, recruited men on the basis of conscription.[17] The effects of this recruitment pattern in both armed forces were however not easily noticeable.

ECOMOG HEADQUARTERS

Although the national contingents had distinct characteristics, the atmosphere at the ECOMOG headquarters was international. The Field Commander and principal staff dealt with the day to day administration of the force and official interactions with the Liberian community at large. This included contact with warring factions, interim government, and holding of press conferences.

Although the headquarters staff members were not directly associated with their respective national contingents, actual interaction between the two was significant. With the exception of Nigeria, the headquarters of the national contingents were also based at the ECOMOG headquarters building. For most contingents, their principal staff officers in ECOMOG were also their contingent commanders. The Nigerian Contingent (Nigcon) headquarters occupied a separate building from the others due to its large population within ECOMOG. Its contingent commander was also not chosen from amongst the headquarters staff.

Whilst allowing for easier administration, the separation of Nigcon headquarters from the rest appeared to create some distance in terms of interaction between Nigerians and troops in other contingents. By being the base for many other contingents, ECOMOG headquarters served as the meeting or contact point for troops from many backgrounds, creating an international atmosphere. It was accessible not only to troops working within the headquarters, but those on different locations, both inside and outside Monrovia, who used this as their administrative base. With the Nigerians in a separate building, the bulk of Nigcon troops tended to interact mostly amongst themselves. This had the effect of reducing the opportunity for greater integration amongst Nigerian troops and their ECOMOG counterparts. This was especially true for other ranks, who (as discussed below), had access

---

[17] Information from questionnaire.

to fewer socialization channels than the officers. However, troops in Nigcon headquarters in the course of each day, had cause to go to the ECOMOG headquarters (which was walking distance), many times. This at least created some daily interaction between Nigcon and other national contingents.

INTEGRATING AND SOCIALIZING CHANNELS

A very important integrating function for the ECOMOG force was the publication of a bi-annual news magazine, 'The Peacemaker', edited by the Public Relations Officers in all the contingents. It reported general ECOMOG activities in English and carried news of the different contingents in both English and French. Much of the information contained in this publication was an analysis of the experiences of the troops in the field, which gave a good insight into the conduct of the operation. Some issues contained papers by officers regarding various aspects of the operation. Others consisted of news of officers at the end of their tour of duty in the various contingents. It is significant that when the nature of the operation changed, especially from peacekeeping to enforcement, activities like this were at a stand still, i.e. there were no publications. The Ghanaian contingent had its own publication, EXODUS, which was devoted to reporting activities of Ghancon, both on and off the mission area. This was the only other publication which existed aside from The Peacemaker. This to a certain extent, confirmed the general opinion of Ghancon as a well organized unit.

The most international atmosphere in ECOMOG was perhaps found in the ECOMOG international officers mess. This served to increase cross-national contact among ECOMOG officers, although troops from the different contingents spent nearly all of their time within the company of their fellow country men. Officers from the various contingents frequently met at the officers mess on a daily basis. In particular, it served as a good socializing point during farewell parties for officers at the end of their tour of duty. The ECOMOG Chief Naval Officer reflected on the crucial nature of these socializing activities between other arms and other contingents to the operation:

> Success in peacekeeping operations has to do largely with personal public relations skills. Relating with men socially is crucial to peacekeeping ... . The international officers mess is a socializing institution. Mess functions are held regularly. Sometimes, to bid farewell to officers completing their tour of duty. ... There is a strong fraternity within the naval group. We hold sports meetings once a month and make new friends.[18]

---

[18] The CNO interview.

For other ranks, the socializing channels were less formal. The cross-national contact amongst this group was supposed to be in the form of weekly sporting events. However, this was very rarely the case, as such sporting activities hardly took place on a weekly basis. The most common channels of communication between other ranks in the different contingents was at public bars when they were off-duty. Even this was limited to other ranks who were within the capital, Monrovia. It was more common amongst Nigerian and Ghanaian other ranks who worked in officers quarters to exchange visits and engage in general discussions. The common language also made this easier to achieve. Nigerian other ranks commented on the language barrier between them and the Guineans:

> Even though we go to the bar to drink with the Guineans sometimes, we don't have anything to say to each other, apart from smile. We act like deaf and dumb people.[19]

Generally, other ranks in each national contingent socialized amongst themselves. Within contingents where troops were from all three services, i.e. army navy, and air force, although there were exceptions, it was the general pattern for each branch to socialize within that group.

CONTACT WITH LOCAL COMMUNITY

Liberians in the capital, Monrovia and its immediate environs were, overall, favourably disposed toward ECOMOG. This could however not be said of Liberians in Gbarnga and areas under the control of Charles Taylor. Many of those in Monrovia, had witnessed first hand, ECOMOG's defence of Liberians and the casualties suffered by them during the enforcement phases. They frequently, freely expressed their appreciation of ECOMOG. The slogan which gained ground in Monrovia was 'Thank God for ECOMOG'. Posters reflecting this slogan were visible right from the Spriggs Payne airport. A radio programme was also aired frequently in Monrovia, called 'Thank god for ECOMOG'. With the passing of time however, this programme began to take the form of propaganda, as presenters often banned people from passing negative remarks about ECOMOG.[20]

The social impact of ECOMOG on the Liberian community was significant in the area of relationships with Liberian women. Young Liberian girls and women engaged in relationships with ECOMOG soldiers in large numbers. The need for such relationships were obvious on both sides. For the Liberian girls and women, the most common reasons for engaging in relationships with

---

[19] ECOMOG Lance Corporal in Nibatt 13
[20] Daily programme on Liberian radio.

ECOMOG troops were financial as well as what some described as the lack of trust between them and the Liberian men due to the war. The former however seemed to far outweigh the latter, so much so that ECOMOG officers and soldiers alike complained of the degree to which they felt they were being used by the Liberian women. For the ECOMOG troops, relationship with Liberian women appeared to be the result of long absences from home. This is especially true for (but by no means exclusive to) troops in the contingents where rotation was infrequent. Many ECOMOG officers and other ranks admitted that the long absences had adverse effects on their social life. In some cases, ECOMOG soldiers had fathered children by Liberian women. The following statements are some of the responses to the question which sought to identify the effects of the mission on the social life of the troops[21]:

> It has vehemently exposed me to moral decadence and habitual inclinations like smoking and drinking.[22]

> ... Increase in the number of my sexual partners and increase in [my] consumption of alcohol.[23]

> The lack of rotation of troops tends to make one feel the absence of his family thereby finding alternative solutions to one's social problems ...[24]

> Presently, a complete answer cannot be provided. However, it has completely messed up my marriage.[25]

The effect of this level of relationship between many ECOMOG soldiers and Liberian women on the operation is not negligible. Whilst some Liberian men condoned this (for different reasons), many were particularly bitter that their women were fraternizing deeply with ECOMOG troops, thereby 'degrading' themselves. Some Liberians accepted this as a pattern which develops in war-torn countries, often citing Vietnam as an example. Some mothers expressed concern about the relationship between ECOMOG troops and Liberian girls:

> The women, especially young girls, are with ECOMOG men. Most of them don't want to go back to school. I think that this is not right and [a risk to] their health. I'm sure that years from now this dreadful disease, AIDS, will be at a peak in our country because they are not taking any precautions.[26]

The NPFL leader, Charles Taylor, was also able to capitalize on this, by warning of the social repercussions of ECOMOG's continued stay in Liberia.

---

[21] Question 25 on the questionnaire – see appendix
[22] Respondent 68 – Nibatt 12 Lieutenant
[23] Respondent N0.19 – Lieutenant, ECOMOG HQ
[24] Respondent No.66 – Lieutenant, ECOMOG Ground Task Force, Monrovia.
[25] Respondent No.70 – Captain, Nigcon
[26] See Arms to Fight, Arms to Protect: Women Speak Out About Conflict, (PANOS London, June 1995), pp.49

This did not enhance ECOMOG's image in the international community where the social conduct of its troops in Liberia appeared to have become inseparable from any discussion of the ECOMOG operations and the peace process:

> Monrovians contrast the aggressive attitude of Nigerian soldiers with the softer approach of peacekeepers from Ghana. The Ghanaian soldiers are accused of one of the greatest abuses – the soaring increase in child prostitution, with girls as young as eight forced into selling sex.[27]

ECOMOG also made an impact on Liberia's war damaged economy. With most of Liberia's major installations severely damaged and frequently under the control of different warring factions, a Liberian economy was virtually non-existent. Under these circumstances, the income of ECOMOG troops had a significant effect on the economy. So did the presence of UNOMIL and other international agencies. ECOMOG soldiers at one time numbering over fourteen thousand, were paid in US dollars. The allowances of the Nigerian contingent alone whenever it was paid, often had a noticeable effect on the value of the Liberian dollar in the black market for example. The abundance of US Dollars in Liberia following the payment of ECOMOG salaries, often had the effect of lowering the exchange rate of the US Dollar to its Liberian counterpart, whilst it increased again as supply diminished.

Overall, the similarities in terms of shared experiences, historical and cultural background appeared to have far outweighed the differences between the national contingents in ECOMOG. This served to forge cohesion within ECOMOG. However, ECOMOG's interaction with the Liberian community had a more noticeable effect on the operation in terms of negative publicity generated by cases of indiscipline and relationships with Liberian girls. This also provided the NPFL with a rationale for opposing ECOMOG's presence in Liberia. This was however the inevitable result of some of the operational problems discussed in the previous chapter, such as infrequent rotation of troops in some of the contingents.

---

[27] *The Guardian* (UK), 13th February 1995.

II

SOURCES OF CLEAVAGE

Conflict between ECOMOG and ECOWAS

In assessing the level of cohesion within ECOMOG, this section discusses the types of cleavage within the force, the types of conflict arising from these cleavages and their effects on the operation. The model adopted by Moskos, in his analysis of the sources of cleavage and conflicts in UNFICYP is relied upon in this examination of ECOMOG conflicts.[28] Much of the cleavage in ECOMOG resulted from organizational politics. There was apparent strain between ECOMOG and the ECOWAS Secretariat in Nigeria. This strain manifested itself in several ways. The bulk of it derived from ECOWAS' inadequate political involvement on the ground in the mission area. It was expected by both ECOMOG and ECOWAS that the latter, which was the political authority in charge of the operation would constantly be present in Liberia, to negotiate with the warring factions and different parties to the conflict, whilst ECOMOG would concentrate mainly on the military/operational aspect of the peacemaking process. This was however not the case. The ECOWAS Secretary-General at the start of the operation, Abass Bundu, was actively involved with West African leaders in the formation and deployment of ECOMOG and travelled to Liberia at the initial stages of the operation. However, such involvement gradually diminished. This created dissatisfaction amongst ECOMOG officials, who felt that they were abandoned in Liberia, by ECOWAS. This issue was magnified by the fact that ECOWAS had no political presence at all on the ground in Liberia, especially during crucial stages of the operation. The posts of political and legal advisers created at the start of the operation were not filled due to lack of funds.[29]

The views expressed by ECOMOG officials and indeed, equally voiced by people outside the organization indicate the significance of lack of political involvement by ECOWAS. According to the Gambian contingent Commander,

> More needs to be done in the political aspect. At the ECOWAS Secretariat, they are the moderators of the military. The politicians must always be abreast of the situation. We are the instrument of the politicians, the end result of their decisions. Therefore, more is required of them. For example, the establishment of a special office to take care of whatever operations.[30]

---

[28] Moskos, *Peace Soldiers* , p. 66
[29] The COO interview. Advisers later came from ECOWAS Headquarters, but they were not based on the ground in Monrovia.
[30] The Gambian Contingent Commander interview.

Commenting on the lack of political presence, General Inienger admitted that rather than focusing solely on the military aspects of the operation, he also had to cope with political matters such as meeting with conflicting parties and negotiating with them.[31] He commented on the need to strengthen the command structure:

> For flow of information within the command structure, there should be linkage between the political authority and the military. There should be military presence at the ECOWAS Secretariat, pursuing the contributing nations.[32]

ECOMOG Chief Logistics officer and the Chief Military Information Officer put their views of ECOWAS more bluntly:

> ECOWAS has chickened out. Their officials do not even come here anymore.[33]

> ECOWAS has no political representative in Liberia. ... ECOWAS seems to have abandoned ECOMOG a long time ago, leaving it without any political direction.[34]

The UNOMIL Commander, General Opande, observed the lack of political presence on the ground in ECOMOG:

> There is lack of political representation on the ground from ECOWAS. The Force Commander is vested with both political and military responsibilities. There must be a clear political presence here.[35]

Amos Sawyer, who supported the ECOWAS/ECOMOG initiative in Liberia, commented on this problem and its effects on the peace process:

> One weakness of ECOMOG is that there is no political office side by side. This is why the UN has been the only one to interpret the political and social processes on the ground, wrongly, sometimes. Peacekeeping has a significantly military and political dimension. The political dimension has been missing here. The Force Commander is saddled with an enormous responsibility. The ECOWAS Executive Secretary has made infrequent visits to Liberia. He is hardly ever seen on the scene.[36]

The effect of vesting political and military authority with one man (i.e. the FC), was illustrated in Liberia. Prominent and ordinary Liberians alike, recalled how General Bakut's relationship with Charles Taylor transcended that between peacekeeper and warlord. Indeed, the prevailing opinion amongst opinion leaders in Liberia was that the somewhat personal relationship which developed between General Bakut and Charles Taylor prevented him from taking necessary precautions even when there were indications of an impend-

---

[31] The Inienger interview
[32] Ibid.
[33] The CLO interview.
[34] Personal interview with the Chief Military Information officer (CMIO). ***Hereafter, the CMIO interview.***
[35] The Opande interview.
[36] The Amos Sawyer interview.

ing NPFL attack on ECOMOG and Monrovia.[37] Whilst many Liberians saw this as a major weakness on the part of General Bakut, some correctly interpreted it as a result of the lack of political presence on the ground.

The one factor that was perhaps understated, and which undoubtedly contributed to the impression of General Bakut as non-responsive to the NPFL's provocation, was his preference for peacekeeping. His participation in the UN Interim Force in Lebanon (UNIFIL), where peacekeeping training placed emphasis on the use of force only in self defence, contributed in no small measure to his preference for this strategy.[38] Clifford Flemister recognized this when he stated in one of his letters to General Bakut:

> I do appreciate the logic of the strategy you are pursuing. In dealing with men and insti-
> tutions of principle, it is the only civilized approach. On the other hand, I am worried that
> the public is starting to become uneasy over what appears to be more of the same; ... a
> good concept becoming diluted through an exaggerated spirit of accommodation. The
> ordinary people of Liberia, and some of higher sophistication and more experience, share
> my doubts.[39]

The diminished political support and involvement by ECOWAS was explained as largely the result of financial constraints within the organization. Some ECOMOG officers admitted that ECOWAS was financially paralyzed, and thus it could not make much impact in Liberia, in terms of running the operation. ECOWAS had agreed to provide logistic support for the operation after the first thirty days during which individual contingents were to provide for their troops. Such support however, did not materialize after the thirty day period lapsed. The troop-contributing governments thus had to continue providing the logistic support for their troops. Beyond this however, ECOWAS' seeming lack of enthusiasm was attributed (in some quarters) to an apparent lack of interest on the part of the new Executive Secretary of the organization, who saw ECOMOG as the personal mission of his predecessor.[40]

Apart from these factors, there were structural problems. ECOWAS was founded as an economic organization although it gradually began to address political and security matters with the adoption of the Protocols on Non-aggression and Mutual Defence. It had no special organ responsible for conflict resolution or peacekeeping. Thus, even if the funds were available to enable ECOWAS take on the responsibility for provision of logistics, it was bound to encounter difficulty in co-ordinating the logistic distribution

---

[37] Amongst those prominent Liberians who expressed such views, were Bill Frank Enoanyi and Clifford Flemister of Citizens' Committee for Peace and Democracy (CCPD). Such views were also prevalent amongst Liberians who closely followed events and those, especially women, who were closely associated with ECOMOG officers and soldiers.

[38] Personal interview with General Bakut in Lagos, April 1993

[39] Letter from Clifford Flemister to General Ishaya Bakut, dated 15 May 1992.

[40] The Nigerian Diplomat interview.

effectively. The lack of such an organ enabled troop-contributing states to completely bypass the ECOWAS Secretariat in the logistic distribution and in the control of the operation.

CONFLICT BETWEEN ECOMOG AND CONTRIBUTING COUNTRIES

The obvious inactivity from ECOWAS shifted the focus of ECOMOG officers to the contributing governments on which they had to depend for logistic supplies and to some extent, political guidance. There were, however, areas of friction in this relationship. One issue which constantly came up was the lack of response from participating countries to ECOMOG demands for increase in troop contribution. Many ECOMOG officers expressed disappointment at the lack of reinforcement of troops by contributing countries. This was seen to slow down the operation and endanger lives of troops. Commentators have confirmed that ECOMOG troops are thinly deployed, particularly in greater Liberia. Mackinlay and Alao for example, remarked that:

> ECOMOG barely controlled a third of the country, its troops occupied weakly constructed positions along the main highways and there was no presence in depth between posts.[41]

Some ECOMOG officers argued that the operation could have been more effective and would have been concluded much earlier, if they had enough troops at their disposal.

Another obvious area of conflict between ECOMOG and contributing governments was what many officers considered to be the manipulation of the force by a number of governments. A lot of the issues raised appear to be consistent with the most frequent complaints levelled by the military against politicians. Many ECOMOG officers for example, were of the opinion that constant interference in the ECOMOG operations by different governments had some adverse effects on the mission. However, the influence from the Nigerian government (whether directly or indirectly), was considered the most important given Nigeria's influence on the entire operation and the size of its contingent. It was thought for example, that the international community sometimes pressurized Nigeria to soften its approach. Commenting on this issue, the ECOMOG Chief Logistics Officer said:

> Political pressures on Nigeria often made Nigeria relax its policy in Liberia. Otherwise, enforcement should have finished the situation once and for all.[42]

---

[41] Mackinlay and Alao, Liberia 1994: ECOMOG and UNOMIL response to a Complex Emergency

Remarking on the politics of the UN and the US, the ECOMOG Chief of Staff argued that:

> ...Both [the UN and US] have attempted to manipulate ECOMOG and destroy its efforts. Enforcement would have stopped Taylor long ago if it had not been halted by the US Since then, different types of politics have been played.[43]

According to the ECOMOG Chief Military Information Officer,

> The UN-US effort is to discredit ECOMOG, especially Nigeria. They are very good in propaganda, they have their machinery and they know what they want. ... They are using ECOMOG as pawns in their own game.[44]

This view is backed by those in Nigerian political circles in Liberia, who stated that Nigeria was pressurized by the US for example to put a quick end to the enforcement operation conducted in response to Octopus in 1993. They argue that this led to a hurried negotiation of the Cotonou Accord.[45] This view is also shared by many members of the Liberian elite, some of who believed that:

> On the political front, it seems that decisions are now being made in Washington through Mamba Point (The US Embassy). Abuja and Congo Town seem to be mere observers in a process which was, until recently, perceived as an African initiative led by the most powerful Black Nation in Africa or the world.[46]

One issue that also created strain between ECOMOG and some home governments concerned the payment of allowances. Officers in the Sierra Leone contingent for example resented the disparity between their rates of pay and those of other contingents. They expressed disappointment at the fact that after agreeing at the ECOWAS meeting which established ECOMOG that the troops would be paid a daily allowance of five US dollars, their government did not keep to this arrangement.[47] Nigcon troops complained about the delay in the payment of their salaries. The lack of timely and adequate logistic supplies was another issue of discontent in ECOMOG. The Nigerians complained about the home governments' delay in responding to requests for logistic supplies, especially military equipment and allowance. Ironically, most of the governments of troop-contributing states were initially under the control of the military. Thus, it often appeared that these military governments placed greater priority on political issues at home, rather than on matters such as the well-being of their troops at home and abroad.

---

[42] The CLO interview

[43] Personal interview with the ECOMOG Chief of Staff (COS) in July 1994. ***Hereafter the COS interview.***

[44] The CMIO interview

[45] The Nigerian Diplomat interview.

[46] Letter from Clifford Flemister to Brig. Gen. S.V.L. Malu, dated March 22, 1994.

[47] Discussion with Leocon officers, July 1994

CONFLICT BETWEEN ECOMOG MILITARY ESTABLISHMENTS OF CONTRIBUTING STATES

The general feeling within ECOMOG was that the military establishments of contributing countries did not have an understanding of what the force was experiencing in Liberia. Nigerians in particular commented on the level of ignorance within the Nigerian military about the ECOMOG operation. They discussed the varying perceptions of the ECOMOG operation within the Nigerian military. At the initial stages of the operation, when ECOMOG embarked on enforcement, many in the Nigerian army were reluctant to go to Liberia, while during the peacekeeping phase, it was seen as a money making venture.[48] The Chief Logistics Officer noted:

> Officers at home are not properly briefed. They believe that with the Cotonou Accord, lasting peace is now at hand. Initially, they felt Liberia was punishment ground. Today, they believe it is land flowing with milk and honey.[49]

Another issue that affected the relationship between ECOMOG and home military establishments concerned the effect of service in ECOMOG on the military careers of the troops. The general opinion amongst officers and other ranks was that the mission was advantageous to their military careers and that they were thus better placed than their colleagues at home. However, it appeared that they held this view for different reasons. For example, the Ghanaian contingent whose national armed forces focused on peacekeeping considered this an advancement of their peacekeeping career. For many of the troops in other countries, they believed that service in an international force would create more opportunities of this kind in the future.

Amongst other ranks in the Nigerian contingent, the possible strain between them and their contemporaries at home was most apparent. Their views were influenced largely by their experience during enforcement. Believing themselves to have been 'battle-tested' by the Liberian mission, many of them considered their contemporaries at home 'inexperienced'. Indeed, some considered themselves to be not only better soldiers than their own contemporaries, but also superior to many officers at home who had no experience of battle.

The response within the Guinean contingent to the issue of the effect of the ECOMOG assignment on their military careers at home was not as positive as that found in other contingents. It was however difficult to assess the reasons for this, given the problem of language barriers.[50] It could well have

---

[48] This was the general opinion amongst officers and other ranks in Nigcon.

[49] The CLO interview.

[50] Observations made at ECOMOG Headquarters.

been that the respondents did not fully understand the question or their responses were not well interpreted.

CONFLICT BETWEEN ECOMOG HEADQUARTERS AND NATIONAL CONTINGENTS

Officers confirmed that strain sometimes existed between ECOMOG headquarters and different contingents. Much of this strain concerned resentment over the tasking and location of contingents. General Iweze recalls how the Guinea Contingent Commander protested over the assignment the Guinean contingent was given at the beginning of the operation, arguing that their contingent was assigned the most difficult jobs. Within the Nigerian contingent for example, officers expressed their resentment of troop rotation when it meant that Brigade and contingent commanders would inherit areas where units which they considered less efficient had operated. This was the case for example when in preparation for troops rotating to and from Nigeria, the Field Commander made plans to swap entire brigades, much to the displeasure of a Brigade Commander who felt that they had worked hard to achieve a smooth running operation along his own axis, whilst the other brigade generally had a sloppy operation.

Overall, there was the tendency for the headquarters to be simultaneously pressurized by different national contingents, who had their own different ideas and practices on how the operation should be conducted. The Force Commander touched on the problem of managing this multinational force where the contingents had different attributes and practices. According to General Inienger,

> Traditions vary within the force, especially between francophone and anglophone troops. They have different ways of training. This calls for a lot of diplomacy.[51]

The Ghanaian contingent for example advocated a softer approach, believing that diplomacy and peacekeeping would enhance the peace effort rather than the use of force. Nigerian and Guinean officers on the other hand expressed support for peace enforcement options when it became necessary.

In attempting to balance these differences, the FC was frequently criticized by officers in the Nigerian contingent, who accused him of bowing to the wishes of the Ghanaians or the Guineans, on a number of issues. Some of these concerned approach and disciplinary issues. According to the Colonel GS, Nigerian contingent,

---

[51] The Inienger interview.

Operationally, the Nigerian contingent is managed by the FC. Administratively, it is managed by the Nigcon Commander. There are differences in management. There are always differences [between ECOMOG headquarters and Nigcon]. ... We are careful not to give the impression that we are not in agreement with the FC.[52]

INTER-CONTINGENT CONFLICT

Although genuine hostility between the contingents in ECOMOG was rare, there were a number of issues which created tension between them from time to time. Much of this was due to differences in orientation between francophone and anglophone countries, and differences in training and doctrine. Whilst the ECOMOG headquarters, particularly the Field Commander often tried to deal with the basic differences between anglophone and francophone troops diplomatically, the individual contingents appeared to be less influenced by this type of pressure. Thus, they spoke freely about the differences between the contingents, although some were more diplomatic than others.

Between the Nigerians and Ghanaians in particular, the strain centred around the issue of the former's preference for peacekeeping and the latter's quick embrace of peace enforcement. Whilst the Ghanaians acknowledged that some differences existed in this regard between themselves and the Nigerians, they were more diplomatic in voicing this feeling along with any others that they harboured about the Nigerians. The Nigerians on the other hand (both officers and other ranks), at any opportunity, referred to the Ghanaians as cowards, who preferred to appease Charles Taylor.[53] Some Nigerian officers went beyond this to claim that the Ghanaians' preference for peacekeeping even when it was most unreasonable to employ this method, was the result of a national agenda designed to support Taylor and aid his cause in Liberia.[54] There was however no evidence to support this claim that the Ghanaian opinion was part of a grand strategy in support of Charles Taylor. As argued in the previous chapter, it appeared that the peacekeeping orientation of the Ghanaians accounted for their softer approach.

In terms of anglophone–francophone differences, the Guineans were often criticized by the others, for their unusual practices. For example, their codes of conduct were considered by many to be sharply different from other contingents. Discipline was thought to be generally low amongst the Guineans. Many actions which were considered an offence in other contingents were

---

[52] The Nigcon Col. GS. interview.
[53] Discussions with Nigcon officers and other ranks.
[54] The Nigcon Colonel GS. interview.

viewed lightly by the Guineans, and in many cases were not considered offences. A Nigerian Lt. Col. for example commented on this issue:

> ... the interaction with officers and soldiers in other contingents is cordial to an extent. The main difficulties observed have been the different codes of discipline and military ethics which the various contingents uphold. You find that what constitutes an offence in the Nigerian contingent may not be so in Ghana and Guinea contingents.[55]

In addition, the social practices of the Guineans were condemned largely by the Nigerians. For example, the practice by Guinean officers, of sharing meals with other ranks and eating and socializing together was condemned by some Nigerian officers as sloppy, hardly professional. The Guineans on the other hand, regarded this as a good bonding exercise.[56] Views about the Malians were not so strong as they were extremely few in number and hardly participated in activities on the field with other contingents. They were all based at the headquarters. The Nigerians however saw the Guineans as very co-operative on strategic issues, and seen as a fearless bunch who would readily adopt an enforcement strategy without dragging their feet.

Although the Senegalese contingent had already been withdrawn at the time of the first field trip, soldiers who participated in the early phase of Octopus with the Senegalese soldiers described them as highly professional. This was corroborated by reports of researchers from the BBC who were present in Liberia during this period.[57] Nigerian soldiers commented on some of the issues that sometimes brought them into conflict with Senegalese soldiers. They were often criticised by the latter, for 'wasting fire power' during the advance to Buchanan. The Senegalese second Battalion (located from Somalia Drive to Johnsonsville) were part of joint operations with Guinea Contingent, Ghana Battalion seven and eight, Nigeria Battalion thirteen, and the AFL black berets, during the effort to repel the NPFL onslaught.[58]

One issue on which perhaps all other contingents were at loggerheads with the Nigerians concerned the latter's attitude to others when it came to the management of the operation. There were complaints that Nigerians were domineering and arrogant. Such complaints were clearly voiced by the Sierra Leoneans in particular, whilst the Ghanaians were more diplomatic in expressing their displeasure with such attitude. Sierra Leonean officers were very critical of the condescending manner in which they were dealt with by Nigerian Brigade Commanders.[59]

---

[55] Respondent No. 34
[56] Discussion with Guinean Contingent Commander (through interpreter).
[57] Discussion with reporters at BBC Focus on Africa.
[58] Records of an ECOMOG Lance Corporal.
[59] Discussion with a group of Sierra Leonean officers at their base at the Freeport, Monrovia in July 1994.

Apart from complaints by officers from other contingents, such attitudes were noticeable in some quarters during participant observation. For example, observing the CMIO (a Nigerian Lt. Col.) and Deputy CMIO (a Sierra Leonean Major) in their day to day operations, one got the distinct impression that the authority which the latter was subjected to by the former far transcended the requirements of military professionalism. It was somewhat different from the type of relationship which existed between Nigerian officers of the same ranks. Whilst much of this may be attributable to the individual personalities of the officers in question, the underlying feeling of superiority was noticeable amongst many Nigerian officers. A moderate version of such a relationship was observed between the CCO, a Nigerian Lt. Colonel, and the Deputy CCO, a Ghanaian Major.

However, the utterances of some of the Nigerian officers as well as prominent Nigerian politicians confirmed that this type of attitude existed and perhaps to a certain extent, why it did. Many Nigerians felt strongly that it was a tactical error on the part of Nigeria, to have allowed the force to be placed initially under the command of a non-Nigerian officer, regardless of the political motivations that lay behind the adoption of such a policy or decision. They argued that, since Nigeria was ready to deploy men and materiel on such a substantial level, its officers should have been given total command of the force and be allowed to make the vital decisions about how these resources should be utilized or employed. In support of this, they argued that the US would not be part of an international force, such as in the Gulf war and in Somalia, and hand over the command of their men and equipment to foreigners. Thus, they believed that this must not be allowed to happen again – Nigeria's voice must be loud in Liberia, and dominate all the vital aspects of the operation. In a lot of respects, Nigerians, saw any challenge to their opinions as an attempt to wrestle control of the force from their hands. It was this sort of view that created strain between Nigerian officers at Nigcon headquarters, and those at the ECOMOG headquarters.

This situation was, perhaps, exacerbated by the fact that many of the other contingents depended on Nigeria for the resources to run the entire operation. Thus they appeared to be in awe of the Nigerians, and allowed them to 'call the shots'. The control which petroleum, (Nigeria's main foreign exchange earner), put in the hands of Nigerian officers was significant. A lot of deals were done, and relationships cultivated as a result of Nigeria's command of this particular resource. The fuel for the entire operation, including that needed for the day to day running of each contingent, their vehicles and electricity for their accommodation was supplied by Nigeria. Thus, this was a subtle form of control over other contingent commanders, and indeed, institutions outside ECOMOG. ECOMOG officers often negotiated items like accommodation, or supply of electricity via generating plants, by exchanging them for fuel. This made for cost effective operations in some respects. This sort of situation also allowed the Nigerians to get away with attitudes like those described above, to members of the other contingents, from time to time.

INTRA-CONTINGENT CONFLICT

For the same reasons discussed in Chapter Five, intra-contingent conflict was most apparent within the Nigerian contingent. This type of conflict existed on several levels. The most common conflict within contingents was between officers and other ranks. The prevalent view amongst other ranks (in most contingents) was that officers benefited immensely from the ECOMOG mission, whilst the welfare of other ranks was largely ignored. For example, many of the soldiers interviewed confirmed that they had been in the mission area continuously without any contact with their families.[60] In a lot of cases, soldiers had been in Liberia since the November 1992 following the launching of 'Operation Octopus'. On the other hand, officers had frequent contacts with their families, both via the telephone, and in person. Other ranks also had limited access to medical facilities, often having to pay for part of the cost of medication. The effect of this became apparent in the Nigerian contingent, with increase in cases of insubordination, where soldiers sometimes reacted badly to officers at check points.

The other level of conflict was between senior and junior officers. Although not as grave as the testimonies of the soldiers, the junior officers complaints also addressed similar issues. According to a Nigerian Lieutenant,

> I have learnt that our leaders don't have the welfare of their troops at heart. They are all interested in making money.[61]

This is also partly the result of infrequent rotation. The effect which such a situation could have was emphasized by a crisis within the Nigerian contingent, where a Captain shot a Major. The former was later court martialled.

This section has revealed many of the cleavages in ECOMOG. Being a multinational force, there were also variations in the levels of internal social cohesion and cleavage within each national contingent. However, the force as a whole appeared relatively integrated despite the cleavages and resultant conflicts. The cleavages were not so significant as to overwhelm the cohesion derived from the common social features of the troops. It now remains to see

---

[60] With the exception of the Ghanaians who stated that they had regular contact with their families.

[61] Respondent No.68 – Nigerian Lieutenant, Nibatt 12

how a combination of the social composition and internal cleavage affected peace creation attitudes within the force.

III

PEACE CREATION ATTITUDES

As has already been established in previous chapters, one of the peculiarities of the ECOMOG operation is that the effort in many respects, sought to create peace rather than to simply keep an arranged peace. This peace creation effort entailed the constant intermix of peacekeeping duties with those of enforcement. The previous chapter already showed that the same troops may have to perform both peacekeeping and enforcement duties intermittently. Subsequently, it illustrated how human and logistical factors can hinder a smooth transition from one phase to another. Human factors were revealed for example, to have created problems in switching from peace enforcement to peacekeeping, whilst logistic and preparatory problems were more closely associated with transition from peacekeeping to peace enforcement.

Questions remain about the type of troops needed to conduct such an operation effectively: Does a soldier require special training for peace creation? Are training in peacekeeping and that beyond soldierly skills required in order to effectively create peace in this manner? Can a well trained soldier under proper leadership possess the flexibility to perform both duties intermittently? A number of assumptions can be made in an attempt to provide answers to these questions and they would depend on the way each of the components of peace creation is defined. For example, if peacekeeping is defined simply as a non-coercive strategy, one might assume that a soldier who imbibes constabulary ethics would make a good peacekeeper. If peace enforcement is seen merely as war, one might also assume that a soldier who is well trained and prepared for combat operations will make a good peace enforcer. Even if both terms were given these simple meanings, it remains to be seen whether both skills can reside with one man and whether he employs them with the same level of effectiveness. It was initially assumed (prior to the field research), that a soldier only required good military training for peace enforcement and that with training in peacekeeping principles, he may employ any of these skills as required, although not without problems. However, the way a soldier, no matter how well trained, perceives and interprets his role, and his attitude to the mission, are undoubtedly crucial to the outcome of an operation.

The question also arises as to whether the findings about the social origins and cleavages in the first two sections of this chapter have any relevance for an understanding of peace creation and attitudes of troops. Although it is difficult to measure precisely, the effects of these factors (i.e. social composition, cohesion and cleavage), on the force's ability, and troops' attitude to peace creation, two factors would give some indication of their impact on the operation. These include a common perception of what peace creation entails, and the development of a common ideology, both of which may have resulted from similar social orientation. Thus, apart from identifying the important variables of peace creation, this section illustrates how individual perception of the troops about these variables can influence an operation significantly.

One of the most significant findings to arise out of the field research was that despite the differences in orientation, training and doctrine between the different contingents, a belief had emerged amongst officers in nearly all the contingents, on the need to blend peacekeeping and peace enforcement as required.[62] Although the sharp differences between the Ghanaian contingent and others discussed above existed, it is significant that despite the peacekeeping orientation of the Ghanaians, a considerable proportion of its officers and soldiers had come to recognize the need for peace creation, albeit reluctantly. This view was brought about by a combination of orientation and experience in the field. The latter appeared to be more relevant in the case of Ghana. The single most important factor which gave rise to this was the intransigence of Charles Taylor. This had resulted in the death of several ECOMOG soldiers that the troops seemed determined not to allow this to happen again. There was still some disagreement however, on the timing of enforcement actions (See below). It is also interesting that there was a recognition of the need to create peace amongst officers of the expanded ECOMOG, even though they were unwilling to take part in operations beyond peacekeeping.

Having made the behavioural observations, an attempt was made to assess the attitudinal commitment to peace creation principles, from officers' responses to the questionnaire. One difficulty encountered in doing this was the problem of measuring precisely, what constituted peace creation. Until this stage, there was an assumption that a soldier would consider peace enforcement to be virtually the same as war. Thus, for a soldier to embrace this peace creation concept, he would be ready to combine his soldierly qualities with constabulary ethics. As such, he would be able to shift from peacekeeping duties to a situation of all out war, and consider expertise in both areas as equally important. Whether he was able to easily abandon his regular military

---

[62] This belief was predominant amongst Nigerians initially and it gradually spread to other contingents. See findings from the questionnaire below.

training and swap this for a constabulary one had been a crucial question from the start. Many of the problems encountered in doing so were discussed in Chapter Five.

This concept was measured from responses to three items on the questionnaire (see appendix): first is question 10, which consists of two items – 'In addition to training in military skills, are additional skills needed for (a) Peacekeeping? (b) Peace enforcement?'; and question 11 – 'Would you say that there are differences between peace enforcement and military operations aimed at defeating an enemy in battle? ECOMOG Officers who provided affirmative answers only to the first of these questions (i.e. 10a), whilst giving negative answers to the other two were categorized as constabulary. Officers who answered yes to all three were seen as possessing peace creation attributes. Those who answered yes to the first and third (i.e. 10a and 11), were judged to have partial peace creation attitudes, whilst those who gave negative answers to the first question, and all others were rated as non-constabulary, to allow for a dichotomous breakdown.

Those officers who were rated as belonging to the same category almost always provided similar reasons for their choices. The 'constabulary officer' saw peacekeeping as requiring a non-combative and non-coercive disposition, a totally different posture from the soldierly skills he possessed. Thus, he saw peacekeeping as requiring special training, different from that which he received as a soldier. In addition, such an officer frowned on the use of force even in the name of peace. He considered peace enforcement a euphemism for outright combat or war and this did not call for additional training to that received as a soldier. He was also of the opinion that a soldier can be an effective peacekeeper if he cannot use force except in self defence. The 'peace creator', who answered yes to all three had the same view of peacekeeping as the constabulary officer. However, he saw peace enforcement as different from war, a necessary operation which was carried out in the name of peace. The reasons for this view are discussed further below. In addition, he thought that a soldier must be taught to exercise caution during peace enforcement in order to avoid the excesses of war. Like the peace creator, the 'partial peace creator' saw peacekeeping as requiring special training and saw peace enforcement as distinct from war. Unlike the former however, he believed that soldierly skills were sufficient to conduct peace enforcement. The 'non-constabulary officer' did not agree that peacekeeping, or peace enforcement required any further training. His position was that a conventionally well-trained soldier under proper leadership, would be flexible enough to perform peacekeeping duties, along with those of enforcement. Within this group however, there was a debate as to whether peace enforcement was different from war. The non-constabulary officer was also of the opinion that a soldier could not be an effective peacekeeper if he could not use force except in self defence.

Of the officer sample, 9% could definitely be categorized as constabulary officers while 47% demonstrated peace creation attitudes, answering yes to all three questions. The partial peace creators constituted 18% of the sample. Thus, 65% of this sample could be described as leaning toward peace creation. It is however difficult to generalize about these findings, given the small size of the sample, and the fact that this sample was predominantly Nigerian (see appendix). The extremely small size of contingents like Gambia, with 1 officer and 9 men, and Mali, with 3 officers and 7 men (see Table 6.1) highlights the difficulty in relying on the general applicability of these figures. However, the fact remains that officers from each national contingent contributed to the data, providing invaluable information on their experiences and views on the operation. This was obtained through observation, questionnaires and interviews. What they had to say about the operation and their perceptions of peace creation are immensely useful in understanding the term.

Table 6.1:

Country	Officers	ORanks	Country Total	% of Officers
Gambia	1	9	10	10%
Ghana	73	1048	1121	7%
Guinea	140	440	580	24%
Sierra Leone	16	348	364	4%
Mali	3	7	10	30%
Nigeria	442	7489	7931	6%
Tanzania	41	733	774	5%
Uganda	53	731	784	7%

Ghanaian officers were generally regarded as constabulary by a cross section of ECOMOG officers, (including the Ghanaians). There was an abhorrence of peace enforcement amongst the Ghanaian officers. However, some of them believed that there was some distinction to be made between peace enforcement and war. An analysis of this is conducted below. In addition, some Ghanaians reluctantly admitted that the need arises sometimes to switch from peacekeeping to peace enforcement, but this must be done only under certain conditions:

> One must know when to switch from peacekeeping. You switch only when your life has been threatened.[63]

---

[63] The COO interview.

Switching to enforcement under such a situation may in fact still amount to peacekeeping, where force is applied in self defence.

The dominance of constabulary ethics amongst Ghanaian officers was attributed by many officers in other ECOMOG contingents, to their training and wealth of experience in traditional peacekeeping. The statements below represent some of the responses to the question asking them to rate peacekeeping qualities in all the contingents.

> ...Qualities in peacekeeping and peace enforcement are separate. Soldiers who have performed in previous UN operations in other theatres, seem to conform to the same practice much easier. In this wise, the Ghanaian contingent whose troops have been on that operation more than twice are good in peacekeeping.[64]

> Ghana is excellent in peacekeeping while Nigeria and others are fair.[65]

> The Ghanaians have been engaged in such [peacekeeping] missions for quite sometime now. Next is the Nigerian contingent. Although both set the pace for others, the Ghanaians are on top.[66]

> The Ghanaians seem to have benefited immensely from their UN peacekeeping exposure world-wide.[67]

Officers who displayed peace creation tendencies advanced reasons for their support of peace creation, particularly their preference for combining enforcement action with peacekeeping. They argued that the threat or the use of force is important in any peace operation and in its planning. According to the Commander of the 221 Light Tank battalion,

> Rebels will ever be rebels. Even though they sign documents 100 times, they can always renege on such accords. Rebels must be treated by concerted efforts of all peace-loving countries through peace enforcement.[68]

Perhaps the most surprising revelation from this effort to understand the troops' acceptance and commitment to peace creation was the fact that the vast majority of those who supported it (and indeed many amongst the non-constabulary officers) had a different perception of peace creation from that earlier assumed in this study prior to the field research. The responses from majority of the officers indicated that they did not consider peace creation to be a combination of peacekeeping and war, because they saw war as distinct from peace enforcement. Many of the officers who portrayed an attachment to peace creation indicated during discussions that they considered both peacekeeping and enforcement as delicate exercises which required deeper understanding and special training. Amongst partial peace creation officers

---

[64] Respondent No. 67 – A Nigerian Lt. Colonel
[65] Respondent No. 19 – Nigerian Lt.
[66] Respondent No. 46 – A Sierra Leone Major.
[67] Respondent No. 28 – A Nigerian Major.
[68] Respondent No. 67 – Nigerian Lt. Colonel.

there was the view that once a soldier received basic peacekeeping training, normal military training was sufficient to conduct peace enforcement. They however all categorically agreed that there is a distinct difference between peace enforcement and war.

The statements from a cross section of ECOMOG officers revealed their perception of what peace enforcement entails, thus contributing to an overall understanding of peace creation. Even amongst constabulary and non-constabulary officers, a significant proportion agreed that there was a distinction between both terms, thus indicating an almost unanimous perception of peace enforcement within ECOMOG. In support of their argument that peace enforcement is different from war, the statements below represent some of these officers' reasons for this view.

The tactics, techniques and psychology applied are different in each case.[69]

Enforcement may require an aggressive and frightening approach and if necessary, light offensive on the stubborn faction. A full [military] operation entails total offensive to incapacitate the enemy.[70]

Peace enforcement aims at disarming and demobilizing the combatants, while military operations aimed at defeating an enemy in battle aim at destroying and killing.[71]

In peace enforcement, total annihilation and destruction of enemy and its military installations is prohibited. But in defeating an enemy in battle, maximum force and means are employed.[72]

Peace enforcement may be necessary solely when the force is attacked and thus forced to defend itself. The aim is not to defeat the attackers who are not considered as enemies.[73]

In peace enforcement, minimum force is applied to avoid casualties and damage, as opposed to military operations.[74]

Military operations as against peace enforcement are devoid of persuasion, diplomacy etc. Peace enforcement is limited in scope.[75]

In peace enforcement, there must be preservation of civilian lives. There is also the need to create an environment for peaceful negotiations.[76]

Peace enforcement is aimed at pressurising warring factions to honour peace agreement. In military operations aimed at defeating an enemy in battle, consequently, the victor forces set conditions on the losing army to obey without options to refuse e.g. Gulf war.[77]

---

[69] Respondent No. 23 – Nigerian Lt. Colonel.
[70] Respondent No.8 – Nigerian Lt. CDR, Naval Task Force
[71] Respondent No.40 – Tanzanian Col.
[72] Respondent 68 – Nigerian Lt.
[73] Respondent No. 42 – Malian Col.
[74] Respondent No. 5 – Ghanaian Lt.
[75] Respondent No. 69 – Nigerian Captain
[76] Respondent No. 4 – Ghanaian Lt. Col.
[77] Respondent No. 1 – Nigerian Navy Captain.

One interesting conclusion that may be drawn from these opinions is that constabulary ethics and peace creation are closely related and as such, peacekeeping and peace creation in terms of their objectives are not so far apart. Officers who displayed either tendency, agreed on the need for limited application of force. The variation is only in degree. The major difference in the views of the constabulary officers and those who supported peace creation techniques is on when to apply force. For example, whilst absolutely seeing the need for the use of force during the NPFL attack on ECOMOG and Monrovia in October 1992, the Ghanaians (largely constabulary), were sceptical about the consequent ECOMOG counter-attack on the NPFL. The Nigerians on the other hand, considered this an attempt to prevent the rebels from launching an attack on ECOMOG, as well as part of an overall effort to create a peacekeeping and peacemaking environment.

Peace creation officers from Ghana, Mali and Tanzania highlighted issues such as the need to use force only when troops were attacked; the preservation of civilian lives; and disarmament and demobilization. However, the general willingness within ECOMOG, to accept the need for peace creation, coupled with the almost uniform view of peace enforcement, made it possible to sustain this type of operation, despite the basic differences between the units. A kind of internal cohesion was formed over time through shared experiences, which became an important determinant of the continuation and success of the mission.

COMMON IDEOLOGY

In addition to the developing cohesion described above, there was indeed a strong bond between the national contingents within ECOMOG, which made the sustenance of the mission inevitable, despite the obvious differences within the force. This bond was largely the result of a common ideology. Although it was difficult to identify a military ideology amongst all the national contingents, common ideological themes were found which helped to explain ECOMOG officers' attitudes to peace creation. These include a strong sense of Pan-Africanism and regionalism. There was a spirit of African nationalism amongst all the contingents and participating nations, which resulted from shared historical experiences. There was a general perception of the ECOMOG operation as a unique one which could set precedence for future missions. Accompanying this was a common desire to record such a successful mission on the African continent.

The latter factor was confirmed not only during discussions, but through the responses of many officers to question 18 which sought to know whether they considered the ECOMOG mission to be considerably different from a UN one. It provided an insight into just how unique they perceived their assignment to be. Over 90% of the respondents considered the mission to be different from a UN one, providing reasons for their views. Some of these are indicated here:

> You don't have to get all the protagonists to accept your involvement.[78] The over burden of the bureaucracy of the UN is avoided [saving time].[79]

> ECOMOG has more commitment, more integration and it is more cost effective.[80]

> Except in Somalia, UN had always preferred peaceful settlement and would want the use of minimum force. ... Peace enforcement is most desirable for African conflict resolution because this is the only language rebels can understand.[81]

> I consider the UN missions different from this because they fail to effect the most effective mandate.[82]

> ECOMOG mission is different in the fact that it does not stand aloof in the resumption of any large scale war in Liberia ... ECOMOG uses force when it is deemed necessary for the general good of all. All these are contrary to UN missions.[83]

The desire to see a precedent set in Africa, coupled with a strong pan-African belief, immensely unified the force. African nationalist issues were brought to the fore both at the official and personal levels within ECOMOG and this factor played no small part in strengthening the resolve of the force, to make the mission a success.

At the official level, strong Africanist views were openly expressed:

> The reality is that the African solution which the White World community espoused while looking toward the Gulf in 1990 is now confounding them because it is succeeding. They are trying to usurp the gains made by Africans, and President Sawyer and his associates deeply resent this. The Liberians continue to look to ECOWAS for a lasting and acceptable solution.[84]

The personal views of many officers further indicated the strength of their commitment to seeing the success of an 'all-African' mission:

> A sub-regional initiative from Africa is as good as any original initiative from developed countries. Despite diversity, ECOMOG troops have successfully operated together. Ideas from within the force are put into practice and success recorded despite adverse cautions on such approach. Despite economic shortcomings, sheer determination by the sub-region

---

[78] That is, consent is not necessary.
[79] Respondent No. 11 – Gambian Captain
[80] Respondent 59 – Nigerian Major
[81] Respondent No. 67 – Nigerian Lt. Colonel
[82] Respondent No. 53 – Sierra Leonean Lieutenant
[83] Respondent 52 – Sierra Leonean Lieutenant
[84] Situation Paper Re Encampment and Disarmament Exercise – ECOMOG Headquarters, Monrovia, December 6, 1991

has earned it recognition world-wide. Deliberate efforts to frustrate the noble initiatives are glaringly seen.[85]

The ECOMOG operation has taught the whole world that sub-regions all over the world can solve their problems, not necessarily depending on the already over-stretched UN.[86]

ECOMOG fosters brotherhood. It has broken the myth that Africans are incapable of solving their own problems.[87]

The ECOMOG mission is a very good initiative. It helps bring unity within the sub-region.[88]

It is a very laudable idea for countries of the West African sub-region to come together to aid a neighbour in distress. Although there are cultural and language problems, the participating contingents do get on very well and learn from each other.[89]

African brothers can be a helpmate for others in period of problems and hostilities, and Africans should not rely too much on aid from western nations.[90]

CONCLUSION

ECOMOG's social composition increased the level of cohesion within the force. The similarities in political, economic and historical experiences played no small part in unifying the force despite the obvious differences. This factor contributed to ECOMOG's ability to carry out an operation which went beyond peacekeeping, to one of peace creation in Liberia. In terms of its social organization, ECOMOG was in many respects similar to other multinational forces. The one atypical feature was its strong African composition. The organizational strains found within ECOMOG were also not unlike those found in other multinational forces. Such strains were not the result of genuine hostilities. Rather, they were largely the result of differences in orientation between anglophone and francophone forces; and differences in experiences amongst anglophone countries. The conflicts that resulted from peculiarities such as the division in command of personnel and other logistic supplies, was the inevitable result of ECOWAS' poor financial state.

Ordinarily, these factors may have made it almost impossible for ECOMOG to function as an organization, let alone conduct a simple peacekeeping operation. For example, despite the sharp divisions at the initial stages, particularly between the Ghanaian and Nigerian contingents in training and

---

[85] Respondent No. 67 op. cit.
[86] Respondent No. 66 – Nigerian Lieutenant.
[87] Respondent No.52
[88] Respondent No. 42 – Malian Colonel
[89] Respondent No.4 – Ghanaian Lt. Colonel
[90] Respondent No. 17 – Nigerian Lieutenant

doctrine, and in their attitudes to peace enforcement, the contingents continued to operate together. National contingents have been known to withdraw from other multinational operations (e.g. UN operation in the Congo) for reasons that were not as significant as this. Thus, although organizational politics revealed internal cleavage, this was not strong enough to weaken the capacity of the force to work together to create peace. The shared sense of African heritage was the overriding factor which forged a common purpose that increased the morale and commitment of the troops to finding an African solution to the Liberian problem.

The common perception of peace creation and the largely favourable attitude to the employment of this strategy amongst ECOMOG officers appeared to have resulted from three main factors. First was the common historical origin and broad African culture discussed above. Whilst this factor served to increase the level of cohesion within the force, it forged a common sense of purpose amongst the contingents. Their beliefs, and desire to see Africa attain prominence on the international scene increased their determination to see the mission succeed. This is linked to the second factor – the size of the Nigerian contingent and the country's influence on many countries in the sub-region. The desire to see an African mission succeed was linked to Nigeria's desire to rise to greatness on the world scene and it had the resources to influence some of the participating states to remain in the operation. Whether this would have translated into an impenetrable alliance is another issue altogether. Lastly, the longer the contingents operated together in the mission area, the more integrated they became. Thus, their views on several aspects of the operation were converging as the operation progressed. Much of this was the result of operational experiences in the field. This should not, however, underrate the effect of the similarities which kept them together even at the times when they had no prior joint operational experience to rely on, and when the variation in logistic provision, doctrine and training patterns served to highlight the cleavages within the force.

CHAPTER SEVEN

Conclusion

In the first chapter, this study identified some of the problems confronting peacekeeping in efforts to resolve post-Cold War conflicts. Perhaps the most significant of these problems is that peacekeeping, in its traditional or wider variant, cannot deal effectively with violent conflict situations which result in humanitarian emergencies, where conflicting parties do not heed calls for peace. In addition, the chapter identified a gap in current peacekeeping literature, as much of it fails to outline a workable concept for constructively addressing such conflicts. This gap has been partially filled through a number of studies, for example, those by Gow and Dandeker, which recognize the need for strategies that extend beyond peace keeping and include a measure of enforcement. Although the present study supports this standpoint, it diverges from Gow and Dandeker's concept of 'strategic peacekeeping' in that it recognizes that a higher level of force may be necessary to control such difficult conflicts, and such force may be employed intermittently with peacekeeping.

The Liberian civil war discussed in this book is an example of those conflicts that result in uncontrollable humanitarian disasters. It has illustrated many of the problems posed by intra-state conflict in the post-Cold War period. Without the constraints normally imposed by superpower rivalry, the Liberian conflict escalated to a serious level. Terror was utilized fully as a weapon of this war, creating more casualties amongst civilians than soldiers, who in many cases could hardly be distinguished from non-combatants. Chapter Three discussed how the horrors of the war were taken beyond Liberia's borders to Sierra Leone for example, and the refugee crisis in neighbouring states, and atrocities against foreign subjects. Early attempts to render humanitarian assistance were futile in this environment. In addition to the carnage, the signs of genocide were an indication that the Liberian conflict could not be ignored by the international community without catastrophic consequences. Rwanda would later illustrate the effects of neglecting such conflicts.

The NPFL rejection of a peace offer, coupled with its threats to attack ECOMOG demonstrated the difficulty in gaining consent for peace operations in intra-state conflicts of this nature. In the absence of consent, peacekeeping – traditional and second generation, were precluded as a response to the Liberian conflict. Prospective peacemakers were then left to choose between using force to stop the carnage, or waiting for the conflict to run its course. The latter option would have meant ignoring all sorts of humanitarian considerations like those, which existed in Liberia and perhaps meant indifference to casualties and tragedies on the scale later seen in Rwanda. The decision to intervene raised all sorts of legal questions such as issues of sovereignty and grounds for humanitarian intervention, many of which were discussed in Chapter Four.

In Liberia, it was clear that for any peacemaking effort to resolve effectively, or at least manage the conflict, then the carnage and the violence must first be stopped. In the absence of the unanimous consent and co-operation of all the parties, a peaceful atmosphere which, would at the very least, enable delivery of humanitarian aid had to be created. This necessitated the use of force. Even then, traditional peacekeeping was first attempted in Liberia. But this, or indeed, wider peacekeeping was not possible, given the attacks on ECOMOG by the dissenting faction. Thus, the problem was how to devise an effective response to deal with the increasing disaster, and to resolve the conflict.

This book has contributed to the search for an effective concept, and approach for resolving complex internal conflicts, through its analysis of the ECOMOG and ECOWAS response to crisis in West Africa. It makes a significant contribution to the literature in four respects. First, is its proposal, and analysis of 'peace creation', which transcends the two generations of peacekeeping in its scope for dealing with such conflicts as Liberia. The book has looked at organizational and practical issues surrounding the implementation of this concept. Second, through its examination of peace creation, it has contributed to the analysis of second generation peacekeeping. Third, it has examined specific regional problems associated with peace creation, and in the process, second generation peacekeeping. Lastly, it has raised questions on the prospects for conducting such operations at the global level, and on the relationship, that must exist between the UN and regional bodies in the conduct of such operations.

CONCEPTUAL FRAMEWORK REVISITED

In assessing the contribution of this book to the search for a viable concept for dealing with complex internal conflicts, it is necessary to revisit some of the conceptual issues discussed in Chapter One, in the light of the analysis of the Liberian experience.

What is 'Peace Creation'?

Peace creation refers to a situation where an intractable conflict results in humanitarian tragedy, thus compelling the use of force to remedy such a situation, with the willingness to abandon this course of action for a political option as soon as the opportunity arises. This would entail the intermittent use of peace enforcement and peacekeeping. The ability of the peacemaker to abandon peace enforcement for a resolution, thus allowing the military to maintain a secure atmosphere, differentiates this activity from other military ones aimed at defeating an enemy or annexing territory.

Was the ECOMOG operation one of 'peace creation'? To a large extent it was, although the regional organization stumbled upon this approach. Peace creation was more apparent in the first enforcement period when ECOMOG abandoned the use of force as soon as it had successfully pushed the rebels back and stopped the carnage. The ECOWAS peacemakers then pursued diplomatic options exhaustively until the NPFL launched 'Operation Octopus'. After successfully ending the killings, ECOWAS did not employ other enforcement strategies such as economic blockade against the factions, as discussed in Chapter Four. In the second enforcement phase, following the NPFL attack on Monrovia and ECOMOG headquarters, the use of force was pursued vigorously by ECOMOG. It was now believed that the NPFL would agree to make peace only by denying it the means to make war. This was largely effective. However, it is necessary to understand the nature of the peacekeeping and peace enforcement that constitute peace creation.

PEACEKEEPING

The first chapter looked extensively at traditional peacekeeping. However, the analysis of Liberia in later chapters, revealed that peacekeeping as it was conceptualized in the 1950s and maintained till the end of the Cold War is irrelevant to many conditions of the post-Cold War era. The nature of peacekeeping in new internal conflicts, as Liberia confirmed, is such that the task of the military is multifarious. From the moment ECOMOG landed in Liberia, it was faced with responsibilities of various dimensions, which included protection of refugees and administering of humanitarian aid. Its role later expanded to the protection of aid convoys, paving of roads to the interior, airlifting of relief food and other supplies, as described in Chapter Five. This was by no means traditional peacekeeping of observation, creation of buffer zones and interposition. Rather, ECOMOG's activity during the peacekeeping phase very much resembled the 'wider peacekeeping' tasks described by

Dobbie, and 'second generation' operations depicted by Mackinlay, Ratner, and others. Thus, peace creation is rather like a combination of peace enforcement and 'wider' or 'second generation' peacekeeping.

PEACE ENFORCEMENT

Although the conventional meaning of peace enforcement discussed in Chapter One is accepted, the analysis of the Liberian civil war and the ECOMOG operation sheds more light on the meaning of this term. The analysis of data from the field research in Chapter Six revealed the views of different ECOMOG officers, about the enforcement operations that they conducted. Whilst some officers saw peace enforcement as hardly different from war, others made clear distinctions between both activities. Many ECOMOG officers indicated that enforcing peace entailed limited objectives, unlike operations designed to defeat an enemy in battle, which may require total annihilation of the enemy, or seizure of territory, amongst other things. Thus, although peace enforcement and war appear similar, they are differentiated by their political objectives, events on the ground, and indeed, the perception of the soldiers and officers involved in their planning and execution. The circumstances under which peace enforcement may be employed are however linked to those surrounding peace creation discussed below.

COMPARING THE COMPONENTS OF PEACE CREATION

Second Generation Peacekeeping and Peace Enforcement

Peace creation clearly has two major functions: to halt human suffering or prevent its occurrence, and to contribute to the resolution of conflict. The first is largely military, whilst the second is multifaceted. In other words, peace creation would require both peace enforcement and second generation peacekeeping. The features of these two activities appear almost irreconcilable. The first excludes consent whilst the other depends on it. As Ratner has pointed out, '... consent remains the sine qua non of peacekeeping, and any mission that includes war-fighting by the Blue Helmets is operating under a different set of conceptual and practical assumptions and constraints'.[1]

In analysing the components of peace creation, this study could not avoid the analysis of second generation peacekeeping. The relationship between peacekeeping (second generation) and peace enforcement during peace

---

[1]   Ratner, *The New UN Peacekeeping*, p.18, see also Chapter One.

creation, as part of an overall peacemaking process is illustrated by Figure 7.1[2] below.

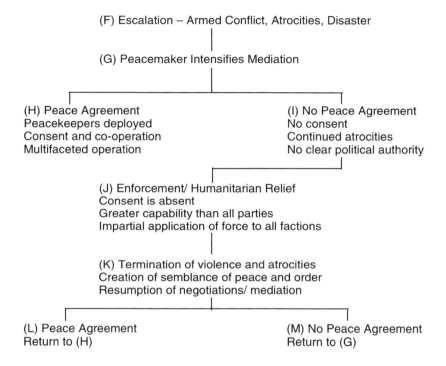

(F) Escalation – Armed Conflict, Atrocities, Disaster

(G) Peacemaker Intensifies Mediation

(H) Peace Agreement
Peacekeepers deployed
Consent and co-operation
Multifaceted operation

(I) No Peace Agreement
No consent
Continued atrocities
No clear political authority

(J) Enforcement/ Humanitarian Relief
Consent is absent
Greater capability than all parties
Impartial application of force to all factions

(K) Termination of violence and atrocities
Creation of semblance of peace and order
Resumption of negotiations/ mediation

(L) Peace Agreement
Return to (H)

(M) No Peace Agreement
Return to (G)

Figure 7.1 builds upon the picture given by Figure 1.1 in Chapter One, concerning the peacemaking process. The above figure explains the role of peace creation after the failure of initial diplomatic efforts. Upon the escalation of disruptive conflict behaviour, the peacekeeping effort following a peace agreement in **H** may be a multifaceted one carried out with the consent of warring parties. The opposite is the case where continued atrocities and human suffering lead to enforcement action in **I**. Here, the operation is not dependent upon the consent and co-operation of the parties. However, its ability to discharge its duty impartially just like in peacekeeping, is crucial to its success. In particular, its ability to embark upon the type of peacekeeping in **H** after the termination of atrocities and peace agreement in **L** will very much depend upon this impartial stance. Throughout this process, the military takes its cue from the peacemakers or representatives of the mediating body. Although the military is in effect acting upon the wishes of the politicians, there is an interdependent relationship between them as discussed in Chapter

---

[2]   Figure 7.1 develops on figure 1.1 from level F. See Chapter One.

One. The politicians or mediators also depend on the military to create an atmosphere where peace may be negotiated.

Thus, Figure 7.1 sends two important messages. First, peacekeeping, albeit in its wider variant, may sufficiently deal with a conflict, depending on its nature. In this case, the process ends at **H**. Second, where a conflict escalates to **I**, the response transcends peacekeeping, to peace creation. The ability to cross from the peace enforcement stage in **J**, back to peacekeeping in **H**, is what this study refers to as peace creation. The one value which would determine the success in crossing between the two is impartiality, as discussed above. This is in contrast with Dobbie's argument that the peacekeeping – peace enforcement divide must not be crossed. Although Gow and Dandeker's concept of strategic peacekeeping implies that this divide may be crossed, it does not go as far as to include the application of peace enforcement at high levels.

IMPLEMENTING PEACE CREATION

Practical and Organizational Problems

This study has shown that the concept of peace creation outlined above meets with serious challenges upon execution. Perhaps the greatest difficulty of peace creation revealed by the study is the problem of reconciling its components – peacekeeping and peace enforcement. Such problems are of political and military dimensions and they had significant effects on the ECOMOG operations. The combination of both peacekeeping and enforcement in creating peace in Liberia raised a crucial political question: How can consent and co-operation of the warring parties be established after having employed force against one or more of them? The main military problem was also linked to this political question: How can troops of conflicting parties have confidence in a force that was previously engaged in battle against them? Conversely, how can peace troops adjust to a peacekeeping mode with rebel forces who killed their colleagues?

This study has discussed the views of parties to the conflict, and of other commentators who argue that this problem can be resolved in a number of ways. First, is the suggestion that impartiality by both the force and mediator can alleviate the political problem of lack of consent and co-operation due to mistrust.[3] It is however difficult to convince a disadvantaged or losing party,

---

[3]   See Chapter One for comments on Gow and Dandeker, 'Peace-Support Operations: The Problem of Legitimation'; and Chapter Four for discussions on the political problems confronting ECOMOG.

of the peacemaker's impartiality as the factions' accusations of ECOMOG at various times indicated. Durch highlights this point when he states that 'in war, partisans often look upon "neutrals" as covert members of the opposition...'[4] In addition, achievement of impartiality was made difficult, if not impossible in Liberia, by the intricate regional issues, which affected the operation. These are discussed below.

The proposal for dealing with the military aspect of the problem of reconciling the components was that both activities be conducted by different forces, allowing the best trained troops for either type of operation to be deployed to a mission area as required.[5] Thus, troops would be rotated periodically, to suit the changing situations on the ground. For example, plans to rotate troops before peace enforcement would focus on deploying troops with combat training and experience and relevant weapons and equipment. A switch to peacekeeping would focus on addressing attitudes of peacekeepers and perception of warring factions. Fresh troops with a peacekeeping focus would be relevant in this phase. The supporters of this view in Liberia believed that deploying enforcers and peacekeepers from different countries would placate factions like the NPFL, who saw Nigerian troops as hostile.

This study of Liberia has shown some of the problems that such careful rotation can encounter. In Liberia, the first problem was of a political nature, as countries whose troops fought to enforce a peaceful atmosphere were reluctant to relinquish control of the operation to the specialized peacekeepers. This was also not unrelated to the organizational problems discussed in Chapter Five and highlighted below. Secondly, the dire financial situation in ECOWAS made such a rotation and indeed, the minimum required rotation impossible. Thirdly, even if such rotation had been possible, smooth transition from one component to the other would have been rendered unworkable, given the unpredictable character of conflicting parties in these complex internal conflicts. The conflicting parties in Liberia still largely dictated the situation on the ground, and thus held what Gow and Dandeker describe as the 'strategic initiative'. The peacekeeping phase was made possible with their consent and co-operation. Thus it is difficult for a genuine peace force to change arbitrarily from this mode to one of enforcement unless a conflicting party reneged on the peacekeeping agreement, embarking on destructive conflict behaviour. It was only after the NPFL assault on ECOMOG headquarters and parts of Monrovia, that ECOMOG could switch to peace enforcement. However, there was some indication before this time, of NPFL preparation for war.

---

[4] Durch (ed.), *The Evolution of UN Peacekeeping: Case Studies and Comparative Analysis*, p.315
[5] See Chapter Five.

Findings of this research indicate that peace creation involves the distinct possibility of both peacekeeping and peace enforcement being executed by the same troops. A co-ordinated effort cannot be ensured in an environment where guerrilla forces could mount attacks regardless of promises made in peace agreements. Assaults like the NPFL's operation 'Octopus' cannot be ruled out in such conflicts as Liberia. Thus, the same troops who participated in peacekeeping may be required to use force. This is all the more important as traditional peacekeeping, which contingents like Ghana specialize in, has little or no place in such operations. Second generation peacekeeping would in any case require all-encompassing training. The best possible option is thus for troops to be trained in all aspects of the operation since it is difficult to separate peacekeeping and peace enforcement into two distinct operations, entrusted in different forces.

The problems involved in executing such uniform overall training were demonstrated in this study's analysis of the organizational problems that confronted the ECOMOG operation in Chapter Five. The tight command and control which peace creation demanded in Liberia was obstructed by several factors as discussed in Chapter Five. Perhaps the most crucial of these factors were the lack of uniformity in training, doctrine, and logistics throughout the multinational force; the influence of politics within the authorizing organization, ECOWAS; and language barriers. Differences in training patterns and capability amongst the different contingents made it particularly difficult to match troops for uniform proficiency during each phase, particularly at the initial phases of the operation. Command and control was greatly hampered by language barriers between the Francophone and Anglophone contingents especially during critical stages in the enforcement period. This was exacerbated by the fact that the Force Commander had no direct control over logistics as they were provided by each contributing government and managed separately by contingent commanders. Not least of the problems was the difficulty created by reluctance of some officers to submit to international command, at times taking orders from their home governments. In addition, the politics of ECOWAS and political rivalries between governments filtered down to the operational level in ECOMOG. Some of these problems however eased gradually, with years of joint operations.

REGIONAL FACTORS AFFECTING PEACE CREATION

Apart from what appeared to be familiar, or at least expected practical and organizational problems, this study has shown that regional peculiarities can have a profound effect on military operations. Through the analysis of the

Liberian case, this book has highlighted some specific issues affecting particularly, second generation peacekeeping and peace enforcement in a regional setting.

The political foundation and military means of creating peace were faulty in Liberia, largely as a result of regional peculiarities. Peace creation implies that the political authority should guide the conduct of the military throughout the operation. In the case of ECOWAS and ECOMOG, the majority of the governments which controlled the mission, particularly the most prominent, Nigeria, were under the control of the military. Thus, the ECOMOG operation was largely a case of the military guiding its own conduct.

This had several shortcomings whilst its advantages were less apparent. From the analysis conducted in this book what was perhaps the main benefit was the quickness with which decisions were reached by these military governments, in response to the situation on the ground in Liberia. This was most apparent when ECOMOG's mandate was changed to one of enforcement. In some cases, decisions were made over the telephone, by just a few individuals.

The flaws of this regional pattern however had more noticeable effects on the operation as mentioned in the fifth chapter. The strong influence of the military in all aspects of the peace mission resulted in what appeared to be total disregard for the use of civilians who would have been valuable in scoring political points, and giving direction to the military operations. There were no civilians on the ground throughout ECOMOG, for much of the operation. Less attention was given to propaganda and the need to gain the confidence of the warring factions, at crucial points.

The involvement of the military in political affairs seriously weakened military professionalism in many of these countries and affected the quality of the force deployed in Liberia. Many of the forces had been severely politicised, leaving what would have been otherwise a professional force lacking in discipline and other qualities befitting a professional force. This problem was most notable in Nigeria, with the largest contingent in ECOMOG. In Liberia, the problem manifested itself in a number of ways. First, disarray in the home military establishment meant inadequate preparation for the mission. The proclaimed impartiality of the force was compromised from the early stages through for example, reliance on a warring faction for logistics items which the force should have been able to provide.[6]

In addition, the level of indiscipline within the force was most glaringly illustrated by the cases of looting, particularly at officer level. The reluctance of the home governments to deter such conduct especially where the offenders were loyal to the military regime served to severely undermine the credibility

---

[6] See Chapter Five.

of the force. This was indeed worsened by the fact that appointment of staff into ECOMOG was sometimes based on favourable standing with the military government, rather than on merit. Thus, with all of these problems, ECOMOG was fortunate to have subdued the rebel forces in Liberia. Indeed, it was an ailing force in many ways which confronted an even more malaise one. A better organized and equipped ECOMOG could have concluded its mission in earlier, aiding the political side of the peacemaking.

Apart from the effects of politicised armed forces, this book has shown how other sub-regional peculiarities affected ECOMOG's ability to effectively create peace. The inherent weaknesses within ECOWAS member states filtered through to the force. First were the inadequacies of the military structures in many of the member states such as lack of qualified staff in the small countries with small armed forces. For example, some countries lacked senior officers as discussed in Chapter Five. Thus, when the rigidly political nature of the organization was brought to bear during the selection of staff officers, the best were not necessarily selected.

A second, and very significant factor was the dire financial situation of the organization, a reflection of the state of abject poverty in many member states. Due to severe shortage of funds, the supply and resupply of logistics were not regular and troops were maintained on the ground without rotation for periods of over two years in many cases. This factor had a noticeable impact on the practical side of peace creation, as troops which ought to have been rotated were kept on the ground to participate in peacekeeping after enforcement. The effects of this were seen in Chapter Five. These same issues – financial and small armed forces accounted for ECOMOG's inability to muster sufficient troops to operate effectively in Liberia. Some countries simply could not contribute more troops without compromising national security, e.g. Sierra Leone and the Gambia, whilst some others could not afford the financial cost of rotation. ECOMOG thus suffered inadequate troop strength at crucial stages in the operation. This problem partly led ECOMOG to employ the services of some of the rebel groups in Liberia, further compromising its credibility.

However, of all the regional peculiarities discussed in this study, one contributed immensely to ECOMOG's ability to sustain the operation against all odds. This was the strong will amongst both politicians and soldiers, to keep the mission going. The findings of the field study indicate that the sense of pride and the belief that Africa's problems must be solved by Africans runs through the military as well as politicians.

The Liberian experience showed that even in the face of humanitarian disasters, potential interveners will only intervene if it is in their interest to do so. The type of response required in such conflicts undoubtedly discouraged interveners, particularly as it did not serve their national interest. The reluctance of the US to intervene in Liberia, its closest African ally, was indicative of the general lack of interest in security matters affecting Africa, highlighting a real problem for the continent. This sent a message that African conflicts are unlikely to attract attention or interest beyond Africa. Thus, it was Liberia's neighbours who were willing, and able to intervene. It was these willing peacemakers, that employed all means necessary to deal with the crisis. Their will to continue to employ a more severe method even after casualties suffered, tested the African will beyond doubt. Whether the will of the African peacemakers would match their capability to conduct the necessary operations, was a different question altogether.

It is doubtful that such will could be found in regions unaffected by conflict. This is more apparent at the sub-regional level in Africa. The reluctance of the extended ECOMOG forces from East Africa to use force if required, is an indication of this. Generally, however, sub-regional powers would seem to be more interested in occurrences in their natural backyards. Outside of these areas, there may not be the desire to intervene. Western and Southern Africa appear to have clear sub-regional powers – Nigeria and South Africa, who if presented with no other option, may be forced to intervene in a deadly conflict in their respective regions. It is a different question altogether, if deadly conflict were to occur in the territory of the sub-regional hegemon. For Central and East Africa however, this may be more problematic as there is no clear sub-regional hegemon. Thus, when the crisis in Rwanda occurred, Zaire, and Uganda, who were affected and perhaps had some interest in intervening, could not muster the men, materiel and funds. Thus it seems there is not always a 'way' where there is a 'will'. It now remains to assess the implications of these for the international community at large.

THE FUTURE: IMPLICATIONS FOR UN AND REGIONAL ORGANIZATIONS

The UN possesses neither the will nor cohesion to conduct this type of operation (i.e. peace creation), with the dogged determination that the ECOWAS employed in Liberia. In addition, some of the command and control problems encountered by ECOMOG have been known to befall UN operations. The UN Secretary-General has noted that the organization 'lacks the political, military, material and financial resources' to meet the enormous demands placed on it.[7] However, the ECOMOG experience clearly shows that this problem is more acute with regional organizations, especially in the Third World. They lack the capacity to conduct effective operations regardless of

---

[7] Boutros Boutros-Ghali, 'Global Leadership After the Cold War', *Foreign Affairs*, March/April 1996, p.88

abundant will. Yet the threat of intra-state conflict has not subsided. There is clearly a need to devise not only a concept for responding to these conflicts, but a context for their application. The optimism shown by Hagglund and others in the immediate aftermath of the Cold War, that a situation akin to peace creation – where enforcement by great power troops would give way to 'less gallant' peacekeepers, has not materialized.

Employing force as part of any operation immediately invites some legal challenges. The few concise definitions of peace enforcement, as well as the UN Charter already indicate that only the UN Security Council may authorize the use of force. The UN Charter itself implies, as discussed in Chapter Four, that regional organizations may deal with matters of international security as long as they do not contradict the purposes and the principles of the UN. Liberia has further confirmed that political will far dominates the provisions of international law. Enforcement of international law depends upon the will of the international community, and that will is dictated by the interest of individual nation states. ECOMOG was deployed and it was able to enforce peace without obtaining the authorization of the UN. The latter seemed content to let the regional organization deal with a problem it was committed to solving, regardless of the legality of the techniques it employed in doing so. This is likely to be a recurring legal problem for the foreseeable future.

Dealing with the problems of peace creation and ensuring the success or effectiveness of an operation, which involves peace creation needs the co-operation of states or third parties with the resources to meet all the political and military challenges posed by the operation. The political challenges posed by Liberia would be best controlled in a situation where a large organization is able, through different groups of states, to issue threats, use force when necessary, wield its power, and make side payments to induce a settlement. Only the UN has the capacity to call on these types of resources. Militarily, the same can be done by the UN, using different states to conduct different types of operations, thus limiting many of the military problems encountered in Liberia. Warring factions would no doubt consider some states as enemies, and others as friends, depending on the role they play in such operations. In West Africa, ECOWAS did not enjoy the luxury of choosing from amongst different nations with the capability of dealing with the ECOMOG operation at different levels. Nigeria, the largest troop contributor was undoubtedly seen as the enemy by the NPFL, and there was no other state sufficiently resource-ful to neutralize this image.

There are undoubtedly a number of obstacles which would face any effort to conduct peace creation at the UN level. First is the financial crisis that appears to have befallen UN peacekeeping for some time. But much more than this, the cycle is completed with same problem of lack of political will, especially amongst the most resourceful and influential members of the organization, to deal with these types of conflicts. Apart from the fact that conflicts in some areas will continue to receive more attention than others if only because of proximity, states will be very reluctant to commit men and materiel to operations in areas which do not serve their interest. Indeed, whether they will be willing to use peace creation even in conflicts where they intervene remains to be seen. Thus, for some time to come, Africans will have to learn to deal with their own conflicts in the best way that they can, with whatever resources they are able to squeeze from the international community. Whether such operations would have solid legal foundations, is another issue altogether. The legal relationship between the UN and regional organizations in managing difficult conflict would require closer attention if regional conflicts are to be effectively resolved.

LESSONS

Under what conditions should peace creation be employed?

Despite the seemingly irreconcilable components of peace creation and the problems of implementation, the conduct of internal conflicts such as in Liberia, (and later, Rwanda) has demonstrated that peace creation is a necessary evil if devastation of these communities is to be avoided. The study of the ECOWAS and ECOMOG response to the Liberian civil war has led to the extraction of some lessons and notes on conditions under which peace creation should be employed.

The first condition is the existence of an intractable conflict, which has resulted in difficult humanitarian emergencies, or the threat of one. It is however far easier if such a situation were always apparent. It may be difficult to prove, or to be persuaded that a conflict situation would result in greater disaster, or to quantify its level of destructiveness before this has occurred. For example, although there had for long been indication of a bloody conflict brewing in Rwanda, no observer could accurately predict the casualty level. Furthermore, issues of sovereignty would be more difficult to resolve if peace creation was attempted on the basis of a threat of humanitarian disaster. In Liberia, it was difficult to dispute the fact that a humanitarian disaster had occurred, and that a state of anarchy had set in. Thus, it was hard to challenge the humanitarian argument of the peacemakers.

Secondly, for peace creation to withstand legal and other criticisms, peacemaking must have been embarked upon on the diplomatic level, and exhausted, without success. It is uncertain whether peacemaking was vigorously pursued before ECOMOG was deployed in Liberia. However, it is arguable that ECOWAS could not wait indefinitely for parties to agree, in the face of such human suffering. The fact that conflicting parties or at least one of them remained intransigent was sufficient to justify the ECOMOG move. Other forms of enforcement such as economic blockade and arms embargo were however not attempted before the military option.

Even when peace creation has been considered the only viable option, a softer approach such as peacekeeping in its wider variant may be attempted, before resorting to enforcement. This does not however preclude preparations for the use of force. The absence of consent would become more obvious if warring factions are given the chance to openly resist peace efforts. There is the likelihood that a peace force that exhausts all other options before employing force would be looked upon more sympathetically by the local community and other observers.

Determinants of Success

No matter how ripe conditions may be, and regardless of the abundance of political will, peace creation may not be successful. From this book's analysis of the Liberian experience, it appears that such an operation would enjoy unqualified success only under certain circumstances. First, the peacemaker plays a crucial role, for without this third party, the operation would be non-existent. Peace creation is part of an overall peacemaking exercise. The overall direction of the diplomatic and military aspects of the peacemaking must rest with the mediator(s).

In particular, when mediation is attempted on a multilateral level as was done by ECOWAS, it is important for such an organization to be cohesive. Divisions amongst ECOWAS members were partly responsible for the prolongation of the Liberian crisis. Political input from the mediator or mediating body is vital as this gives direction to the military operation. Whilst the mediator is dependent on the military to create and maintain an atmosphere where it can conduct negotiations, the military in turn, relies on the mediator for direction in the area of operation. This is why the lack of political presence on the ground in Liberia was seen as a setback for the operation by many within and outside ECOMOG, who felt that this enabled ECOMOG to dictate the pace of events at times.

In addition, impartiality, is important for a strong mediatory base, as well as for the success of the military operation. Applying the same rules to all parties and both in diplomatic and operational matters could serve to build the confidence of conflicting parties and lend credibility to the peacemakers.

However, regardless of the sincerity of the peacemaker, the perception of warring parties may be different. Allegations of partiality created problems for ECOMOG in Liberia. Whilst the mediator may be impartial, it is however possible that the mediators would not be total outsiders to the conflict. Guinea and Sierra Leone for example, seemed to have genuine interests in the resolution of the conflict given the refugee crisis created in their countries. Thus, it is unlikely that peacemakers from within a conflict-ridden region would be neutral. It does not however follow that neutral states cannot be impartial peacemakers.

Militarily, the force seeking to create peace must be superior to the combined forces of the warring factions. Only then can it be sure of attaining its objectives. Such military superiority must undoubtedly entail amongst other things, numerically superior and well trained men, efficient command and control system, effective administration of logistics and re-supply channels. The need for a high level of military professionalism in the peace force was illustrated by the operational flaws in the ECOMOG operations as discussed earlier in the book and in this concluding chapter.

Map

LIBERIA

JSCSC\ACADEMIC\LIBERIA.PPT 315/97

Questionnaire

Please fill in the spaces and place a tick in the relevant boxes.

A. BACKGROUND INFORMATION

1. Nationality   _____

2. Unit Assignment in ECOMOG   _____

3. Military Rank   _____

4. Regular or Reserve   _____

5. Length of Present Tour in ECOMOG   _____

6. Length of Service in Country's Armed Forces   _____

7. Is Country's Army an all-volunteer force
    or based on conscription?   _____

B. ATTITUDE TOWARD MISSION

8. What is ECOMOG's mandate in Liberia?

    _____
    _____
    _____

9. In your opinion, which strategy was better suited for the fulfilment of this
    mandate?

    Peacekeeping ☐   Peace Enforcement ☐

10. In addition to training in military skills, are additional skills needed for:

    a)   Peacekeeping?   YES ☐   NO ☐

    b)   Peace Enforcement?   YES ☐   NO ☐

11. Would you say that there are differences between Peace Enforcement and military operations aimed at defeating an enemy in battle?

YES ☐   NO ☐

If you have answered yes, please list the differences:

_____

_____

12. Can a soldier be an effective peacekeeper if he cannot use force except in self-defence?

YES ☐   NO ☐

13. What do you see as the problems of switching between Peacekeeping and Peace Enforcement in one operation?

_____

_____

_____

14. Which of the two strategies in 13 above has been more effective in Liberia?

_____

15. Do you think this ECOMOG assignment helps your military career at home?

YES ☐   NO ☐

16. Will you readily take part in a similar mission in future?

YES ☐   NO ☐

17. Do you think that more efforts of this nature should be put into making peace in African conflicts?

YES ☐   NO ☐

18. Do you consider this mission to be considerably different from regular UN Missions?

YES ☐   NO ☐

If you have answered yes, please state the differences:

_____
_____
_____

C. VIEW OF OTHER CONTINGENTS

19. How would you compare the soldierly qualities of the various national contingents in ECOMOG?

_____
_____
_____

20. How would you compare their peacekeeping qualities?

_____
_____
_____

21. Do you think that the cultural differences between the contingents have some effect on the performance of the force?

YES ☐   NO ☐

22. What are the effects of language barrier?

_____
_____
_____

23. How do you rate morale within ECOMOG generally?

_____

_____

_____

24. How would you rate your level of interaction with soldiers in other contingents?

_____

_____

_____

D. SOCIAL EFFECTS OF MISSION

25. How has your involvement in this mission affected you socially?

_____

_____

_____

26. Do you have frequent contact with your family?

YES ☐   NO ☐

27. Does the pay leave you better or worse off than you would be in your home country?

BETTER ☐   WORSE ☐   UNCHANGED ☐

28. Overall, would you say that your living conditions while serving in ECOMOG have left you better or worse off, or no different than normal?

BETTER ☐   WORSE ☐   UNCHANGED ☐

29. What aspects of your living conditions would you like improved?

_____

_____

_____

E. GENERAL

30. What in your opinion are the lessons of the ECOMOG mission?

_____
_____
_____

Index